Contents

The publishers would like to thank the *Irish Examiner* and RTÉ's *Drivetime* programme for kind permission to reproduce the columns within this book.

Notes from the Margins

Fergus Finlay has contributed a weekly newspaper column to the *Irish Examiner* for the past decade, and broadcasts a weekly radio column on RTÉ's *Drivetime*. He is the bestselling author of a number of books, including his political memoir *Snakes and Ladders* and *President with a Purpose*, about Mary Robinson's election campaign. He worked for many years at the forefront of Irish industrial relations before moving into politics, where he was adviser to Labour Leaders Dick Spring and Pat Rabbitte. He is now CEO of Barnardos, Ireland's largest children's charity, and has been an active member of the disability movement all his adult life. He is married to Frieda and has four daughters and a grandson.

Notes from the Margins

A Decade of Irish Life

HACHETTE
BOOKS
IRELAND

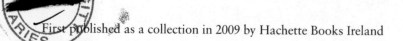

First published as a collection in 2009 by Hachette Books Ireland

1

A CIP catalogue record for this title is available from the
British Library.

ISBN 978 0340 99315 6

Typeset in Sabon by Hachette Books Ireland
Printed and bound in the UK by
CPI Mackays, Chatham ME5 8TD

Hachette Books Ireland policy is to use papers that are natural,
renewable and recyclable products and made from wood grown
in sustainable forests. The logging and manufacturing processes
are expected to conform to the environmental regulations of the
country of origin.

Hachette Books Ireland
8 Castlecourt Centre
Castleknock
Dublin 15, Ireland
A division of Hachette UK Ltd
338 Euston Road, London NW1 3BH
www.hbgi.ie

Посвящается Эмме,
которая всегда идет к своей цели,
несмотря на препятствия на ее пути

For Emma,
Who always gets to where she wants to go,
no matter what obstacles are in her way.

Foreword

When Fergus Finlay resigned from the position of then Labour Party leader Pat Rabbitte's chef de cabinet a little over four years ago to become chief executive of the children's charity Barnardos, he said: 'I will be a political animal until the day I die but I will now leave partisan politics at the office door.'

For once – for an extremely rare once – Fergus could have been found wanting in his trademark precision. He might have been committed to leaving partisan *party* politics at the office door with his move to Barnardos, but there was no way he would ever have been capable of leaving partisan politics to fade from his core focus.

Because he is partisan. He is as much so now as he was the first day he immersed himself in the politics of this country, amplifying the voices of the voiceless, articulating the needs of the marginalised, fighting their corner when few in Government or opposition seemed to care, and he has exploited every opportunity to do so consistently for many years, with considerable success.

If that is what partisan politics means, then I am partisan, and I am with Fergus Finlay.

It has nothing to do with party-political affiliation. It is about doing the right thing. Many, many families throughout the country have good reason to be grateful to him for his unrelenting, ceaseless commitment to fighting the good fight for those who most need that support. Not that he would want or expect any gratitude for what he has been doing all his adult life. He does it out of an innate abhorrence of injustice, and he does so with an integrity and intellectual capacity and vigour admired by even his most avowed critics.

I would not pretend to know Fergus very well, though what I do know of him I like and admire very much indeed. What I also know of the man is of someone whom you would dearly wish to have on your side, and someone to be feared if you were corrupt, feckless, or reckless with the fate of the country resting in your hands.

It has been a privilege to have him as a columnist for the *Irish Examiner* for the past ten years, a decade during which Ireland changed profoundly, almost to an unrecognisable degree. Changes which he charted, and frequently challenged in his characteristically articulate and thought-provoking way.

While, in recent years, he has become more publicly recognised for his campaigning on disability and children's rights issues, he has been one of the real forces for change in Ireland for over three decades. His commitment to trade unionism, social equality, and the Northern peace process has been outstanding and an example to us all.

Among many achievements in a remarkable career, he was responsible for the establishment of the Commission on the Status of People with Disabilities in 1993 and it was his brainchild two years later to establish the International Body on Arms Decommissioning, one of the key pieces in the complex jigsaw that finally brought peace to Northern Ireland.

He has been consistent in championing the rights of

minorities and the overarching principles of democracy in a way that sets a standard that far too many at all levels of our public life fail to attain.

His has been one of the progressive voices which shaped modern Ireland and we would be much the poorer without his contribution. That independent, forceful, commanding and erudite voice has been articulated for over a decade in the columns of the *Irish Examiner* and it is entirely fitting and appropriate that they now appear together within the covers of this book, providing an invaluable insight into the way we were, the way we are and the way we should be.

Tim Vaughan
Editor, the *Irish Examiner*
May 2009

Introduction

My father used to say that you worry about your kids until they reach the age of sixteen – and then you start getting frantic about them. Over the years I've learned that there was a lot of wisdom in that remark, only now I tend to apply it to these columns. I start worrying about them on Friday, and I'm usually frantic by Sunday night (the deadline is Monday morning). What if there's no news, nothing to react to, nothing to write about? What if I simply have nothing to say?

Thankfully, the Irish political system, and the weird and wonderful way in which Irish public policy works, has never let me down. In recent years (unlike my years working in politics – now there's a comment in itself!) my day job has brought me into direct contact with dozens of people who live on the margins of Irish life. Brave people, sometimes beaten people. People struggling in all sorts of ways, and trying to cope with systems that are inflexible and frequently unfeeling. Sadly, there's always something to write about. Sometimes, it's possible to have a bit of fun, often all too easy to get mad, with politics itself.

I've mainly tried over the years to tell the stories of people who live at the margins. One thing I have learned from many years of experience in politics, and nowadays in trying to help people to make lasting changes in their lives and the lives of their children, is how hard a struggle it can be when there is no one to listen to your story. And in the world we live in, it's important that these stories are told. They mightn't change anything – but it's always been my view of a civilised society that it is prepared to listen. And maybe sometimes to reflect. I have huge admiration for people who struggle against the odds, and I'm in their debt every time they allow me to share their stories.

For that reason, I've been really grateful to Tim Vaughan, and the rest of the team in the *Irish Examiner* that I've worked with over the years, for giving me the platform. The only instruction Tim ever gave me was never to send in a column about how hard it is to write a column – something all columnists do sooner or later. And if I've ever got into trouble with touchy politicians about something I've said – and some of them are touchy, believe it or not! – he and his colleagues have been a rock of support. In more recent times I've been given a similar opportunity, with a similar brief, by *Drivetime* on RTÉ Radio One. Mary Wilson and Marian Richardson, the guiding spirits behind that programme, are inspirational people to work with, as are the producers who cope with my odd hours of recording the column, and the need to do a second, or sometimes a fifth, take. The one thing they have in common with the Irish Examiner is that they never suggest a change that doesn't improve the final product.

I'm also grateful to Hachette Books Ireland, and especially to my editor Ciara Considine, for suggesting this book. I hope I haven't tried their patience too much. I'm completely indebted to all my colleagues in Barnardos, who put up with me in the course of the day job and

carry me through any challenges with their professionalism and their total commitment to children and families. They're simply the best bunch I've ever worked with.

Finally, my four daughters, my son-in-law Tony, and
my grandson Ross are not just a source of continuing
inspiration, they have also taught me a lot over the years.
There is one person in particular who has given up a lot
of Sunday nights to watching me pace the floor in
desperation when a column just wouldn't kick off in my
head, and who has saved my bacon time out of number
by saying quietly 'Why don't you write about ...?'
Thanks, Frieda. You know what you mean to me.

Fergus Finlay
May 2009

Seen But Not Heard

This Thing Called Charity
(1999)

Charity suffers long, wrote Saint Paul. Charity is kind, it lacks envy and arrogance, is not easily provoked. Charity bears all and endures all. It is the greatest of the virtues.

So how does charity conspire to turn human beings into a sub-species, to rob them of rights and dignity, and to subject them to the unspeakable cruelty of the charitable?

And how do we manage to always turn a blind eye? Anyone who has watched the *States of Fear* series on RTÉ can only end up wondering. The abuse and cruelty suffered by children at the hands of those who were trusted with their care is only part of the story. The untold part is how it could have happened.

The truth is it was done for us. Our way of dealing with illegitimacy, with mental or physical disability, with unwanted children, was to put coppers in a tin cup and close our eyes. We gave to charity, and we relied on charity. We never knew that charity was building prisons and torture chambers in our towns and villages. Many of the children in them were there as a result of a court order, and most were condemned by the courts to stay until they were sixteen. None of them were ever charged with a crime – except the crime of being unwanted.

They had no rights. Even to put it like that seems banal, when you consider the way in which they were routinely degraded and brutalised. Many were known and addressed by numbers, not names. Beatings – often brutal, savage beatings which drew blood and required stitches – were commonplace. No form of treatment was regarded as too cruel.

And it was done in our name. Brutality and abuse carried out by nuns, brothers, priests and laypeople were paid for by us, through the coppers we put in the tin cups and the taxes we paid. It was supervised for us by a bureaucracy and political system whose principal concern was to ensure that the walls were high enough and the doors double-locked.

We have investigative journalism now. We have a political system that prides itself on transparency. We talk all the time about the rights of the person. We prosecute people for abuse, and we no longer spare members of the clergy from investigation.

But to what extent is there any real accountability yet? How much have things actually changed?

I'm tempted to say go to St Ita's in Portrane (it's about fifteen miles from some of the most expensive real estate in the Western world) and see for yourself. Except that you won't find it easy to get in, especially if you have a camera with you. And you might be surprised to discover that a doctor tried to carry out medical experiments on patients there – two years ago.

But you don't have to go that far. Let me give you a small and more mundane example from my own experience. It's an experience that thousands of parents all over Ireland could replicate – and go a lot further with.

I have a daughter with Down's Syndrome. Mandy is her name. She's lovable a lot of the time, though not always. She's twenty-five now, and until she was sixteen her mother got a monthly allowance from our local Health Board – some small recompense, I suppose, for giving up a career to become a full-time expert in learning disability. Once a year, in return for this pittance, we had to satisfy the local health board that Mandy hadn't been cured of her Down's Syndrome. Now she qualifies for the Disabled Person's Maintenance Grant in her own right – and she is legally liable to be asked to see a medical referee at any time, so that the state can be sure she isn't getting the allowance under false pretences.

In all those twenty five years, no one on behalf of the State has ever asked us if Mandy is happy. We have never been invited to comment on the services she receives (we would, if asked, praise those services highly for effort). We have never been invited to participate in any planning that might be going on about her. Nobody has ever told us that as a citizen of her country, she has inalienable rights.

We are reasonably assertive people, and we don't need anyone to intervene on our behalf or on behalf of Mandy. That's just as well – because there's nobody there. That's why thousands of parents live in fear for their children's future. They know they have no rights in the eyes of their own society, and they dread what charity might end up doing to them.

I don't want in any sense to compare that situation to the horrors that occurred in Goldenbridge and countless places like it. I want to make a different point. Charity still rules in attitudes to vulnerable people. And charity doesn't have any room for rights or accountability.

This year, for example, according to the Estimates for the Department of Health and Children, a total of £125 million will be paid directly by the Department, or through Health Boards, to 'homes for mentally handicapped persons administered by voluntary bodies'. Great, isn't it? Sure aren't we doing a lot? Hang on a second. I'm not asking you to think about whether the sum of money involved is enough to provide a decent full life (it isn't, by the way).

But think about this for a second. Who runs these bodies that you're giving this money to? When did you last see any newspaper reports about their annual accounts? Who are the people, and what is the money spent on? Who inspects them, and who reports to us about standards of care and the rights of the people who live in these 'homes'? Who is accountable?

The answer, essentially, is nobody. We still give the money, and we still close our eyes. There is no independent body empowered and obliged to go into Ireland's institutions (and they still exist) to ensure that the rights of Irish citizens are being fully protected. There is no one to whom anyone can complain if those rights are being trampled on, and no means of automatic redress.

The National Disability Authority, in respect of which legislation went through the committee stage last week, was supposed to be such a body. It might be yet, given an awful lot of political goodwill and commitment. The original Bill was a watery thing, and it has been improved a bit by committee work. But the real teeth the NDA needs, if it is to promote the concept of rights instead of charity, are still not there.

In a week in which Ireland won an international

Disability Award (and Mandy was in the United Nations, helping to represent her country, incidentally, when it was given out), it may be worth emphasising once again that we may have come a long way.

But my God we have a long way to go before we have ended the 'silent crisis', as Kofi Annan called it. We could begin by getting rid of this thing called charity.

Real Rights at Last?
(1999)

The Government is to appoint an Ombudsman for Children. So it appears from announcements and front-page newspaper stories this week. Three cheers might be in order for a long overdue development. But I think I'll withhold my congratulations until I see the legislation. Anyone can make an announcement, after all – and Frank Fahey, the Minister for Children, has never been behind the door when it comes to getting his name in the papers.

According to the stories, the Ombudsman for Children will monitor the implementation of the UN Convention on the Rights of the Child. A complaints procedure will be established, with the power to investigate individual complaints in relation to both public and private bodies. The Ombudsman will also have the power to comment on the need for administrative or statutory reform.

When established on a statutory basis, the Ombudsman for Children will have contact with children on all matters relating to their welfare. It will be an independent office responsible to the Oireachtas. Although its decisions will not be legally binding, it will be able to take legal action on behalf of children and the outcome of such action would be binding on those it was taken against.

Yeah, right. This is the same Government that has steadfastly refused to appoint an Ombudsman for people with disabilities. I've spelled out here before the way in which the Government has refused to allow any real independence for the National Disability Authority. The legislation underpinning that body has been watered down to ensure that there is no independent forum for making complaints, no right to initiate legal action, no reporting to the Oireachtas.

That's why, as reported in this newspaper during the week, parents of people with disabilities are reduced to preparing long and wearying legal actions against the State – and taking the risk themselves that they won't have huge legal bills at the end of the process.

Incidentally, when is it going to dawn on people that the State is using the law to batter parents in this way? Particularly where the education of young people is concerned, there is a clearly established constitutional right. It was spelled out in detail by Judge O'Hanlon of the High Court in the landmark O'Donoghue case, and has never been challenged by the State in the Supreme Court. It is therefore the law of the land.

Instead of applying the law, the State consistently invites parents to sue. That's why you'll have read in yesterday's *Examiner* that the establishment of essential facilities for children with Attention Deficit Disorder in Limerick came about as a result of an agreement between the parents and the Department of Education made on the steps of the High Court. If the Department was intent on applying the law, they would never have forced those parents into the High Court.

What the State is doing is simple enough. Let parents apply for a service. Refuse it. If the parents threaten to sue, tell them you'll fight them. You can afford the lawyers, they can't. If the parents go ahead anyway, fudge and procrastinate until the issue reaches the steps of the court. Then settle. The State always settles these actions – it has to, because it's in the wrong, and knows it.

But why? Why hasn't the State decided just to implement the law? Why does it constantly seek instead to use its unlimited muscle to frighten parents? More than a hundred such cases are still outstanding. All of them will be settled – all of them will result in an improvement in services. And all of them will be fought up to the steps of the High Court.

That's why, when I hear the Government saying they're going to create a powerful, independent advocate for the rights of children, my reaction tends to be more cynical than enthusiastic. I will take a lot of convincing that this Government has more than cosmetics in mind. An Ombudsman for Children, along the lines announced, would have the right to take the legal actions, and the risks, on behalf of the young people involved, rather than their parents. I don't see this Government, based on its track record, allowing that to happen.

And it's not as if we don't need it. There have been enough documented cases of child abuse and neglect over the past few years to establish beyond doubt that there is a case for a children's advocate in Ireland. And more – there is an undeniable case for putting the resources in place to ensure a proper inspectorate for all our social services. We need to be happy that someone is watching the watchers in this area. Too often, the social services are stretched to the point where sloppy practice and skewed priorities can end up doing more harm than good.

It's not just in the areas of abuse and neglect that we

need constant reminding. Too many children in Ireland are being deprived of the opportunities of a decent education by inadequate facilities. Too many still go to bed hungry at night because of family poverty. Too many suffer the stress of marital breakdown without anywhere to turn.

Hardly a month goes by in Ireland without a child being sentenced to a totally unsuitable prison environment because there's nowhere else to send them. Hardly a month without a judge pointing out the duty of the State to provide proper facilities and services.

And other practices abound. It's common enough in Ireland to employ youngsters in pubs, hotels and restaurants. It's not unusual for kids to have no safe place to play, no access to creative outlets. There are parts of Ireland – mainly, it has to be said, in the cities – where sports facilities are still woefully inadequate. Alienation among young people, allied to a complete disinterest in civic matters, is a phenomenon which cuts across all class lines.

I'm not saying that the appointment of an Ombudsman would solve all these problems. What I am saying is that in one of the twenty richest countries in the world, there is really no excuse for turning a blind eye to

---

Footnote: Last week, I wrote about the railways, and got a number of letters on the subject. Most of them were kind enough to agree with what I wrote – and none of my correspondents tended to blame the train drivers for disruption. Irish Rail was less impressed with the piece. I did, however, get a letter from five retired train drivers who told me I was wrong to say that the maximum pension they could get was £54 a week. In their case, with up to forty years' service, they were getting £38 a week! Maybe some of my erudite readers could explain how any public company could feel justified in treating its long-term employees in this way.

the rights of children. We've signed up to a UN Convention – not only do we have a moral duty to live up to it, we even have the resources to do it. When we see the legislation, then – and not until then – will we know the Government is serious.

Somewhere Over the Rainbow
(2003)

Do you know what a rainbow is? Do you know that girls have been treated in the Sexual Assault Treatment Unit in the Rotunda Hospital in Dublin with an amount of alcohol in their systems that is normally found in the morgue? Do you know what a Wild Thing or a Rodeo are? Do you know what 'MLDAs' are? Do you know that a doctor in Dublin told the Dáil recently that he treated a fifteen-year-old girl who was in a deep coma within an hour of drinking half a bottle of neat vodka? Have you ever heard of a Skoal Bandit?

Do you know the connection between all these things?

I don't want to pretend it's a simple or straightforward relationship. President McAleese has recently highlighted our peculiar relationship with alcohol. There's no doubt in my mind that she was perfectly right to do so, and that she did it in a thought-provoking way. I have equally no doubt that it is a multi-faceted issue.

Many of us drank too much when we were younger. Few of us are in a position to judge or condemn anyone who has a difficult relationship with drink.

But what does astonish and horrify me is the fact that there are now drinks that have been manufactured with the sole and specific purpose of appealing to young people, of getting through their defences. They are marketed directly at young people. Incidentally, drinks marketing people never refer to young people directly in their meetings and video conferences. They call them MLDAs. It's short for 'minimum legal drinking age' and it allows the marketing people to develop plans without thinking that their own teenage sons or daughters might be hooked by them. Using jargon is often a good way of fooling your conscience.

One of the most 'successful' drinks aimed at young people – its American manufacturers would be very upset if I said it was aimed at teenagers, so I'll let you be the judge of that – is a product called Aftershock. The company that manufactures it calls it a 'cordial', which is defined in my dictionary as 'a stimulant or tonic'.

Aftershock comes in a cool square bottle and pretty colours – pink for girls, blue for boys and green for a mouth-freshening effect. Many barmen in Dublin, and presumably elsewhere, know how to make a rainbow with Aftershock. You do it by carefully pouring a shot of each colour into a tall glass. Drink it quickly and the colours will stay separate.

Drink it quickly and you'll have had three shots of one of the strongest drinks on the market. Aftershock is 40 degrees of alcohol – that's the same strength as neat whiskey, and stronger than vodka or gin. It's three times stronger than wine or beer.

It's one of the most popular 'catch-up' drinks among young people – if you want to get out of your mind quickly, there's a variety of ways you can do it with Aftershock. And they are helpful at pointing them out.

Not on the bottle, mind you. You won't find any

indication on the bottle of what's inside. There's a website address, but even the website is not too informative about exactly what Aftershock is. It does tell you quite clearly how to drink it – this incredibly strong drink. You pour it neat into a shot glass, 'take it in one', and then take a deep breath.

And if that's not strong enough, the good people who manufacture it have ways of helping you along. There's a recipe for Wild Thing – that's mixing Aftershock with one of the Irish cream drinks and a vanilla liqueur. Or Rodeo – Aftershock and a shot of bourbon. The website, not surprisingly, recommends that you should 'hold on tight'.

Aftershock is only one of the drinks that are specifically aimed at very young people. Some of the others are not quite as strong, but are made very sweet to encourage addictive and easy drinking.

All of them make their own contribution to what is now an epidemic of underage drinking, with deadly consequences. All of them make a lie of the claims of some drinks manufacturers that they believe in responsible drinking and marketing.

It was Dr Colman O'Leary, a consultant at the Mid Western Regional Hospital in Limerick, who told the Oireachtas Committee on Health recently that crash drinking among the twelve-to-fifteen age group was a major concern. He referred to the fifteen-year-old girl in a deep coma from neat vodka, and he went on to say that he would like to take pictures of these young people in a comatose state, having soiled themselves, and show them to themselves and their parents.

Dr Mary Holohan, director of the Sexual Assault Treatment Unit at the Rotunda Hospital, told the

Committee that 60 per cent of females seen at the unit had alcohol taken. Many of them believed they had been the victims of the so-called 'date rape' drug, rohypnol, but it was seldom, if ever, found in the blood tests.

What was found was enormous amounts of alcohol. 'The toxicology service has remarked to us that levels of alcohol in the samples they test for us are only seen in samples from one other source: the coroner's office,' Dr Holohan added.

This had not changed over the past decade, she said, but the pattern of alcohol consumption had. 'Spirits are consumed at home before going out. Mixed-sex groups of young teens drink in parks – the boys beer and the girls undiluted spirits,' she said.

Apparently, one of the reasons girls favour undiluted spirits is in the belief that they are less fattening. How big a worry is that when you end up in casualty, I wonder? Dr Eamon Brazil of the Mater Hospital told the Committee that they had to deal with about ten drunk patients a day. Alcohol consumption accounted for up to a quarter of all A&E attendances at his hospital, he said.

Which brings me to Skoal Bandits. Skoal Bandits are a kind of chewing tobacco. They're a form of snuff, sold in sachets, and quite popular throughout Scandinavia. Like all chewing tobaccos, they are very strongly associated with mouth cancer.

In the mid-1980s, when Barry Desmond was Minister for Health, he discovered that Skoal Bandits were about to be launched on the Irish market. He took the decision immediately that there was no good reason why a cancer-causing product not already legally here should be allowed into the market. And he banned it, simply, directly, using a provision of the 1947 Health Act.

That provision has never been used for any other purpose. I believe it should be used to ban alcoholic products that are specifically designed to hook very young people. They are a form of exploitation and abuse of young people, and the State has the power to end it.

I don't favour that form of compulsion as a rule. But everyone involved in dealing with the consequences knows that there is an age at which young people are especially vulnerable to exploitation. If we choose to ignore that fact, many of them won't survive their first experiments with the poison that alcohol can be.

The Smell of the Pillow
(2003)

The following scenario is unimaginable, isn't it? A religious brother now in his seventies is arrested and charged with a series of horrible crimes. They include both physical and sexual abuse of the children in his care, who ranged in age from ten to fourteen. The crimes with which he is charged cover a period of ten years in the late 1950s. Over twelve days in the criminal courts, grown men break down in tears at the sight of their abuser. He is still powerful looking, still arrogant, still confident in his denials. But their testimony tells, as one by one the men recount the terror and the pain they felt at his hands.

One phrase sticks in the jury's collective mind. 'I can still remember the smell,' one witness says, 'as he pushed my head into the pillow.'

It becomes clear as the trial goes on that this man operated with virtual impunity. Each of the witnesses revealed that they had confided in other brothers, but that it had never made any difference – except in one case, where the witness was beaten by the brother superior for telling lies, while his tormentor looked on with a smirk. 'And he raped me that night,' said the witness, 'before the welts had gone down on my bottom.'

Eventually the trial ends. It takes the jury less than an

hour to find the brother guilty, and as he is led away to begin a twelve-year sentence, each of the men who had testified against him experiences the beginnings of catharsis. They resolve though that they will not let the matter rest there, and with the aid of a firm of solicitors, they set about lodging a series of High Court actions against the guilty brother and the order who shielded him.

The solicitor who is handling their case is very confident that after the man has been found guilty, and with the accumulation of evidence that he was protected, there is every chance that the men will win their High Court action. 'But of course,' he tells them, 'in the old days we would have sued three co-defendants – the brother, the order and the State that put you all into that orphanage in the first place. But under the indemnity deal that was done a few years ago, it is the State and the taxpayers that will have to pay. This won't cost the order, or even your abuser, a red cent, and we won't be suing them.'

Unimaginable? Unfortunately, it's not only imaginable, it's what would happen. The particular criminal case I outline above might never have happened (although the quotations are true, taken from other cases with which I am familiar). But if it ever happened in the future, the indemnity we have given to the religious congregations will fully protect them from any potential liability.

How did we manage to do that? I read one commentator at the weekend saying that the moment the Taoiseach apologised to survivors of abuse, and the moment a redress fund was set up, it was always going to involve large amounts of taxpayers' money. According to this analysis if the opposition wanted to save taxpayers' money, they should have questioned the terms of reference of the redress fund.

That sort of analysis completely misses the point. As far as I'm aware, nobody objects to survivors of abuse being compensated – and in large measure – for the suffering they underwent. It was suffering caused by State neglect and by the inhumane attitude towards vulnerable children at the time. But it was suffering perpetrated by individuals, and all too often those individuals were shielded and protected by the orders of which they were members, and their deeds covered up. In any normal civil action arising from that kind of abuse, there would be three co-defendants – the abuser, the order and the State.

Now there is only one. In return for an amount of money that I believe will only ever exist on paper, and very little actual cash, the religious orders, and any individuals within those orders who have questions to answer, have bought themselves an indemnity for all time and in all circumstances.

After the indemnity deal was done, in June 2002, the religious orders notified the Department of Education that there were 2,640 cases outstanding in which they and the State were possible co-defendants. In the absence of an indemnity, those 2,640 cases must have represented an appalling vista for the congregations. Each one would have to be fought or settled. If the orders couldn't plead the statute of limitations, and depending on the severity and duration of the abuse involved, the orders could have been looking at damages running to hundreds of thousands of euros in each and every case. If one were to take an average settlement of €100,000, the bill would have exceeded €250 million. Legal costs would have doubled that to €500 million. And that's not counting the cost of the never-ending publicity attaching to such cases (although I suppose they should be used to that by now).

So we should be very clear about one thing. It may well be that the congregations genuinely wanted, at some point, to make a contribution towards the redress due to victims. It may well be that they were at one point inspired by a feeling of contrition or penitence. But what they achieved would make the most mercenary capitalist proud. They made a contribution that involved little or no real sacrifice on their part, and in return they secured a deal that protected the vast bulk of their assets into the indefinable future.

They suckered the State. On behalf of all of us, a minister and a civil servant entered into a deal in principle that resulted in the State being exposed to a completely unlimited liability, and at the same time they precisely, to the penny, limited the exposure of the religious congregations.

Could they have done better? The answer is I don't know. They certainly caused no estimate of the exposure of the congregations to be carried out. They sought no audit of the assets of the congregations. At critical points in the negotiations, they excluded necessary legal advice.

In other words, they didn't try. They told the congregations how much they would accept, they told them how far the indemnity could go. And they told them all that before the negotiations even began.

I believe that evidence will emerge to show that they had plenty of advice, from officials in the Attorney General's office, that the course they were following was dangerous and wrong. Perhaps that was the very reason the AG's office was excluded.

And as for the AG himself, what are we to make of all the belated bleating on his part that he was left out of the loop? His colleagues spent last weekend pointing out to the media that his bleating was most muted when it should have been loudest, and he is collectively responsible for this bad deal whether he likes it or not. As a result he is, to borrow a phrase he once used about someone else, something of a broken reed.

Forgotten People
(2004)

My friend Aileen Atcheson has written a book about times past, about things that are gone and people forgotten. It's called *Castles Falling* and deals with all the memories of her native town, Clonmel. The buildings that have fallen into disrepair and ruin, that once marked out a thriving industrial and commercial life. The famous and not-so-famous names connected with the town, from Bianconi to the late, great broadcaster Tommy O'Brien, whose 'Good evening listeners' was the preface to an hour of pure pleasure for many years.

Every town in Ireland should have a chronicler like Aileen, because there is so much we easily forget. It's not just the great names, the famous old buildings, that we need to remember. All too often we bury the memories we're ashamed of.

The other day I listened to a man called John Griffin on Rodney Rice's *Saturday View* programme. He recounted his time in the Baltimore Fisheries School, one of the institutions under investigation by the Laffoy Commission. His story, of cruelty almost beyond description, and the dignity with which he recounted it, made me cry. His was one of too many stories yet to be told, largely because the Government that set up the Laffoy

Commission stopped caring about it the minute it was established, and left it to the tender mercies of a bureaucracy whose instinct is always self-preservation.

The absence of any political drive behind the Laffoy Commission – a fault almost certainly going to be repeated in the case of its successor under Judge Ryan – ought to be a source of shame to the Government and the minister involved. The value of the work already undertaken by Judge Laffoy is there to be seen in her third interim report. Dealing with the institution in which John Griffin's childhood was stolen from him, she has this to say:

Experience of life in Baltimore School ... was so harsh and deprived by the standards of today as to verge on the unbelievable ... the large dirty dormitories; the poor quality beds with flea infested and urine saturated mattresses and bedding; the refectory, which doubled as an oratory, and in which the drinking utensils ... ranged from cracked enamel mugs to pottery mugs to jam jars; the primitive and inadequate sanitary accommodation which included outside dry closets; the primitive and inadequate washroom which was serviced with hot water if a cart load of dry turf was to hand but not otherwise.

On bathing day the bath water was changed after five or six boys had bathed. There were no toothbrushes or toothpaste, combs, soaps or personal towels. The clothing and the bedding was verminous. There were outbreaks of scabies ... the pupils were not merely hungry, they were literally starving. They were compelled to supplement their diet by eating raw vegetables and vegetation — potatoes, turnips, mangolds, carrots and sorrel, by eating barnacles at the seashore and by scavenging, begging and stealing in the village of Baltimore.

> *... A picture emerged which is consistent with the presence in Baltimore School of a sexual predator, probably a homosexual paedophile, who systematically preyed on and sexually abused vulnerable children in a pervasive and indiscriminate manner, regularly and over a period of time; a perpetrator whose modus operandi was the inducement of fear and apprehension in the victim ...*

The Governors of Baltimore School during all this period of savagery (which lasted up to 1950, the year I was born) were the Bishop of Cork and Ross and the parish priest of Baltimore, and the school was subjected to regular inspections by Departmental Inspectors.

It is perhaps not surprising that the boys in this school, and others, were invisible in their communities, and forgotten for years. We didn't want to know – and maybe we still don't – because it is so hard to cope with the truth that we let it happen.

The abused boys and girls whom Laffoy was trying to help aren't, sadly, the only ones. A debate took place last week in the Dáil about another generation of forgotten people – the emigrants who left Ireland in their tens of thousands at around the same time, and many of whom are now living in poverty and misery in the UK and elsewhere.

Pat Rabbitte moved the motion, and my regret is that the powerful and emotional debate that followed didn't receive the attention it deserved. In his speech, the Labour Leader pointed out that between 1949 and 1989, well over 800,000 people were forced to leave Ireland (including 55,000 in 1955 alone). That's about a fifth of the present population of the State.

It has been estimated that those emigrants sent back

more than €3.5 billion in present values, and that their contribution was a mainstay of our struggling economy throughout some of the blackest years. We have given them almost nothing in return.

Among the speeches made in the debate was one by Emmet Stagg, one of the most powerful and honest I have ever heard in the Dáil. Here are just a few paragraphs:

I was born in 1944 into a family of fourteen children on a fifteen-acre farm in County Mayo, which was typical of families in the area at the time. Ten of the family emigrated. We had no running water, showers, toilets, or electricity and had a limited diet. Meat was seldom on the table. Tuberculosis was rampant. There was a savage school regime and unaffordable fees if one was to go to second-level school. Third-level education was for doctors' sons.

There was no option; a son or daughter had to emigrate. The first one to go was the hardest. A cardboard suitcase was purchased and all they brought with them were two shirts, some socks, working clothes, shoes and minor personal belongings. A going-away 'do' was held the night before. It was not called a party. It was more like a wake. I remember a succession of them. The next morning there was the leaving of the house, the hackney to the railway station, the tears and misery heaped on misery. The station in Claremorris was filled to capacity with other victims of the great Republic. There were more tears and heartbreak.

A sixteen- or seventeen-year-old raw green youth was dispatched into the unknown. A new and dreadful reality then dawned. That brother or sister was gone forever. A new form of death had entered into our being. A hole had been created in our family and community. Our small community of seven houses eventually emptied completely. Our great Republic forced them out in tens of thousands. They travelled in cattle boats, stayed in doss houses, queued in the early morning frost for a chance of a job and were paid in pubs. They laid the sewers, built the roads and houses, drove the buses and, as nurses, cared for the sick. Most came back when they could afford it. They all yearned for home.

The more we bury memory, the more we repeat our mistakes. And we're doing it still – instead of the €18 million needed to provide some sustenance to our forgotten emigrants this year, we're giving four. We've forgotten already.

Timmy
(2005)

The teachers knew that Timmy was supposed to be starting school, but they were too busy with the new intake of kids to notice that he never turned up. Not the first day, nor the second, nor the third. His mum had been to the school to enquire about what he needed, and she had seemed absolutely determined to bring Timmy herself. One of the teachers knew the family, and when she saw Timmy's mum on the street, she stopped her to ask why Timmy hadn't started.

That's when Timmy's mum started to cry. She couldn't send Timmy, she said. She hadn't the price of the uniform, and she couldn't afford new shoes for her son. And because the teacher was sympathetic, it all came out. She was being terrorised by a money lender. Ever since Timmy's dad had left, she just hadn't been able to keep up with the bills. The teacher knew that Timmy's mum loved him desperately and wanted nothing but the best for him. But she had passed the point of coping. And it's such a loss, because Timmy is bright. He seems to be bursting to learn.

Margaret, on the other hand, a little girl the same age as Timmy, hasn't spoken for two years. It's hard to say how intelligent she is, because even when she is encouraged to play, she does so silently. There's a sadness in her eyes that you should never see in a four-year-old.

Both of Margaret's parents are on methadone. The last four years, ever since Margaret was born, have been chaotic for them. They've done everything they can to quit the drugs to which they have both been addicted since they were sixteen. They were together then, and in its own way it's a small miracle that they're still together. Margaret is the glue. Although they can't really cope with their own lives, they never miss an appointment at Margaret's play group. They have both said they would willingly give her up if it was a way of guaranteeing a better life. But once, Margaret heard them saying that and became hysterical. The sadness in her eyes deepened from that moment on, and the staff in the play group are convinced that Margaret believes she is going to lose the only mum and dad she has ever known.

And there's a third kid. Robert, four, and already a problem child. He lives with his grandparents, along with three brothers and sisters. He never had a dad, and his mum is in and out of hospital. She suffers from chronic deep depression, and has several times tried to take her own life. The grandparents, already well into their sixties and living on a combined pension, do everything they can. But with four kids who need clothes and heating and school gear and lunches every day, it's harder and harder.

They simply don't know what to do with Robert. He's disconnected from the rest of the family, uses foul language that no four-year-old should ever have heard, and has regularly hit his two sisters. Recently, he tried to bite one of the other kids in the play group. There's no way the staff there are willing to give up on him, but they know he needs a lot of intensive, one-to-one help. They're doing their best to find it for him, but there's a very long waiting list and no guarantee it will be the right type of help.

Poverty is the thing that binds these children together. These are true stories, by the way, though none of the children's names are real. Poverty is the thing that puts them beyond the pale, that makes services hard to come by, that puts them at the end of every queue. Poverty excludes them. And they know they're excluded. They feel it. Even at four.

If I knew them all, I could tell 148,000 stories like these, some better maybe, some worse for sure. Because 148,000 children live in consistent poverty in Ireland. That's every seventh child we have.

We tend not to see it. It's hidden away from us, especially if we drive fast enough past the places where it is most concentrated. And many of us don't really experience it. We think of poverty as a thing of the past – and if we feel poor ourselves, it's only because the neighbours seem to have so much more. And if we do occasionally see poverty, we reckon there's someone to blame – a shiftless dad, a drug-addicted mum.

But here are two simple thoughts. Consistent poverty, the kind that affects every seventh child in Ireland today, means you're cold a lot of the time. It means you're hungry more often than not. It means you wash in cold water, and sometimes sit in the dark because the electricity has been turned off. It means you've been bullied, and could well turn into a bully yourself.

And the second thought. The causes of poverty are many and complex. Yes, not all parents are ideal (and not all parents got much of a chance themselves). But there are thousands of loving parents in Ireland who simply can't afford to give their children the basics we take for granted. Income supports are too small, and services are still too poor and inadequate. Despite all our wealth, we haven't got around to breaking the cycle of poverty. As a result, poverty and the exclusion, marginalisation and alienation that go with it are likely to be life sentences for a great many of the children who are poor now.

When we think about poverty in Africa, we understand it readily enough. And frequently we're moved by the size of the problem. Here, in our own place, perhaps it ought to be the shame of the problem that moves us.

Because we can fix this. We have the resources to ensure that every kid in Ireland gets the best possible start in life, whatever their circumstances. Yesterday, the Taoiseach launched an important programme in Tallaght aimed at breaking the cycle of poverty through early intervention and family support. Today, the organisation I work for, Barnardos, is launching a national campaign to highlight the fact that poverty really does exist for nearly 150,000 children in Ireland, and that it hurts.

We're doing it because we really believe that if we become aware of the issue, if it can be put on the political map, it's a solvable problem. And guess what? Solve the problem of child poverty and we'll be taking a giant step to bring down crime figures in the future, to bring down drug addiction figures, to end anti-social behaviour, and to reduce the amount of money we spend on treating mental health problems.

We have a saying in Barnardos – every childhood lasts a lifetime. A childhood of poverty, of the kind of poverty that excludes children from their peers, that makes them hate themselves and the world, leaves scars that in many cases never go away. Timmy, Margaret and Robert may carry those scars forever. And we could fix that. Not overnight, maybe, but in a reasonable time. Wouldn't it be worth trying?

Fixing Ferns
(2005)

Here's a daft idea. Instead of building 300 kilometres of roads next year, let's build 280 instead. And use the money we save to make sure that nothing like the Ferns scandal can ever happen again. Let's make our kids safe.

Because we'd save an awful lot, not by stopping the roads building programme, but just by slowing it down a little. It costs about €4 million to build one kilometre of road. If we were to build 20 kilometres less a year, we could devote €80 million to ensuring that our kids never had to live alone with the fear of a sexual predator. Or live with the consequences of contact with one.

What could we do with €80 million, if we saved it this way (or any other)? What do we need to do?

First of all, we need to complete the investigations. We need to know in how many other dioceses there are still people hiding under the authority of the church. Not just diocesan clergy, either, but all of them, no matter what their order, no matter what their position. The church that has held such a central position in Irish life for so long needs to be cleaned up, once and for all.

Why they haven't done it themselves baffles me. Why does it have to be dragged out of them, inch by inch? Every one of our priests, many of them caring and compassionate men, have been damaged by the drip-drip of sensational and ugly revelation. The overwhelming desire to protect the institution, and to continue to exert control in the face of terrible abuse, has perhaps fatally undermined the moral authority with which they hope to continue to deliver their message.

Last week, I met Father Gerard McGinnity, the priest who reported serious concerns about Monsignor Michael Ledwith in Maynooth. He was doing exactly the right thing, and was one of the very few priests who did. He has been punished by his church ever since. Ledwith was believed at the time, although he has now been defrocked. The priest who told the truth about him, who behaved honourably towards the students in his care, was destroyed.

That can never be allowed to happen again. At least publicly, the signs are that the hierarchy are now willing to face up to their responsibilities in full. That must be measured and tested with a full and rigorous examination of the past, not just in the Dublin diocese, but throughout the country. If we don't come to terms with the past, then we'll repeat it over and over.

But the future matters too. The second thing on which we need to spend some money is a massive public awareness campaign. Children must be told, again and again, that they have nothing to be afraid of when they have a story they want to tell. They must be told that they're not alone. They must be told that the feelings they have, of fear and guilt and shame, are the same feelings that every other child has.

This is the real cruelty of the child abuser. Every child who is sexually abused is put into a state of terror first. The abuser always sets out to exert maximum power over the child he abuses, partly because there is additional gratification in that, and partly because it helps to keep the abuser safe. The breaking down of that power can only be achieved if every child knows that it is safe to tell what is happening to them. They must know that they will be believed, that they will be taken seriously, that they won't be interrogated, that they won't be forced to face their abuser and point the finger at him.

Public awareness is vital, and we need a massive television and advertising campaign aimed at putting children in a position of strength and confidence. But even that is not nearly enough. Education is another key part of the response.

We have programmes now in our schools. But they're not mandatory at primary level, and they're run on a shoestring at secondary level. Every school in Ireland, primary and post-primary, must have a dedicated, trained and professional teacher whose job it is to ensure that every child in that school knows how to protect themselves from unwanted advances, and how to approach people in authority when they need someone to talk to. Silence is the abuser's friend, and getting through the barrier of silence must become a core objective of our education system. That also means breaking down all the barriers that still exist around open and honest discussion about this topic.

We're very good at guidelines in this area. We've all been calling on the church to make sure their guidelines are in place, but we seem to have forgotten that the State as a whole believes that it is possible to protect our children with guidelines too.

The entire system of child protection in Ireland is built on guidelines. They might work if they were resourced. But there is plenty of evidence that the system of investigation and protection is stretched to breaking point, and has been for some years. We have to put a lot more resources into this area, within the health boards especially, if we are to put a real and sustainable culture of child protection in place. That too will cost money.

Finally, there is the issue of reporting. The Minister for Children, Brian Lenihan, said on television on Sunday that he wants to create a culture where there will always be reporting of abuse. But it is laws that create culture, and we must change the law now.

Right now in Ireland, if a teacher (say) has information in his or her possession about a murder, and that information would be useful to the police investigating the crime, and if the teacher keeps that information from the Gardaí, he or she could be charged with being an accessory to the murder. But if a teacher has information that could lead to the arrest of a serial abuser of children, and keeps that information from the relevant authorities, that can be seen as the exercise of appropriate discretion.

It makes no sense. We must have mandatory reporting of sex abuse if we are to protect children. Every professional who knows about a child being abused knows about other children at risk. Because people who abuse children don't stop at one. So there must be no dilemma about this. Mandatory reporting is the only way to ensure that information about sex abuse will be put into the hands of people trained to deal with that information. Mandatory reporting is the only way of ensuring that every case of suspected abuse is properly and independently investigated by people who can make informed judgements.

We cannot persuade children and young people that we are determined to protect them, that we will always believe them and take them seriously, if we then fail to act on what they tell us. If we really want to protect them, we have to act now. We know what the past was like. We can change the future.

Stephen
(2007)

I work with a remarkable woman. I won't tell you her name, because it might help to reveal the identity of the boy she told us about at a function the other night. But she has spent all her working life working with boys like this. And she, like all her colleagues, never gives up on them. This is Stephen's story, as she told it. Stephen isn't his real name, but his story is true in every other respect.

Stephen lives with his parents and older brothers in a council house on a sprawling housing estate. The roads have no names, and numbers have been removed from doors in order to confuse the police when they come in search of stolen cars. Crime is high in the area, with many of the neighbours serving prison sentences for drug dealing, weapons possession and theft.

Stephen's parents have never done time. But they're young, unemployed and untrained. They live on social welfare, disability and child benefit. Stephen's dad has had a few jobs, but he never manages to hold them long. When employers find out about his depression and dependence on street drugs, they change their minds about him. There is a year's rent arrears on the house, but the street drug dealers get priority when debts have to be paid. They always get paid first.

Every morning when Stephen arrives at playschool, his head is lowered and his eyes are fixed on the bowls of cereal, all ready on the table. His body is rigid with tension. As soon as he reaches the table, he pours milk into a bowl until it overflows, then starts to eat rapidly with one hand while gathering cereal from other bowls with the other. He curses at anyone who comes near him or complains that he has taken their cereal. While he's eating, he can lash out at anyone who comes too close. Sometimes he complains of a pain in his tummy, but it usually subsides after he has eaten several bowls of cereal.

After breakfast he finds his favourite toys, and likes to have a grown-up near him while he plays. But they must use a soft voice, as any loud noise makes him angry and agitated.

Stephen appears well dressed. His clothes fit and are warm enough for the cold spell. His hair is naturally curly and is kept short. It is only when one sits close to him that you can see the head lice moving on his scalp. He scratches constantly and is clearly annoyed that the scratching doesn't stop the itch. Close up too it is possible to smell Stephen's unclean clothes and skin. But gradually Stephen responds to the story a grown-up is reading. When he lifts his head you can see the dark circles under his eyes from late nights. He never smiles.

Stephen's day improves after breakfast. He likes to play with the sand, driving trucks through sandcastles. He tolerates the company of grown-ups but as yet has no interest in the other children. He's jealous of toys that any of the others show an interest in, and on his sadder days he'll hit any child who steps close. On better days Stephen's vivid imagination and advanced verbal skills are obvious. He sings, rhymes, listens to stories and makes up his own. Those days are rare, but wonderful.

Sometimes Stephen tells stories from home. He tells a grown-up when he has seen his mum cry or witnessed his dad hitting her. He tells stories about his dad's drinking and sleeping all day long. He confides, sometimes, about how scared he can be. But he always asks the grown-up not to tell his mum what he has said.

Through it all, he loves his mum and dad. But that doesn't stop him sometimes getting tearful when the bus goes up his road to bring him home. At home, he spends most of the time in his room with his brothers, because they have been bullied on the street, so they're kept indoors. They are all pale from lack of fresh air and nutritious food. They virtually live on cereal and bread, to the point where they find it hard to digest other food, and they're often sick with vomiting and diarrhoea.

Stephen's home is one of thousands. There are sweet shops and a pub within walking distance, and a field where stray dogs run. There's broken glass there too, hundreds of empty beer and cider cans, and hypodermic syringes. Situated two miles from Stephen's house is a large shopping centre. Among other things, it has a cinema and a McDonald's. Stephen has never been in either.

My colleague works with Stephen as often as she can. She will never give up trying to help, trying to give him the skills and the confidence to break out of the cycle of poverty and put his undoubted talents to use. Just as Stephen is one of thousands of children who live in poverty in Ireland, my colleague is one of hundreds who work, day in and day out, with children like Stephen.

My colleagues are part of what is sometimes

sneeringly referred to as 'the poverty industry'. But they don't mind that – the sneers are water off a duck's back to them. The only thing they care about is breaking through the vicious circle, and trying to help kids make it against the odds.

The only time they get upset is if it proves to be impossible to reach what's inside every one of those kids.

And of course the poverty industry is made up of a number of agencies, charities, non-governmental organisations – call them what you like – all of which have the same aim. The aim of ensuring that this rich country doesn't forever ignore and forget its most vulnerable citizens. They all deserve support, perhaps at this time of year more than any other.

Stephen and his family are citizens of Ireland. But they're weighed down by the stress of trying to cope in a world that doesn't understand them. As my colleague put it, they are held under a blanket of poverty, unemployment, addiction, mental illness and lack of education and parenting skills. Stephen too is enfolded in this blanket. He is a bright, creative, funny child whose sadness and anger overshadow his every gesture and every word. The poverty of his home has damaged his innocence and his spirit. Although those who work with him are determined to ensure it doesn't happen, that damage may be indelible.

I'm telling you this story, I suppose, because of the time of year it is. There's a lot of Stephens out there, and a lot of organisations working with them. For many of them, Christmas Day will be just as bleak as any other day of the year. In whatever way we can, we're trying to ensure that isn't so, just as all the other organisations, agencies and charities are trying their best too.

Stephen has lived a pretty full life already. He's seen and experienced a lot. Enough to make him distrustful, cynical, angry. Enough, maybe, to cause long-term damage.

And Stephen, by the way, is five.

An Ugly State
(2007)

In a democracy, there is no uglier spectacle than the power of the State being used against its own citizens. In fact, it's not even compatible with the notion of democracy. Only totalitarian states operate as if the interests of the State were more important than the needs of the people. Of course, in any democracy, the State is often involved in making choices, and frequently difficult ones.

The common good demands that the State gets involved in arbitrating or mediating between different interests, and that always involves winners and losers. In a democracy, the winners will often, though not always, be the more vulnerable. In a totalitarian state, the powerful will always win.

We have seen two examples in the past week where the power and influence of our State were deployed to make sure vulnerable people lost.

In one situation, people who have been sexually abused by teachers have been denied any form of redress by the State and threatened with financial ruin if they seek to take a case. In the other, families of autistic children have been told that a State which has historically under-provided for their children's needs still knows best and will allocate only what the State considers appropriate.

Every teacher is a public servant. Their salaries are paid by the State; their conditions of employment are set by the State. It is not possible to pay a teacher more or less, or treat a teacher better or worse, than in the conditions laid down by the State. But much more important than that, every teacher provides a public service, perhaps the most important and long-lasting public service there is.

They don't save lives, of course, but they form them. For better or worse, they influence the course of young people's lives, often forever. A good teacher will often be counted among the most important influences that most of us can remember.

They do all this on behalf of the State. The investment made by the State in education is critical to the development of a society and an economy. Decisions made by the State over generations in relation to education are among the most formative and influential possible – in years to come, for instance, historians will trace the foundations of the Celtic Tiger right back to the decision to introduce free second-level education.

But a bad teacher can destroy lives. A teacher who uses the authority and control their position gives them to abuse children can, and does, leave scars that never heal. The man who abused Louise O'Keeffe in Dunderrow National School, near Kinsale, was a public servant employed for the specific purpose of helping to shape her young life and equip her for the future. His name was Leo Hickey, not just any teacher, but the principal of the school.

And the State has no responsibility for this public servant.

The State has argued successfully in the courts that it did not employ Hickey and cannot be regarded as liable for the actions that devastated the lives of Louise O'Keeffe and others. Instead, Hickey was hired by the local school, through whatever structure was in place at the time. The courts may be prepared to accept this legal technicality, but it is a fiction. Anyone who is involved in a school board, at whatever level, knows it is not possible to buy a pencil for the school, never mind hire a teacher, without ultimately accounting to the State for it. Every penny spent by a school must be reported annually and nothing of any substance can be spent without the permission of the State.

But then, having won its case against Louise O'Keeffe, having established in the eyes of the law that it was not liable to her, the State set about punishing her for daring to suggest it had some responsibility for the terrible things a public servant had done to her.

The State is now pursuing her for costs amounting to €500,000 and has threatened every individual it knows who has been similarly abused that they, too, will be punished if they seek redress.

This is the State that has apologised to people who have been abused in religious-run institutions largely funded and inspected by the State. This is the State that has insisted on paying the lion's share of the necessary redress to the people who were abused because, in the Taoiseach's words, the State didn't want to bankrupt the religious orders. This is the State that has failed to take any action against politicians who have defrauded taxpayers of millions and broken half a dozen laws. This is the State that has paid out tens of millions to soldiers who have lost hearing as a result of their employment. This is the State that has wasted hundreds of millions on vanity capital projects.

The State may have law on its side in the case of Louise O'Keeffe and other people who have suffered gross abuse at the hands of public servants, but there is no justice in this action, and no morality.

The State may not care about people who have been abused in school, but it still knows best about how to meet the needs of its most vulnerable citizens. So it has argued, successfully, in the courts against the family of Seán Ó Cuanacháin. Seán is six, and has autism. If the State is awarded costs in this case and pursues them, his parents' search for a proper education for their son may cost them their home.

I'm not going to go into the rights and wrongs of different forms of education for autistic children here. The one thing that is absolutely indisputable about the development of young people with autism is this: early intervention is essential, and education must be intensive and geared to their specific individual needs. If that doesn't happen, the prospect of good development is hugely diminished. And it didn't happen, and won't happen, in Seán's case because the State has decided it doesn't want to guarantee it. The State knows best what's good for Seán.

It doesn't matter that in our constitution 'the State acknowledges that the primary and natural educator of the child is the family'. All that means, it seems, is that families can provide whatever education they can afford themselves. If they believe they can rely on the State to listen to them about their children's needs, they should forget it. It might tell you in the constitution that you know best what your child needs, but that's tough. The State will decide what's appropriate.

Many families of young people with autism were hoping this time it would be different.

But the very fact that the State was prepared to drag this family through sixty-eight days in the High Court should have told us all we need to know. The State has argued in the past that its responsibility for education should only extend to those whom the State regards as educable. Clearly, that mindset has not changed.

We need to be angry. But the behaviour and mindset behind these cases should make us more than angry. We should be afraid of a State that acts this way.

Welcome to the Republic

It Could All End in Tears
(1999)

Half a million people, all willing to invest hard-earned money to play their part in the future of Telecom Éireann. Banks willing to take a risk so customers can make that investment. Who knew there was such unbounded patriotism in Ireland, such willingness to sacrifice in the national interest?

If only! The Telecom flotation has nothing to do with the future of the company. It has nothing to do with the national interest. It is nothing more than a transfer – a present – from national resources to the middle classes. People with a bit of disposable income, or a willing bank manager, are putting themselves in the way of adding a few bob to what they have already.

They're backing a racing certainty, just exactly the same as if they had a hot tip at the Curragh. If the bet works, the vast majority of people with shares will off-load them at the first possible opportunity. The institutions – the Dutch insurance companies, the Arab banks – will end up owning Telecom in the end.

There's nothing wrong with that, from the perspective of the punter. But there's an awful lot wrong with it from the point of view of Ireland.

First of all, the whole thing has been based on bogus

messages. The ads beamed at us day after day, cajoling us to play our part in the future of Telecom, are as cynical an exercise in manipulation as I've ever seen. It would have been vulgar, of course, for those ads to have featured a spiv whispering behind his hand to the audience. 'Roll up, roll up, for the chance of a lifetime. Valuable company going cheap, and loans available. Buy a bit, and sell it on quick – you can't lose. And you don't have to worry about what happens in the end. Get out quick and spend your winnings!' Tacky, but true.

Second, we were being urged to go out and buy something we already owned – a company in which Irish taxpayers have invested hundreds of millions of pounds. That investment is what has made this company such an attractive punt. It has turned Telecom into a genuine national asset, one of the most modern and sophisticated telecommunications companies in the world. The fact that Telecom has been able to hold onto most of its market share in the face of the most intensive competition is testament to that – and another reason why major financial institutions should be willing to take your shareholding off your hands at a premium.

Third, the main reason why this bet is almost bound to be a sure thing is that Telecom is being sold cheap. The best efforts of highly qualified advisers are being bent to ensuring that the starting price of shares is fixed at a level that's guaranteed to go up. Good news for the punter, that – but if it works, it will mean that taxpayers are subsidising punters. I can't think of a good reason why taxpayers should be willing to forego a dividend that could help to strengthen and transform our infrastructure into the future. But there you are – punters, it seems, matter most.

Fourth, writers in this newspaper have already pointed out who the real winners in this will be. Bank managers, whatever their sterling qualities, have never been known as philanthropists. The fact that they have been falling over themselves to dish out money to customers to buy these shares surely tells us something about the banks' vested interests.

I have a long enough memory to recall the way AIB treated this State during the ICC crisis in the mid-1980s. Their privileged position in the Telecom flotation seems inappropriate recompense.

The one thing we can be sure of, of course, is that there weren't too many bank managers entertaining poor or unemployed customers – the kind of customers who could well benefit from the bonus that will come from a successful flotation. In this mid-summer bargain sale, you have to have a decent income before you're welcome in the shop.

Fifth, of course, there's any number of ways in which this could go wrong. Shares can fluctuate, the radio ads say (you'd have to have very keen eyesight indeed to see the same message on the TV ads). What happens if these shares don't take off?

It's going to be deeply embarrassing for the Government if there isn't a good premium – and don't be at all surprised if there isn't a mass middle-class movement demanding compensation for lost profits.

But more important, a flotation that doesn't work as predicted will not only place a cloud over Telecom's immediate and medium-term future. It will also put a spoke in the wheel of all of the Government's future privatisation plans.

None of this is an argument against privatisation per

se – even though I have my own views on that. It may well
be that this Government has a coherent philosophy aimed
at turning middle Ireland into a share-owning society. I
doubt it – I reckon that when they looked at the options
for securing the privatisation of Telecom, they simply
went for the one that they believed would be most
popular.

But this Government certainly has privatisation on its
mind. Aer Rianta, the ESB, ACC, ICC and the TSB are all
on the block. The manner in which the privatisation of
Telecom has been conducted will raise demands for
similar opportunities for punting when the next
companies are ready – but with far less likelihood of a
quick profit. The popular flotation of Telecom may well
become a rod with which the Government's back is
beaten.

And what of the rest? I have found it striking that
there hasn't been a peep from the opposition, especially
the left, about what's going on. One senior left-wing
politician said to me recently that it's a bit like Northern
Ireland – you might have your doubts about the course
that's being followed, but it doesn't seem wise or patriotic
to speak up.

There's another way of putting that, of course. We'll
keep quiet as long as it's popular. If it goes wrong, then
we'll start attacking the Government. I can envisage some
even joining in the chorus for compensation. But if you've
nothing to say when the going is tough, you don't deserve
to be listened to when the going gets a bit easier.

We need a debate about privatisation. I'm not saying
we need knee-jerk opposition, much as I'm tempted. But
we need to know why it's necessary. How the interests of
the whole community will be served by it. How resources

generated by it will be wisely applied in all our interests. How it guarantees the future viability of essential utilities and services. Who wins and who loses. How we can ensure that there's no corruption involved.

I hope the future holds fine for everyone who has borrowed money to invest in Telecom shares. And above all I hope they repay the banks as soon as they get out – otherwise tears are guaranteed to follow the champagne. But this is no way for a country to develop its long-term future.

The Luddites We Trust with Our Lives
(1999)

Militants. Luddites. People implacably, and unreasonably, opposed to change. That's those bloody train drivers for you.

I've met those train drivers. In fact, I know a number of them very well. I've met a few militants in my time too. And train drivers are neither radicals nor militants. You won't find a more decent bunch of men anywhere. They have the railway in their blood, and they care passionately about the traditions of rail.

So why are they always being painted as trouble-makers, constantly being harassed and vilified? And why is it happening when profits on the railway have increased by 150%? The publication in the last couple of days of CIE's Annual Report makes it clear that rail is making something of a comeback. After generations of neglect by successive Governments, the railways are beginning to be seen as part of the solution to some of the more pressing problems created by rapid economic growth. Problems like dense traffic, longer and longer commuting times, rapidly escalating house prices in the suburbs – any attempt to deal with these issues will include, somewhere along the line, the development of a modern and sophisticated rail service.

That will include a core of professional, well-trained, flexible train drivers, capable of taking responsibility for the safety and comfort of hundreds of passengers, dealing with every contingency that arises.

And some contingencies are more dramatic than others. About one in every three train drivers, at some time in his career, has witnessed a suicide. And there can be no more horrible way to witness a suicide than to be the driver of the train that is used by the victim. Many of the drivers who have been involved in such incidents have been deeply traumatised by them – in some cases for years afterwards.

Naturally, you'd expect that a company which has to deal with tragedy like this on a regular basis (and it's very regular) would have a counselling service to which drivers could turn. You'd be wrong. The driver who is involved, as an innocent participant, in the suicide of another person is on his own. If he needs help and support, he gets it from his own colleagues – nowhere else.

Most train drivers seem to earn around £26,000 a year. A modest enough salary for what they do. But that's only half the story. In fact, the basic pay of a train driver is around £14,000 a year – about £270 a week. That's what they get for a 40-hour week, and it's the only element of their pay that's pensionable. At the end of a lifetime of service, the highest pension to which a train driver can aspire is £54 a week.

So how do they earn nearly double their basic salaries, on average? By working nearly double the hours the rest of us work, that's how. That includes every Saturday and most Sundays. It includes rosters which can take them on and off duty at any hour of the day or night. I've seen rosters which allow drivers no more than three or four Sundays off a year.

Tough, you might think, but that's life. Think about this. You're sitting comfortably on the 7.30 a.m. train from Dublin to Cork, reading your *Examiner* and watching the countryside whizz by. Would you feel quite as comfortable knowing that the man driving that train had been on duty since 1.30 in the morning, after maybe four or five hours' sleep, and had already worked three trains while you were in your bed? It happens – and a lot more than you'd think.

And what's even worse, in the drive to get profits up further, the management of the railways wants to make it happen more often. Some of the elements of the package that these 'Luddite' train drivers are resisting include the following elements.

It's proposed to do away with all the overtime arrangements, and bring their salaries up to a figure of around £25,000 a year. Of that, only about £17,000 (at best) will be pensionable. I don't know of any other category of public service workers who have pensions calculated on only a proportion of their regular weekly wages, but that's what train drivers are supposed to accept.

In return, they will be expected to work up to a 48-hour week without overtime, and within incredibly complex rosters that will never allow them to plan family weekends or any kind of decent time off.

As further steps in the development of a modern and sophisticated rail service, and as a fundamental part of the changes they are looking for, management are also determined to increase the number of miles a train driver can travel. There are experts in rail safety who believe that any journey longer than 200 miles is dangerous without a change of driver. Irish Rail wants drivers to agree that they can manage total mileage of more than 400.

They are also reducing the training period. For years it has been recognised that the proper training period for drivers is 72 weeks – not a lot, you might think, given the increasing complexity of the machinery, the risks associated with more and more traffic, and the over-riding importance of safety. Now, apparently, Irish Rail management thinks that 48 weeks is enough to equip a school-leaver to take responsibility for a fast-moving locomotive with 300 passengers.

It doesn't surprise me in the least that changes like these have led to massive resistance among train drivers, and to splits among the unions representing them. What does surprise me is how easy it is to dismiss these concerns as some kind of old-fashioned and greedy resistance to change.

I have a lot of admiration for the management of CIÉ and especially for Michael MacDonnell, the group chief executive. He is a committed public servant, dedicated to a transport service which fulfils all its economic and social functions. He took on a hard job when he went to CIÉ and he devotes most of his waking hours to it – and he has succeeded, to a considerable extent, in instilling a new respect for the operations of the company.

But I wish he'd take a long hard look at what's happening every day in Irish Rail. I believe it's not too much to say that there's a danger of safety being compromised in the interests of more profit, and that simply isn't acceptable.

What's even less acceptable, in my view, is the way train drivers are being scapegoated. A very heavy-handed approach, in industrial relations and public relations terms, has been used to paint them as backward. They're hard-working men, with families, who are fed up to the back teeth with the way they have been treated.

The next time the trains are stopped on a Sunday, and you can't get to the football or hurling match you've been dying to see, don't just blame the drivers. They have been driven to the only recourse they have, because their management refuses to treat them as partners in the change that's undoubtedly needed. Divide and conquer is no longer a basis for intelligent industrial relations – except, it seems, in Irish Rail.

Surely Not Again
(1999)

There's a lot we need to discuss. Lots of areas in which it would be helpful to see all the options laid out. Dispassionately, fairly, accurately. How we can distribute tax more effectively. How we can substantiate rights in a wealthier society. How we can deal with critical environmental challenges. How we should address the issue of immigration.

We could use a Green Paper in all these areas – and a lot more. A Green Paper is supposed to set out options and choices. It's supposed to analyse the issues. Above all, it's supposed to stimulate discussion and debate.

Publishing a Green Paper is not leadership, for that reason. It can be a tool of leadership – it's a foolish leader, after all, who completely ignores the mood of his troops when making decisions. There will be no decisions in a Green Paper – the decisions follow the debate, and are usually contained in a White Paper. The decisions in the White Paper may slavishly follow the mood – or they may challenge it.

So when the Government lets it be known that it's going to publish a Green Paper on abortion, it's safe to assume that there will be no decisions in it. Only choices, to be debated and discussed. The Government will make its decisions later.

But by publishing the Green Paper, they're starting a process. And it's just as safe to assume that the process will have only one end – another referendum. What question will be put in that referendum? I'll tell you – it will be the question posed by whoever the Government is most afraid of. Whoever shouts the loudest, or whoever strikes the most fear into the hearts of some vulnerable or independent TDs.

The question I want to ask about this is why? Who really believes we need another detailed debate about abortion?

The pro-life movement doesn't – the last thing they want is open debate. They want decisions and they want them now. And the pro-choice movement, though smaller and less vocal, doesn't want debate either.

I should say where I'm coming from in this argument (if I don't, the usual anonymous letter-writers will pigeon-hole me anyway). Throughout all my involvement in politics, I've been troubled by the issue.

I've never been able to see it in black-and-white terms. I wouldn't find it easy to advocate termination of pregnancy in any readily available way.

But I know this for certain. I have four daughters. If any of them ever had a crisis in her life, and needed my help in carrying out whatever careful decision she made, there's no Government in the world that would prevent me offering them any help I could. If they ever had to decide there was only one recourse for them, I would want them to know above all that their parents will be there to help.

Of course I would want them to think long and hard,

to look for and accept professional counselling and advice. The one thing I *wouldn't* want is for them to be forced to look at the explicit anti-abortion propaganda that apparently constituted part of the 'counselling' offered by the agency at the centre of this week's High Court judgement about improper abortion procedures. I can think of nothing more hateful than to expose troubled and vulnerable young people to that sort of stuff.

I might as well make another confession as well. My attitude to this issue over the years has been heavily influenced by the tactics of some elements of the so-called pro-life movement. I've never got more evil correspondence from anyone, nor heard more strident personal abuse from anyone, than I have heard from some of the extremists of that point of view. It has become clear to me over the years that there is no lie they're not prepared to tell, no tactic they're not prepared to stoop to, no level of intimidation beneath them.

They practice the politics of fear and hate – the easiest, and the worst, politics of all – and I would never want to be on the same side of any argument as they are.

But the bottom line has to be that there is no black-and-white answer to this issue. Everyone in politics knows that – and I suspect a huge majority of the Irish people know it. We used to think it was simple, but life taught us all that if you make a blanket rule, you end up doing immense human damage.

Thus, we (the people) thought in our wisdom that we had solved the problem in 1983, by equating the life of the unborn with the life of the mother. We learned soon enough that that simple formula, literally applied, could put young girls and women at enormous risk.

The Supreme Court interpreted the equation differently,

as we all know, and arrived at the conclusion that any risk to the life of a mother – including the risk of suicide – gave the mother the absolute, unfettered right to end her pregnancy.

In effect, that judgement gave women a right that can never be exercised in a jurisdiction where no abortion services are available. We dealt with that, as a people (we thought), by deciding in a further referendum in 1992 to give women the absolute right to travel for abortion, and all the information necessary to enable them to secure legal abortions. We decided, as a people, in the same referendum, to leave the Constitutional reference to equality between the mother and the unborn alone.

So the abortion referendum now to be foisted on us again, if it happens, will be the *fifth* time the people have been asked to decide – already once in 1983, and three separate questions in 1992. As a people, we have developed a view, and put it in the fundamental law of the State. It may not be a perfect view – it may even be entirely cynical – but no one can say that the Irish people have not considered this issue carefully, and dealt with it in their way.

So why are we being asked to tear ourselves apart over this again? Only one reason: the so-called pro-life movement hasn't yet got the answer it wants. And a cynical Government is sufficiently afraid of them to subject the rest of us to another bitter and divisive debate, which will either lead to no solution or an immensely cruel one.

I don't know the perfect answer. I believe that the right thing to do at this stage is to put the Supreme Court judgement in the X Case into law, and to provide for legal terminations in Ireland in properly regulated circumstances. But I can't find it in me to argue that we should any of us be prepared to go to the stake for that solution in this imperfect world.

The one thing I'm certain of is this. If the so-called pro-life movement finally get their way this time, the country I love will be a sour, bitter place, incapable of attracting the allegiance of thousands of people like me. This time, if never again, we have to shout louder than them.

The White Man's Burden
(2000)

Since the foundation of the State, Ireland has run a very effective immigration policy. It has been all the more effective because it's not written down anywhere. It's not based on legislation or statute; no one person is politically accountable for the policy; and best of all, it's operated in secret.

The policy has three main ingredients. They are never stated explicitly, but they are the three driving elements of an approach that has stood the test of time. The ingredients are these.

First, immigration is a matter of national security. It's not an issue of humanitarian concern, economic imperative, or international obligation. It's about protecting our borders. That has the delightful consequence that everyone involved in operating the policy can assume wide powers, and they are almost entirely unaccountable. They don't have to explain, don't have to apologise. They don't even have to tell. That means they can be as arbitrary as they like.

A couple of years ago, I got a phone call from a Scandinavian woman. She was married to a Dublin man, had lived and worked here for twenty years, ran a successful business employing more than twenty people, and had three children, all born in Ireland. And she was about to be deported. For no reason other than that her work permit had expired, and some entirely anonymous official had decided she had been here long enough. Her deportation would be entirely unconstitutional, because it would mean the break-up of her family. That didn't seem to bother the people in what was then called (I wonder is it still?) the aliens section in the Department of Justice. They weren't accountable, and didn't have to give any reasons.

One phone call to the then minister's office put an end to that particular piece of nonsense, but I often wondered afterwards how many other people had been harassed in that way. People who have impunity to harass others always – this is a rule of nature – end up abusing their power.

The second ingredient of this tried and tested policy is that it is designed to ensure that no one ever enters Ireland who might conceivably at any time in the future end up as a drain on the State. That risk, naturally, applies to everyone – so everyone who wants to come here, no matter what their skill or profession, is suspect.

And the third ingredient – the most successful of all in terms of its visibly measurable impact – is that the primary purpose of the policy is to keep Ireland white. We may deny it to our heart's content, but we have run an explicit policy of ethnic cleansing in Ireland for more than seventy years. We've done it in secret, and we have cloaked it in verbiage – but that has been our primary goal.

And by and large, it has been a case of mission accomplished. Ireland is ethnically pure. And of course, because we have never set it out as an explicit goal of policy, we can claim to be liberal and welcoming, notwithstanding.

But now we have been found out. It has become clear that the Irish State recognises only two kinds of 'aliens' when they land at our shores – refugees and illegals. Every other civilised country in the Western world recognises a third category – legal immigrants. But not us. If you can't prove that you're going to be tortured or killed when you return home – if all you can prove is that you're going to be poor there, but could make a living and a contribution here – then our message is: 'Home you go. We'll keep you here for a while – we won't let you work, mind you – but we'll let you live in an agony of suspense until, inevitably, we pack you and your children off home anyway.'

This is an easy enough policy to change. The real issue though is that the policy, operated so effectively for so long, has left us with a legacy of xenophobia and intolerance. This is expressed in a variety of ways. The most benign of them is the simplistic belief that if we keep sending money to the developing world, that somehow absolves us from our responsibilities.

Then we have the 'urban legends' that are now springing up around the issue of immigration. Every immigrant who lands in Ireland is entitled to a mobile phone. Immigrants are given a £2,000 grant to buy a car. Taxi drivers are making a fortune by picking up families in Larne and dumping them in the middle of Dublin. This nonsense is now so pervasive that people who should know better are routinely peddling it.

The more pernicious rumour-mongering would have it that it isn't possible to get a Corporation flat, or a job, because immigrants have taken them all. We have to wonder how long it will be, in this climate, before someone gets beaten up or killed because of the colour of their skin.

The political system is paralysed in the face of all this. There are several reasons. Some politicians see self-interest in pandering to it. Some are afraid of being deemed illiberal if they spell out a rational policy too clearly. Only a few are involved in trying to form and lead a debate. I would include Liz O'Donnell, Ruairi Quinn, Brendan Howlin, Gay and Jim Mitchell among that number. There are others too – but so far, courage has not been sufficiently matched by coherence. I wonder is there a case here for a cross-party selection of TDs to come together, even on an ad hoc basis, and try to agree a common position?

Because the truth is that nobody could better Liz O'Donnell's description of her own Government's approach as a shambles. Some days they're hoping the problem will just go away, others they're pandering to fear and ignorance, and others they're proposing off-the-shelf solutions. We need solutions – and we need to start from the point of accepting that it's not illiberal, or racist, to suggest that proper solutions will always include some element of control.

Above all we need to define, and establish, the category of legal refugee. We need to establish reasonable conditions, on the basis of which people can apply for visas to enable them to come and work and live here. Those conditions can, without being unfair to anyone, quite properly include the kind of information on which a reasonable judgement can be made that the intending immigrant has a reasonable prospect of making his or her own way here.

We all know that you can't land in America or Australia or Canada and demand entry and the right to work. You have to apply in advance, and satisfy their authorities that you have a reasonable prospect of being needed. That's not unreasonable.

What is unreasonable is the system that forces everyone to lie. People claim asylum and refugee status here only because there is nothing else they can do. I would have no problem with a system that turned people down for visas because they failed to meet reasonable criteria. We all ought to have serious problems with the system that rejects people because they fail to satisfy impossible criteria.

Anyone for Cheltenham?
(2003)

You're probably familiar with the Horse and Greyhound Racing Bill of 2001, I suppose. You're not? You haven't studied it and used it as a model for the management of your own finances? I can't believe it – sure that Bill is a perfect example of how things could be done. And should be done, if only everyone had the wit and imagination of the two principal authors of that dynamic piece of legislation.

Well, I suppose I can't blame you if you're not up to speed. Although it was a really revolutionary piece of legislation, it kind of snuck through the Dáil. The debate was full of witty remarks and congratulatory references to Istabraq, Ted and Ruby Walsh, and other legends of the turf. There was no real dissent anywhere in the house, from either left or right.

Which is a bit odd, considering the ground that bill was breaking. It did two things really, neither of which seemed that exceptional on the face of it. It set up a body called Horse Racing Ireland, which would in future deal largely with the administration of horse racing in Ireland. And it set up a thing called the 'Horse and Greyhound Racing Fund' for the purpose of giving support to horse and greyhound racing.

No big deal there, you might think. This fund, and the Bill that underpinned it, was the brainchild of two people – first the Minister for Finance, Charlie McCreevy, a keen racing buff anxious to see the industry placed on a sound footing (the tax-free status applied to many forms of livestock income by Charles J Haughey isn't enough, apparently). He was ably supported by his colleague Joe Walsh, also a man to be found at race meetings throughout the country (and abroad, indeed, if his national duty of supporting the industry requires him to make that sacrifice).

But what was to be in the fund? These are tough times, after all. We must cut our cloth to suit our measure. Mustn't we?

Well, no. That only applies if you're in a queue for health care, or if you have a learning disability. Under the racing legislation, every penny collected in betting tax is ploughed straight back into the sport.

Isn't that great? A guaranteed income. Except there's a problem. The betting tax yield is going down. People are betting on the internet now, because you can avoid tax that way. In order to protect the betting industry here, Governments have to reduce the rate of tax they will apply. So that will reduce the amount of tax revenue coming in, and therefore that will reduce the amount they will be able to give the industry. So what seemed like a great idea mightn't work after all.

But Charlie and Joe had a solution. They picked the amount of money that was raised in 2000 – about £46 million – and they put a formula in place which would guarantee either the amount of tax raised each year, or £46 million increased by the rate of inflation – whichever was the larger. As Joe said in the Dáil debate at the time,

'We need to keep the latter as a guarantee, as for obvious reasons connected to potentially fast-moving changes in the off-course betting market, the rate of Excise Duty on betting may, at any time in the future, have to be adjusted downward from the current 5 per cent in order to maintain our competitiveness.'

So what the Dáil was asked to do by these two gentlemen of the turf was to earmark every penny raised in betting tax and plough it back into the industry. And just in case not enough was raised, the Dáil was asked to pass a law which guaranteed the money anyway. If the betting tax didn't cover it, the Exchequer would pay the balance. The only restriction on the money would be that after about €250 million was spent on horse and greyhound racing, the minister of the day would have to put a regulation before the Dáil (they're normally nodded through) to keep it going.

It's not that easy to find out how much the industry got last year. Although the legislation says it should be accounted for by the Department of Agriculture, it has actually been transferred to the Department of Arts, Sport and Tourism. If you look at the Book of Estimates for that department, you'll find it all right: €46.35 million in current spending and €21.58 million in capital, making a total of almost exactly €68 million. Next year (the year of cutbacks everywhere, remember?), the current spending is planned to increase to €55.63 million (that's an increase of exactly 20 per cent) although the capital projects won't be on the same scale. There will only be €8 million in capital.

And do you know the really good news about all this? Well, the really good news is that they were able to raise the prize money this year. Total prize money for the year was €46 million, an increase of 11 per cent over last year in National Hunt racing and an increase of just over per cent on the flat.

Lo and behold – the exact amount of taxpayers' money they were given, they gave out in prizes. And who did they give the prizes to? How many impoverished, disabled, elderly, poor and infirm horse-race owners and trainers benefited? How many people on the very margins of our society were able to live their lives with a little bit more dignity as a result of all that prize money?

JP MacManus was one of them. John Magnier was another. And there were many, many more. Thank goodness our money is dedicated by law to such needing and deserving causes.

Why am I telling you all this? Is it because I'm a begrudger who thinks the racing industry shouldn't be supported? No, it isn't. I don't object to the support, because the industry is good for Ireland. It employs thousands of people, and attracts thousands of visitors here. No, I want you to know about the degree to which we support horse racing for this reason.

It proves that we can afford to do the things we feel we should. It proves that we can afford to make choices.

And it proves that the people who tell us otherwise are cheating us, day in and day out.

I could have given you other examples. In the last couple of years, Charlie McCreevy has put massive tax incentives in place to support the so-called SSIAs. It's costing hundreds of millions a year. He has put massive tax breaks into the law of the land for people who want to build private luxury hospitals, or student accommodation, or car parks where people can leave their cars to get on buses.

We can afford to do all that – and lots, lots more – because he and Bertie Ahern tell us we can. But we can't afford €25 million a year to give people with severe and profound disabilities some basic human dignity. And to give their parents some hope. Telling us we can't afford that is the greatest political lie we have ever been told.

Born in a Stable Doesn't Make You an Ass
(2004)

So, this referendum on citizenship. Its only purpose is to bring us into line with every other European country, right? And that's because Europe wants a common set of rules about citizenship, ok? And in the process, we're going to do away with an abuse that has hundreds of people claiming Irish citizenship who have no connection with the country apart from an accident of birth, isn't that it? And we need to do that because the maternity hospitals are being over-run by all these non-nationals, and the senior staff of the hospitals have pleaded with the Government to change the law? And the whole issue has nothing to do with immigration, right? There's no racist intent behind it, and no possibility of a racist outcome, isn't that clear?

No. No. No. No. No. They're the answers to all those questions. There is no common set of rules in Europe. No one has ever suggested there should be. If there is abuse at any level of our existing system, no attempt has been made to establish it. And this referendum will allow an entirely new abuse to be created. Our maternity hospitals are not being over-run, and their staff have never asked for the law to be changed. And as for racist intent, the truth is that this referendum will go ahead, assuming the

Government forces it through the Dáil, for one reason and one reason only. To enable Fianna Fáil candidates in the local elections to say that they're doing something about immigration, and no one else is. The things that will be said on the doorsteps will play to people's fear about a complex and sensitive issue, and an all-out effort will be made to make this issue seem more pressing and important than all the other issues people will raise.

Here's an extract from a leaflet already doing the rounds of one of the Dublin constituencies. (I won't name the Fianna Fáil candidate for now, in case she has genuinely misunderstood the issues involved.) But if this is what they are prepared to put in print, I'll leave it to your own imagination to guess what will be whispered at the doors.

> *Concern continues to be expressed about the number of Asylum Seekers and Refugees entering this country as a result of our economic prosperity and this issues represents a challenge for us all. Asylum applications must be processed in compliance with international obligations. I believe that Fianna Fáil has a comprehensive understanding of the issues and that it is taking measures both legislative and administrative to deal with this matter efficiently.*
>
> *I reject the 'open door' policy which is advocated by the parties of the left and accept that all states need effective laws to deal with entry, residence and departure of non-nationals in the interests of the well-being of society. I warmly welcome the Minister for Justice's recent announcement of the Government's intention to hold a referendum on the right to citizenship for all persons born on the Island of Ireland and the right of residence for their parents.*

This referendum has nothing to do with rights of residence of parents. There is no party in Ireland, left or otherwise, that advocates an open door policy on immigration. But you see how easily they link the issue of citizenship and the issue of immigration. You see how easy it is to brand anyone who is against the change on citizenship as being in favour of opening the flood gates of immigration.

But still they deny there is any racist intent behind this referendum. The Minister for Justice gets violently angry if anyone suggests there is. Yet still, on the *Sunday Supplement* on Today FM on Sunday, he was unable to provide any figures at all for the number of late-pregnancy arrivals in Ireland. He gave global figures for the number of babies born in Ireland to parents who are non-national, but was unable to say how many of those parents are living and working in Ireland in perfectly ordinary circumstances.

And in the middle of all his other figures, he managed to drop in the assertion that 787 babies were born in Irish hospitals last year to Nigerian parents. He offered no figures as to the number of American, Canadian, French, Australian or British babies born in Ireland last year – only Nigerian (or black, if you want to use another term). And no figures about the number of those Nigerian parents who are living and working here perfectly legally. And he gets huffy when people suggest there is inherent racism, and certainly political cynicism, behind this proposal.

What are we really concerned about where immigration is concerned? Are we really terrified of being over-run by people with different skin colour, different languages and religions, different habits and culture? Are we really convinced, despite all the evidence to the contrary, that they get rights we don't?

Last year, 2003, our population increased by around 62,000. Net immigration (the difference people arriving and people leaving) contributed less than half that, with the balance being made up by newborn babies (Irish ones!). The total number of immigrants – people arriving in Ireland – was just around 50,000.

But guess what? 17,500 of them were Irish people coming home. 7,000 were from Britain, 7,000 were from the rest of the EU, and nearly 2,000 were from America. The rest was made up of New Zealanders, Australians, Canadians, and a scattering of people from most countries of the world. Some were here as students, many as health workers, some as managers. Some are seeking asylum.

Altogether, the Central Statistics Office estimates that around 4,000 people emigrated to Ireland from countries in central and eastern Europe, and about 3,500 from countries in Africa. About half of all our immigrants last year were under the age of twenty-four. On the basis of our existing law – without making any change whatever – only a tiny proportion of all these immigrants (apart from the returning Irish) will ever qualify for citizenship unless they pass all the naturalisation tests we already have.

At the risk of boring you to death with figures, let me give you one final one. We are talking about 7,500 people coming to Ireland last year, out of a total population of 3,980,000. You can work out the percentages for yourself. And they are running shops, garages, restaurants, working in our hospitals, as everything from doctors and nurses to nightwatchmen. A few, no doubt, are up to no good – but there are a few (let's say) Irish citizens about whom we could say the same thing.

In short, there's nothing to worry about here. Sure, immigration can cause problems and difficulties for various public services. Over time, we adapt to that as we adapt to everything else. And sure, we need to keep an eye on it so things don't get too stretched.

But do we need to change our Constitution, to send a coded signal to the rest of the world that a country that has been saved in the past by emigration is going to be harsher than anyone else on immigration? Only a truly miserable government would ask us to do that.

Guantanamo, Ireland
(2007)

Last week I wrote here about a Government proposal to introduce a network of detention centres for asylum seekers. This week I'm perplexed. Why do we need a network of detention centres? We already have them. To all intents and purposes, we are already incarcerating anyone who comes to Ireland seeking refuge. We put them in places that we don't call detention centres, and we leave them there, sometimes for years.

What we actually call these places is direct provision accommodation centres. I went to look at one of them during the week, and I have to say I left the place shaking with rage. The notion that we could treat families this way, and still call ourselves civilised, leaves me baffled.

I'll describe what I saw in a minute. First of all, this is what the Department of Justice has to say about them. That Department published an annual report last year, and you can search it from top to bottom without finding any description of how an accommodation centre is run, what it's like to live in one, how human and family rights are protected, how sanity is maintained. If you search hard enough on the Department's website you'll find a value for money report that explains how further 'efficiencies' can be generated in the treatment of asylum seekers.

There is a helpful link on the Department's website that brings you to the home of the Reception and Integration Agency, the government agency charged with the welfare of all asylum seekers. In a variety of different languages on their site (www.ria.gov.ie), they set out the rules for anyone seeking refuge here:

Your photograph and fingerprints will be taken when you lodge your application.

When your application for a declaration as a refugee has been lodged, you will be given accommodation in a reception centre in Dublin ... for an initial period of ten to fourteen days.

You will then be relocated under the 'Dispersal Scheme' to an accommodation centre outside of Dublin. There are currently fifty-eight such accommodation centres throughout Ireland and you will not be given any choice with regard to the location of the centre to which you are dispersed. You may have to share your bedroom with other asylum seekers.

You will be expected to remain in the accommodation centre to which you are dispersed ... You may only move from this accommodation with the permission of the Reception and Integration Agency ...

Your accommodation will be full board, i.e. bed, breakfast, lunch and dinner.

As your accommodation will be full board, the only income you will receive from the State shall be a personal allowance of €19.10 per week and, if you have children and they are accompanying you, €9.60 per week for each child ...

You will not be allowed to seek or enter employment while your application for refugee status is being processed.

You will not be allowed to carry on any business,

trade or profession while your application is being processed.

You will not be entitled to third-level education or to vocational training while your application is being processed.

There are more such rules. In fact, the entire asylum process goes on for page after page. If you want to apply, you'd better be familiar with the rules. It will never be enough that you fit the definition of an asylum seeker (and you're going to have a hell of a job persuading anyone in the system that you do, given the rejection rates).

That means you have to be willing to go where you're sent and stay there, live on the paltry income you're given, eat what's provided for you, and take your place in the queue for all sorts of essential health and welfare services. Try to improve yourself through learning, and you've broken a fundamental rule. Try to augment your income and you've broken the rules. Stay out overnight, get drunk once in a while, try to cook some of the food you're used to at home, and you've broken the rules. In short, if you want to seek asylum here, you must be willing to enter a prison.

I told you earlier I went to see one of these centres last week. I didn't know we had fifty-eight of them in Ireland, did you? I knew about Mosney, and one or two others. But there are no signposts to any of these places. They're not on bus routes, or in the heart of any of our towns. They're all located in places where a blind eye can be turned to them.

I won't tell you where this particular centre was, because I don't want to stigmatise anyone. They know I was there anyway, because the uniformed security guard

at the gate demanded my identity and purpose. I refused
to tell him what I was doing there other than that I
wanted to see it, and handed him my business card. I
thought at first he was going to refuse me entry, but he
seemed to think better of it and let me through after he
had taken down the registration number of my car. For
some reason, it seems, not only must asylum seekers be
discouraged from coming and going, so must any Irish
citizen with an interest.

It's hard to describe this place. Imagine a caravan
park, entirely surfaced in concrete, with about 150
smallish and identical mobile homes lined up in fifteen
rows of ten. They're no more than about twenty feet
apart from each other, and there's nothing between them
but concrete. No grass, no garden furniture, no
playground or swings, no clotheslines. Absolutely
nothing but one mobile home after another. Each mobile
home is capable of accommodating a small living area
which must function as sitting room, dining room and
kitchen, a bathroom and two tiny bedrooms.

The entire area was spotless. Spotless and barren. I
don't know whether the people who lived there took
responsibility for the cleanliness, or the numerous
security guards who were patrolling while I was there. I
can just imagine it being shown off as a showcase, it was
so clean and tidy.

One hundred and fifty of these tiny mobile homes
accommodate up to three hundred families. The rule that
says you may have to share your bedroom with other
asylum seekers is literally, and liberally, applied. There is
no family privacy, no comfort, nowhere to allow your
children to play, nowhere to sit and talk. And many of the
families there have been there for years, the euphoria of

initially arriving in Ireland long since replaced by despair, depression, and a pervading sense of hopelessness and alienation. No community exists there. Just people in jail.

We, the people of Ireland, own these places. Our money built them. But like so much else we don't want to take responsibility for, we've 'contracted out' the management of these centres to the private sector. Although I can't yet be 100 per cent certain, I have reason to believe that the 'manager' of the place I went to see is the person who runs the security contract. Wouldn't that just say it all?

Where's the CEO?
(2007)

A civilised society should have a good health service, able to make its sick people better and to treat them with respect and dignity. That's why I've never begrudged whatever proportion of my PAYE goes into our health service. Over the years I've had a lot of professional experience of the dedicated people who manage the system, and they are totally committed to the health and well-being of the people of Ireland. I've no fault to find with them, though I have huge sympathy with the size of the task they have.

And in addition, throughout my adult life, I've invested year after year in maintaining my status as a VHI subscriber. That too I've always regarded as a good investment – not because I'm interested in jumping queues, because I'm not, but because it's another way of contributing to the development of a health service that really works hard for all of us.

In my innocence, I've always assumed that because we have made, and are making, this investment, we have created a working safety net. If you're sick, you can turn to the health service. They'll make you better. And the VHI will help in that process. Together, the health service and the insurance will function as a sort of one-stop shop

– you place yourself in their hands, and a team will click into place to sort you out.

The irony in all this is that I've never personally needed either the health service, or my VHI membership, until now. I've watched and supported others who needed access to care, and my family as a whole has had plenty of reason to be grateful to both the availability of a national care system and the VHI. But until a month ago, I had no personal reason to question what is going on within the system.

Now, I have a question I want to ask, and it's this. What in God's name is going on?

Let me explain. You may remember I moaned a few weeks ago about a back pain. Well, it never went away. In fact, it got worse to the point where my local general practitioner, who had put up with me manfully for long enough, decided I needed tests. And here's where I made my first discovery. There's nowhere you can go for tests.

Well, that's not entirely true. If you've buckets of cash or loads of insurance, or don't believe in the national health system anyway, you can probably ring one of the super-duper private clinics on the south side of Dublin (a bit tough if you live anywhere else, of course) and book yourself in.

But if you just want to go into a hospital, owned and paid for out of your taxes, you can't. You can't go in the front door of a hospital and ask to be admitted – that's just for visitors.

If you or your doctor thinks you might be sick but isn't sure, there's only one way in – through Accident and Emergency. So your doctor gives you a letter (it's like the first day at school), and you go to the A&E department of, in my case, a major teaching hospital. And there you take your place with people who are wounded or bleeding, and clearly in a worse way than you are yourself, and hope to God someone notices you.

I was lucky, or maybe I picked a quiet day. Within eight hours I had been seen by first a nurse, then a doctor, then another nurse to take lots of blood out of my arm, then the doctor again to conduct (in a very charming way) a variety of unpleasant examinations, then a series of X-rays, then more discussion with the doctor in charge.

Within the eight hours there was a lot of waiting time, so I explored the hospital. Half of it is old, half new, but it's well designed and laid out. It's particularly well sign-posted. At every corner you can find directions to almost anywhere within the hospital, and to almost any function.

Except one, I discovered. There's no sign-post anywhere to the chief executive's office, although I'd be ready to bet that such a large organisation as a modern teaching hospital couldn't function without a chief executive. When, overcome by curiosity, I asked at one of the reception desks where the CEO's office was, I was politely asked, 'Why do you need to know that?'

Anyway, all the blood tests, X-rays and physical examinations proved one thing – I needed some more tests. That's when the system really began to test my sanity.

The doctor with whom I had dealt throughout the day explained to me that I would need, ideally, a CT scan and an MRI scan. If I was in an immediate life-threatening situation, that could be arranged within the hospital, but since I wasn't, and especially since I was a VHI subscriber, it couldn't.

At least not without a delay of months (unless in the

meantime I descended into a life-threatening situation, of course). In the meantime I'd be doing everyone a favour by using my VHI to purchase the additional tests elsewhere – namely, in the super-duper private clinics I hadn't wanted to go to in the first place.

But I went to them – yes, to two of them. That's because it turned out, when I went looking for appointments, that my VHI would cover a CT scan in one of the clinics, but not an MRI, and an MRI in the other clinic, but not a CT. (If you can follow all this, you're probably not sick enough to need the tests in the first place!) Beautiful places, both clinics, and lovely staff, and all the tests completed in a few days.

The good news is that ultimately, the tests revealed that there's no specific reason I shouldn't be still writing this column in thirty years' time (at least, dear Editor, I hope that's good news!). The other good news is that we have a health system that is staffed from top to bottom by good and professional people, who treated me exceptionally well and courteously.

But why isn't it possible to go to one place – preferably a place we (the taxpayers) own and have built – to get your tests and to get better? Nobody will give you a reason – it's just the way it is.

The truth, though, is that political decisions of the last few years, presided over by our current Taoiseach and Minister for Health, have been geared to ensuring that the drift is towards 'competition' (although it's so artificial it's unreal) and the free market in health.

Right now, the whole thing is about the public sector existing to enable the private sector to be as profitable as possible. And the key mechanism for ensuring profitability is to offer people the choice between waiting in pain or paying (over and above their taxes) for relief. That's not what its managers want – it's what the politicians want. And a health service that is increasingly geared towards the generation of profit for some of the players is not our health service any more. It's about time we took it back.

Ireland's Pride –
Ireland's Shame

Avoiding Prohibitive Expense
(2000)

The Government keeps telling us to look at the big picture – forget the sleaze and look at the achievements. Right, let's do it. And forgive me for getting on my own hobby horse, because I want to look at the big picture from the perspective of people with a mental handicap.

There is a range of rights in the Constitution – equality before the law (we've all seen how that can be applied), the right of private property (a big one that) and so on. Only one right exists that could be called social or economic – the right to a free primary education.

Only one group of people in Ireland has to battle through the courts to get access to this right – people with a mental handicap. There is no record of anyone with a mental handicap ever losing such an action. But that does not prevent the State from forcing them and their families into the courts on a daily basis.

That makes them unique. No one has ever had to challenge the failure of the State to make provision for a child's education on grounds of sex, nationality, colour, or any other grounds. (Imagine the outcry if they did have to!) The main argument advanced by the State, in many cases involving people with a mental handicap, is that the person concerned is ineducable. Another argument sometimes put forward is that the resources required to offer an education to a person with a mental handicap would be so considerable as to make it impractical – in other words, a waste of money.

There are a number of cases still awaiting judgement in front of the courts on this issue. On past record, the State will lose every one of them it doesn't settle. But the cases will go on, because nobody in Government seems able to shout stop.

Apart from that one positive right, the other main right that people with a disability (including mental handicap, but also the entire range of other disabilities) have is the right to be protected from discrimination. This right is not in the Constitution, but in law.

All are supposed to be protected by the two main pieces of legislation which are intended to outlaw discrimination in general – the Employment Equality Act (which deals with discrimination in employment) and the Equal Status Act (which deals with discrimination in the provision of services).

In both these acts, discrimination is supposed to be illegal if it happens on the grounds of gender, disability, sexual orientation, race, membership of the Traveller community, religious beliefs, age, marital status, family status or victimisation.

But there is a specific clause in both acts in relation to disability. Where disability is an issue, both acts say that employers or people providing services must make reasonable efforts to meet the needs of people with disabilities – unless it costs more than a nominal amount to make those efforts. No discrimination can be alleged if there is any issue of costs involved.

This issue of nominal cost is unique to people with a

disability. No one could claim, for instance, that the cost of providing, say, a women's toilet should entitle them to discriminate against women. The word 'nominal' has no legal meaning in this context – the dictionary definition of a nominal sum of money is 'virtually nothing'.

The reason this clause is there, and the reason it applies only to people with disabilities, is because when the first of these acts, the Employment Equality Act, was passed, it was referred to the Supreme Court by President Robinson for a test of its constitutionality, because there was an issue in the Act about possible discrimination against teachers arising from the religious ethos of schools.

The Supreme Court found nothing wrong with the sections referring to teachers and ethos, but it struck the Act down anyway. The main reason advanced by the court was that in imposing an obligation on employers to make special provision for people with disabilities, and in placing a potential financial burden on employers, the Act could interfere with the property rights of employers!

The consequence of this bizarre judgement was that the Government of the day decided to water down the protection afforded to people with disabilities under that Act, and the subsequent Equal Status Act, to ensure that no challenge could be made by anyone whose property rights might be infringed by having to make 'reasonable accommodation' for people with disabilities.

The tragedy of this is that it effectively deprives people with disabilities of recourse to the Equality Authority, which was set up by the legislation to replace older agencies, and given a very wide remit. The Authority can, for example, institute legal proceedings on behalf of anyone who claims to have been discriminated against under any of the grounds in the Act.

As can be seen, however, it is almost impossible to establish discrimination against a person with a disability if there is any cost involved.

Instead, people with a disability have to rely on the toothless National Disability Authority, a body established by this Government with no powers whatsoever to provide redress for people who are struggling with an uncaring bureaucracy. The NDA is chaired by the chief executive of a service-providing agency, and staffed by former employees of the NRB – hardly a recipe for radical independence.

In summary, the result of this is that people with disabilities are treated differently again. Those with a mental handicap have to go to law to assert their one constitutional right – none of them can rely on the law if they are discriminated against.

Sure, the Celtic Tiger has made a bit more money available for services. A couple of weeks ago the Taoiseach launched a 'major initiative' aimed at bringing people with disabilities into the mainstream of Irish life. But the law and the courts conspire on a daily basis to ensure that they are kept on the margins. Apart from the single constitutional right already referred to, which is frequently disputed by the State, and the watered-down protection from discrimination described in law, people with disabilities have no other legal rights.

When the Department of Finance was asked to agree that people with disabilities generally should have a legal right to a professional assessment of their condition and the needs that sprang from it, this was their answer:

The Department of Finance cannot accept these recommendations which imply the underpinning by law of access to and provision of services for people with disabilities as a right. This right, if given a statutory basis, would be prohibitively expensive for the Exchequer and could lead to requests from other persons seeking access to health and other services without regard to the eventual cost of providing these services.

This statement appears in the report of a Government working party drawn up to monitor progress on the implementation of the *Report of the Status of People with Disabilities*. It's the nearest we have to official policy in relation to positive rights.

That's the big picture for people with disabilities generally. Cosmetics, and a few bob here and there from the rich man's table. But equal citizens of a republic? God bless our innocence.

Keep the Blank Cheque, Minister
(2001)

Siobhán and Brendan are the real names of a married couple I know. I won't use their surname. They had a small but successful business, a nice house, and a happy, normal family. Then Brendan went into hospital for a routine operation, a treatment that shouldn't have caused any difficulty or major risk.

It went wrong, and Brendan came home, eventually, with many of the capacities of a child. He had been cared for after his operation in hospital, and then in rehabilitation. But now, severely brain damaged, he was his wife's responsibility.

And hers alone.

So she coped for as long as she could. Lifting, changing, feeding, minding, exercising this sixteen-stone bewildered man. Dealing with his outbursts, his pitiable attempts to help himself, his bottomless sorrow at what had happened to him. And while she coped with him, the business went, and they became dependent on the goodwill and charity of the State.

Eventually, when she was herself almost broken, Brendan was admitted to a brain injury unit where he could get the full-time care she had been supplying on her own. And now, because she no longer had to care for him, the State took away her carer's allowance. Because she was still married to him, determined to remain so, they would not give her a lone parent allowance.

So Siobhán works wherever she can to support her children. She doesn't complain – in fact she's the sort of woman who would instinctively want to cheer you up. She has been through hell, while her husband lives in a sort of limbo.

And she has had no one to speak up for her.

This all happened to Siobhán and Brendan over the last couple of years – it is only in the last few months that he was admitted to the unit he lives in now. It happened to them in one of the richest countries in the world.

Brendan has a disability. It has taken away far more than his life or his livelihood. It has taken away most of the rights he enjoyed as a citizen of Ireland. There was a time when Brendan had plenty of people willing to speak up for him. As a businessman, an employer, a taxpayer, a leader in his residents association, he was never short of support.

Until he really needed it. That's when Brendan and Siobhán discovered the difference between the rights of a citizen and the dependency of a person with a disability.

In this, of course, they have something in common with Jamie Sinnott. He has been defined by the Supreme Court, effectively, as too old to be educated but too young to be awarded his own damages. Brendan lives in an often remote and strange world, with the boundaries drawn by his condition. As if Jamie Sinnott hadn't enough boundaries, the Supreme Court decided to add a few more.

Jamie Sinnott, of course, had his mother to speak up for him. But who did she have?

That is really the question confronted by people with

disabilities and their families year in, year out. Things happen, all the time. There's no one watching, though there should be. And the net effect of a lot of those things is that the situation of people with disabilities gets worse and worse.

Because they have no rights – especially not the right to have someone speak up for them.

The most offensive thing that has happened to people with disabilities in the recent past was not the Supreme Court judgment, bad as that was. The most offensive thing was Dr Michael Woods saying he had more or less a blank cheque to look after them.

Rattle the tin outside the church gate and Michael Woods will fill it to the brim. He won't recall the Dáil. He won't even discuss legislative responses. But he will do whatever it takes to 'look after' people who only want the dignity of being heard in their own right.

People with disabilities and their families don't actually want to bankrupt the State. In a lot of cases, they want to make a contribution they are debarred from making. But there is a fear in the system that if they are given any statutory right at all, they will use that to drain the resources of the State away.

But just look at some of the things the State is capable of. And these things all happened within the last couple of years.

Before Nice, without consulting us at all, our Government argued trenchantly against a proposed Charter of Fundamental Rights and Freedoms, which the European Commission wanted to include in the Nice Treaty. Article 26 of that Charter says, 'The Union recognises and respects the right of persons with disabilities to benefit from measures designed to ensure their independence, social and occupational integration and participation in the life of the community.'

In the Finance Act, the Government introduced a new tax break, without any debate or discussion, which will have the effect of subsidising private practice for educational psychologists and speech therapists. These are two professions in which there is a nationally recognised and critical shortage, which makes life far more difficult for people with disabilities. As a result of the direct actions of the Government – and again, no one was consulted – the shortages in both professions will grow, and the waiting lists for their services will lengthen. That means there are people whose chances of speaking or communicating, or being properly assessed, have simply disappeared.

The Government has appointed hundreds of resource teachers to help improve the education prospects for people with disabilities. Every one of those teachers is what they call 'whole-time temporary'. Nobody's educational needs for the next five or ten years can be planned on that basis, because at the first puff of a wind of recession, those jobs will disappear without trace.

The Government couldn't do any of that, nor allow the other cruelties in the system, if people with disabilities had a legal right to an assessment and to the services that flow from that assessment. Everyone associated with disability knows that even those who are receiving services are getting the services that providers decide on. In very very few cases are services determined by need. In the vast majority of cases, they are determined by resources.

All because there are no rights. All because there is no one to speak up.

In looking for a recall of the Dáil, people with disabilities and their families are saying that they want the Government to stop, right now, treating them as charity cases. Stop promising to buy us off with your blank cheque. Stop patronising us, telling us that you know best. Stop the dependency. Stop the indignity.

People with disabilities overcome all the time. They do it by climbing barriers – a lot of which we put in place. And they are making only one demand now. Stop admiring our struggle. Stop patting us on the head. Join the struggle. Help tear down some of the barriers we have to climb.

That's all. It's inconceivable, isn't it, that the Government will continue to turn a blind eye to that demand? Isn't it?

Mary and the Compo Culture
(2002)

Katherine Sinnott went to the courts last July and she obtained compensation for the fact that Jamie did not have an assessment of needs when he was a child, did not have access to services throughout the years. I believe that we would be far better off for the future with the Jamie Sinnotts in this world to give them an assessment of needs and proper access to services rather than compensating them twenty-four years later because they didn't get it. And that's the difference between the compensation route and the enforcement route. We want compliance without compensation to ensure that we change Ireland.

I wonder did anyone else sit bolt upright when they heard Mary Wallace, the self-styled Minister for Disabilities, say all of that on *Morning Ireland* last Wednesday. Did anyone nearly get sick with disgust? Was anyone shocked and astonished that a minister could stoop so low?

Several times in the course of the interview, Mary Wallace referred to the compensation route. Several times she referred to her objective as being the noble (if difficult) one of changing Ireland.

The meaning and innuendo were clear. Mary Wallace wants to change Ireland, others want compensation.

She should be forced to resign. And before she is, she should be forced to apologise for the disgusting and untrue impression she tried to create. She should be forced to apologise to Katherine Sinnott in particular, and to the disability movement in general.

She was utterly wrong even on the basic facts – but that didn't seem to matter. What mattered was the need to cover up the complete, total and contemptible mess she has made of the Disability Bill. And in setting out to cover her tracks, she offered a gratuitous insult to a woman whose shoes she isn't fit to tie, and tried to insinuate that the only difference between her and the disability movement is that people with disability are only interested in compo.

Colin McNab isn't looking for compensation. He is four, autistic, and needs help. He and his parents have spent four weeks in the High Court trying to get an education. Four weeks! Can you imagine what that will cost if they lose? And the State has fought this four-year old and his parents every inch of the way. They have even now persuaded the judge in the case to rule that the Government's own Task Force on Autism Report must be treated as hearsay – because the Government has refused to publish it! And this shower expects us to believe that they want to change Ireland!

As a matter of simple and well-known record, Kathy Sinnott didn't go to the courts last July and obtain compensation for anything. She went to the courts (the Supreme Court, to be specific) because the State dragged her there. Not only that, but the State demanded that the Supreme Court should take compensation off Kathy Sinnott, and the Supreme Court complied.

Kathy Sinnott never went to any court to look for

compensation. After years of trying and failing to get her son the basic constitutional right of an education, she went to the High Court to try to enforce his rights. She did so at enormous personal cost and risk to herself. She won, and in the process established a new interpretation of what public policy should be in relation to the education of people with learning disabilities. She, and the High Court, gave the families of people with learning disabilities hope that they wouldn't have to fight any more to get their children the education to which they were entitled.

And the State decided they couldn't wear that. They appealed, and dragged a brave woman to the Supreme Court to have that interpretation overturned. They told the Supreme Court that it would cost the State millions and millions if the State had to be obliged to give an education to people over the age of eighteen. And the Supreme Court, which now contains members who believe that our Constitution was written to regulate an economy rather than civilise a society, agreed with the State.

Kathy Sinnott wasn't alone in a number of respects. I don't know of any parent who has ever gone to court looking for compensation because their child was deprived of a service – and I will bet Mary Wallace can't name one either. I know hundreds of parents who have fought for years through all sorts of bureaucratic obstacles to try and get essential services for their children – ranging from a basic education down to such things as incontinence pads.

Kathy Sinnott also wasn't alone because the outcome of her case galvanised hundreds, if not thousands, of other families. The gross injustice of her situation and the callous way in which she was treated by her own Government outraged the entire community, and raised the anger of the media throughout the country.

In fact, the outcome of Kathy's case created such a dynamic that the Minister for Education was forced to publish a detailed set of promises – enhanced measures, he called them – to try to calm the storm. His promises included seventy additional psychologists, the establishment of a group of senior officers, the setting up of an independent and autonomous National Council for Special Education, the holding of a Special Needs Education Forum, and especially the publication of a Disabilities (Education and Training) Bill. Although not one of those promises has been kept (naturally), it did calm the storm for a while.

But people with a disability have decided they are not going to be walked over any more. And when, finally, Mary Wallace did publish the general Disability Bill – the one she says will change Ireland – people with disabilities read it. They read it carefully in all its legalese, even though she didn't bother publishing an explanatory memorandum with it. And they realised that far from changing Ireland, it will change nothing.

There is nothing in this Bill – nothing – except a copper-fastening of old attitudes, a message to public bodies everywhere that they needn't worry too much about the rights or needs of people with disabilities. Page after page of the Bill drips with contempt for them. The Bill is riddled with opt-out clauses, with provisions that make it clear that everything – everything – in the Bill is only enforceable if resources are available.

So people with disabilities, on one of the worst nights in Dublin for many a year, came to the Mansion House in their hundreds, overcoming obstacles far worse than the weather, and told the minister to stuff her Bill. In her insensitivity, she had made the biggest mistake of all – she had begun the process of possibly making disability an election issue. More sensible figures in Government clearly spotted the mess she had made, and forced her to climb down a bit – although not nearly enough.

And in the process, she further branded people with disabilities as compo-seekers, subliminally comparing them to chancers on the make. It would be laughable if it weren't so scurrilous. How could anyone vote for a Government likely to contain people like Mary Wallace?

Cheated Again
(2002)

The Government, unbelievably, has done it again. They've published an Education Disability Bill which is a transparent and contemptuous effort to yet again cheat people with disabilities. If you didn't see it with your own eyes, you wouldn't credit it.

This time it looks like they intend to ram the Bill through without any consultation whatever. If they get away with that, it will represent one of the longest strings of broken promises of any Government in recent history.

I wouldn't blame you if you found yourself bewildered by another row about another Disability Bill. Let me explain.

The Government and the Minister for Education Dr Michael Woods were rightly under huge pressure after the Sinnott judgement in the Supreme Court. We won't go into all that in detail again. Suffice it to say that the court, at the request of the Government, put sharp limits on the only constitutional right people with a disability thought they had, the right to an education.

There was public outrage about it, and about the fact that the Government had dragged Kathy and Jamie Sinnott into the courts in the first place. In order to assuage public anger, the Government promised, finally, that they would produce two bits of legislation. One was intended to deal with the rights of people with disabilities throughout most of their lives, the other was to deal with the rights of people with a disability in that part of their lives they spend in education.

We know what happened to the first bit of legislation. It was so bad that if enacted it would actually have made the situation of people with disabilities worse rather than better. The disability movement rose up in disgust and forced the Government back to the drawing board. Everyone in the disability movement knew that if that Bill was put into law, it would be many years before any Government would address the issue of their rights again.

The reaction of an angry movement, which knew immediately when it was being conned, may be the reason why Dr Woods is trying to sneak this new Bill through before anyone finds out about it. It was put into the Senate Office late on Monday night by the Government Whip in the Senate, Donie Cassidy. Despite an angry reaction from all the opposition groups and independents, none of whom had seen it before, it was rammed through over Tuesday and Wednesday, and can now go straight to the Dáil.

This is an outrageous way to treat people with disabilities, and it's an outrageous way to treat the Dáil and Seanad. The only reason they are doing it is a try-on – to try to position the Government so they can add people with disabilities to the list of those for whom this Government has delivered. It won't be true.

What makes it even more dishonest is two things – the background and the Education Disability Bill itself. Only last Friday, Dr Woods told the media he was publishing the Bill in 'white paper' form because 'he wanted to press ahead without delay with consultation and enactment'.

This must be the consultation he promised on 2 August last year when he announced that 'the Government has also approved [his] proposal to establish a Special Needs Education Forum which will be convened during September. The Forum will provide a valuable mechanism for groups, organisations and individuals to contribute to the elements which will make up the State's comprehensive response to the needs of people with disabilities. Full details of the Special Needs Education Forum will be announced in due course and interested parties will be invited to participate. The proceedings of the Forum will help to inform the drafting of the new Disabilities (Education and Training) Bill.'

That Forum never happened. It didn't stop Dr Woods from promising it again (no date this time!) in a press release at the end of September. When asked about the promised consultation in the Dáil in October, he announced that 'arrangements to hold the special needs education forum are proceeding in my Department. My objective is that the forum should take place in early November 2001. The discussion at the forum will be considered in the context of the debate on the Disabilities (Education and Training) Bill which I hope to publish as soon as possible.'

Despite all these promises of consultation, the truth is that this education minister has in fact point-blank refused to meet any of the major bodies who represent people with disabilities.

But broken promises shouldn't be any surprise from Dr Woods. Among the other commitments he made after the Sinnott judgement, when he was on every branch of the media waving an 'open chequebook', was the recruitment of seventy additional psychologists to reduce the appalling waiting lists for assessment that every school in Ireland has to deal with.

As recently as last week he assured the Dáil several times in response to questions that 'the National Educational Psychological Service is expanding its service in a phased and orderly manner as additional psychologists are recruited. The Civil Service and Local Appointments Commission is currently organising a recruitment competition for additional psychologists in NEPS. This competition is now nearing completion ...'

But when I checked with the Civil Service Commission, what did I discover? Since the minister announced seventy more psychologists last August, not one extra person has been appointed. The Commission is now nearing the end of a competition that it has been asked by the Department to organise, for twenty additional psychologists. With any luck, they might be in place next September, leaving us fifty short of the minister's promise more than a year after he made it.

In this area, the minister has so far only kept one promise – and that's the Bill now being pushed through. Most people with disabilities will wish he hadn't. It's yet another con job.

It pretends to establish a new right to an appropriate education for children, whom it defines in an entirely arbitrary way as 'not less than 3 nor more than 18 years of age'. In fact, it qualifies their existing constitutional rights even further, depriving children and their parents of the kind of choices they have now. The Bill is full of what I call 'we know best-ery', the philosophy that has dominated the Department of Education's approach to this issue for as long as I can remember.

A couple of weeks ago, the Department of Education and its minister were spending tens of thousands of euro pursuing a High Court action which threatened to bankrupt the family of a four-year-old autistic boy, Colm McNab. Now they are ramming through legislation, and refusing all consultation in the process, to pigeon-hole the Colm McNabs of Ireland forever.

And naturally, although Dr Woods says grandly that this is a 'rights-based Bill', the Bill is riddled with get-out clauses when it comes to resources and money. It's another disability measure effectively written by the Department of Finance. In the eyes of this Government, rights are whatever they say they are, and whatever they say they can afford. Once again, people with disabilities are being cheated.

One Finger
(2003)

I love the Spire. Especially in daylight, its first sight, from O'Connell Bridge or Henry Street, can be breathtaking.

But more and more I think it could be most useful as a symbol of the Government that has ruled us through all the time the Spire was being conceived, designed and created. Increasingly when I see it, it reminds me of a single finger, upraised against the sky, telling the people of Dublin and of Ireland exactly what its Government thinks of them.

This is a Government that does more than raise the finger to the citizens of its republic. It turns a blind eye, and it speaks with a forked tongue. Those three characteristics might sound like clichés, but they are becoming more apparent by the day.

As you read this, the Government and some of its acolytes will be hosting a reception in the Mansion House. The Taoiseach, no less, will preside over the affair, which is designed to launch the 'European Year of Disabled Persons' in Ireland. Among the things he will announce will be a series of grants for projects that highlight the purposes of the year. (However, grants for capital projects, or which involve the employment of staff beyond 2003, won't be considered. So if you were

113

thinking of using the money to provide some much-needed service for people with disabilities in your area, sorry about that.)

We will all be encouraged to celebrate though, to remember that people with disabilities are among the most courageous, determined, and graceful citizens of our land.

And the most discriminated against.

You may have seen or heard about the independent report into conditions in Drumcar, one of the larger centres for people with severe intellectual disabilities in Ireland. These are very vulnerable citizens of our republic, and they are routinely restrained in straitjackets or locked in secure units, at serious risk to their lives. The people who run Drumcar, the John of God Fathers (who provide some of the best services in Ireland) commissioned the report that made these shocking revelations. They admit frankly that without resources, there is little they can do to improve the appalling conditions in which their patients are sometimes held.

Is that worth celebrating?

Drumcar isn't the only place. Much has been written about St Ita's Portrane over many years. Report after report, and Government promise after Government promise, has promised to do something about it. Money has been set aside, commitments have been given that it would no longer be used as an entirely inappropriate home for people who need shelter and support. But the money hasn't been spent, and as recently as the last couple of weeks more people were admitted there – a last resort, because there was nowhere else for them to go.

Is that worth celebrating?

Throughout the whole of 2002, the Government was

engaged in 'consultation' – seeking to devise a piece of legislation to replace the entirely discredited Disability Bill it tried to ram through before the election. All of those involved in the process are entirely agreed about what they want. They want the rights-based Bill the Government promised in its election manifestoes, they want enforcement of those rights, they want accountability and inspection of services. All these things were promised when the original Disability Bill was withdrawn. But guess what? They haven't been able to reach any sort of agreement yet.

Is that worth celebrating?

After the Jamie and Kathy Sinnott case, the then Minister for Education made a whole series of promises. You might even remember he talked about having an open chequebook. Structures were going to be radically changed. Psychologists were going to be employed, to finally get the National Educational Psychological Service up and running and to eliminate the shameful waiting lists for basic assessments. The bottlenecks that have led to incredible shortages of occupational therapists and speech therapists were going to be eliminated, by the simple (and entirely achievable) device of doubling the numbers in training. But I guess I don't need to tell you that hasn't happened either.

Is that worth celebrating?

Over the last couple of weeks, many organisations around the country have had to send out letters to countless parents of people with learning disabilities, telling them that 'because of the lack of funding there may not be a service available for your child from September'.

Could you imagine the uproar if the parents of children *without* learning disabilities got letters telling them that there wouldn't be educational or training places for their children this year? I often wonder why, when services for people with disabilities are threatened, it seldom makes the front pages of the papers. If similar threats were made against school services for children without learning disabilities, it would be all over the front pages of the papers.

But the arrival of those letters hasn't encouraged parents to celebrate.

Before the last Budget, the organisations representing people with learning disabilities made urgent, even frantic representations to the Government. On the basis of the Government's own figures, there are hundreds of people in dire need of residential care, of education and training, and of respite care. (Respite care means giving parents, often under extreme stress, a break.) The Government acknowledged the representations, and refused to allocate one extra penny in the Budget. Not one extra penny. When questioned in the Dáil on the matter, the Taoiseach, bless him, expressed sympathy and regret.

Is that worth celebrating?

So instead of celebrating, instead of joining the festivities in the Mansion House, parents will be protesting outside. They will be trying to make the point that disability is about barriers. People with disabilities aren't sick. They are people who have had barriers placed in their way. The only thing they ask of the rest of us is a bit of help to tear those barriers down.

Later this year, the Special Olympics World Games will be held in Dublin. It will demonstrate just what people with disabilities can do, and it will demonstrate it to the whole world. It will happen because of a gigantic effort by a lot of people. And it will happen because throughout our community, at corporate, community and individual level, people have said they want to help to tear down the barriers.

But in one of the richest countries in the world, our Government has decided to make an example of people with disabilities. That's why, for the first time in my memory, there wasn't a penny in the Budget for new places or services. The message was – if the Government was tough enough to ignore people with disabilities, despite the visible level of community support, they were tough enough for anything.

It wasn't even necessary – there is more than enough money to solve any problem we choose to solve. But that doesn't matter to this Government. And that's why parents have to protest rather than celebrate outside the Mansion House at 9.30 this morning. It's not too late to join them, and show solidarity with some fellow-citizens who are being elbowed aside.

And later, maybe, you could walk on down and have a look at the Spire. See what it reminds you of.

The Death of Peter McKenna
(2005)

When Peter McKenna died, he was alone, in terrible pain, and frightened. He didn't know what was happening to him, because he couldn't. He'd had a recent stroke. He was blind. And he couldn't communicate. The bottom half of his body was blackened as a result of blood poisoning. When he had arrived in Beaumont Hospital earlier that evening, they discovered that he was completely dehydrated. Those supposed to be caring for him hadn't even had the wit to see that he was in terrible thirst.

Peter was almost certainly going to die reasonably soon anyway. All his life he had had Down's Syndrome, and at the age of sixty he had been in the grip of Alzheimer's disease for a couple of years. The end of his life – a life that had been happy for all that – was near enough. But it could have been an end accomplished with dignity. In peace and comfort. It had none of those things.

Peter's family have lived with the circumstances of Peter's death ever since. I have talked to them again and again. In every conversation, there is one unspoken thought. Was it their fault? Could they have done more for Peter? What measure of guilt do they have to carry as a result of Peter's pain and distress?

The thought is theirs. It has never been mine. Nobody

118

could have done more for Peter than his family did. They fought to protect him, to achieve the highest standard of care for him. If they had been listened to, and treated with the respect they deserved, Peter would have died in peace.

Although, as I said, the thought of their guilt was unspoken in all our conversations, they finally expressed it on *Prime Time* last week. You might have seen the programme (at least I hope you did), the devastating exposé of conditions in Leas Cross Nursing Home. Dan and Mary, Peter's brother and sister, featured on the programme. And they both said the same thing. What must Peter have thought of us in his pain? Why did they abandon me?

They never abandoned him. Which is not to say he wasn't abandoned. I think of Peter often, and when I do I think of him as a citizen of Ireland. A brave and happy man, a man of character, a man with profound disabilities.

What is it about disability, especially intellectual disability, that makes it easy to rob a person of his citizenship? Because that is what happened to Peter. He was deemed inadequate to be a citizen, and that's why he died in pain.

Peter was sent to Leas Cross by the people entrusted with his care, and he was sent despite the strong objections of his family. Because he was a ward of court, a court ordered him to be sent there, on the advice of professionals. A dying citizen of Ireland, with a high level of dependency, was sent to a place that was utterly incompetent to deal with those dependencies.

The day before he went to Leas Cross, Peter was taken by ambulance to Beaumont Hospital because he had a urinary infection. There, a catheter was inserted into his penis, an event that would be traumatic for any man, but must have been many times more so for Peter. Once it was inserted, he was taken to the care of complete strangers, away from the routine that was vital to him.

When he died, a fortnight later, the catheter was still there, untended, untreated, uncleaned. Almost certainly, it was the failure to deal properly with the catheter that caused the blood poisoning that brought him to die in pain.

In that fortnight, Peter was visited only by his family, and by one or two of the staff who had cared for him prior to his departure to Leas Cross (they were, it is important to say, off duty). All were seriously concerned about the obvious deterioration in his condition, and all their concerns were waved away by the seemingly professional staff who were on duty.

Why did all this happen? How did it happen? If we don't find out, could it happen again? Are there standards in place to make sure it doesn't? Is anyone accountable, in any way, for what happened to Peter?

Well, we may soon enough know some of the answers. After months and years of pressure, with some outside help, Peter's family have managed to secure an investigation into the circumstances surrounding Peter's last few weeks as a citizen of our republic. That investigation is complete, and will be published soon.

Or will it?

As I understand it, these are the facts. The investigation was carried out by Martin Hynes, a public servant of long standing. If I'm any judge, he is a decent and compassionate man, the sort who would be thorough and painstaking in conducting an enquiry of this sort.

His work was carried out in private, and I understand he reviewed extensive files and posed many questions to everyone involved.

Some time ago, he submitted a draft of his report to the HSE. That draft was sent, in the interests of due process, to each of the parties mentioned in the report. I gather it was also checked by lawyers. Naturally, of course, Peter's family weren't given it.

When the parties involved had an opportunity to comment, Martin Hynes finalised his report. Peter's family were given to understand that the report would be published this week, and were made aware of some of its contents, although again they weren't shown any of it. They do believe, however, that the report raises serious questions and draws certain conclusions. In other words, there is accountability in the report. The degree of accountability will only be clear when the report is published.

But now, it seems, just as the finished report is ready for publication, someone has decided that, again in the interests of due process, the parties mentioned in the final document must be shown it again. At the least, this will mean a further delay.

This report must be published. There must be no question of any legal devices being employed to prevent publication or to water down its contents. If necessary, the report should be presented to the Minister for Health and published through an Oireachtas Committee, thus giving it the full protection of parliamentary privilege.

Perhaps it is the case that the system is ready to give a full accounting in Peter's case. Perhaps there won't be the usual hiding behind the law, behind professional reputations and bureaucratic imperatives. Perhaps the system will recognise, just for once, that the death of a vulnerable citizen and the circumstances surrounding it should be an occasion of openness and shame, rather than yet more secrecy and 'due process'.

I believe in due process. I regard it as a cornerstone of our system of justice. But increasingly I find this thought nagging at me. How is it that people with money and influence always get due process? And people like Peter McKenna seldom do? How is that?

Or will it be different? This time, could Peter teach us all a lesson about what citizenship means?

Gifted Students
(2006)

In the early 1990s, a long time ago, two women decided to pay a visit to Trinity College in Dublin. Neither of them had been a student there, but it seemed a logical choice, because at the time there was some publicity about the college's attitude to access. The women had one simple question to ask. If you believe in access, what about access for students with an intellectual disability?

Simple, but revolutionary. The two women who asked the question had just been through a dispiriting journey around Ireland. Mary Boyd and Frieda Finlay (yes, related to this column by marriage) were (and are) mothers of young adults with an intellectual disability, or mental handicap as it was called then. As their children reached adulthood, both women realised that there seemed to be few, if any, services available for them. So, with several other mothers, they decided to investigate the level and quality of service available throughout the country for young adults. When they started their research, their primary expertise was that they had had more than fifty years of what we would now call twenty-four/seven experience of intellectual disability. They lived with it, around the clock.

In their travels around Ireland they found that,

essentially, most people with an intellectual disability went to school until around the age of eighteen. Most were in special schools, whose standards varied from extremely good to pretty poor. There was no standardised curriculum, no way of measuring progress, no certificate at the end to prove that the young people involved had reached any standard at all. And after they left school, if they were lucky they got a place in a sheltered workshop or training centre. If they were very lucky, they got a place in a sheltered workshop or training centre with a commitment to ongoing education. But for the majority, such education as there was ended at eighteen.

They wrote a far-sighted and visionary report, called 'Working and Living'. In it they outlined what they saw as a crisis in philosophy, resources, management, staffing, and above all political will in the entire area of disability service, and they developed a set of proposals for new structures and management set-ups in the whole area of training and employment. (Many of the ideas they outlined then, and campaigned for at conferences all over the country, are part of the mainstream way of developing training and employment services now.)

Two of the women, Frieda and Mary, became convinced that they needed to go further, and to concentrate on the area of education. At that time, the idea of a person with an intellectual disability in third-level education was considered absurd. And standards in second-level were patchy at best. Frieda and Mary came to the conclusion that the solution was to be found in a national body, based in a university, that would combine education and research.

Education programmes capable of maximising the potential of people with intellectual disabilities would ensure their integration into a third-level campus. It would enable other students to learn about them. It would enable research to be conducted into the best methods of training and educating people with intellectual disabilities. These methods could then be transferred to other education settings, improving the standards at second-level and opening more doors for the students.

Frieda and Mary wrote all this up, into a paper called *The Belfield Centre*, because originally they believed they could persuade UCD to adopt their idea. UCD, essentially, wasn't interested, so Frieda and Mary took to the streets. Neither had any experience in public speaking, but they went to every conference they could – 'gatecrashing' they called it – and tried to interest anyone at all in their ideas.

They got some support, but an awful lot of scepticism. The most positive response was when they finally got to speak to the Dean of Studies in Trinity College Dublin, Professor George Sevastopulo. Rather than dismiss them out of hand, as some others had done, he gathered some other academics around, and began asking them the questions. Could Trinity do this sort of research? Did the college's commitment to access extend to people with an intellectual disability? Was there the remotest possibility that there might be something in Frieda and Mary's idea?

Little by little, the response that started to come back was 'why not?'. Several of the academics involved – Noreen Kearney, PJ Drudy, Sheila Greene, Robbie Gilligan, Mona O'Moore – all began to take an interest. Noreen Kearney was the first to take up the cudgels, and in later years PJ Drudy became the main champion of the idea within the college.

So the two mothers began a political campaign, that led ultimately to a decision by Niamh Bhreathnach when she was Minister for Education to allocate some money for a building and a little more for a proper feasibility study.

Eventually, and despite a change of Government, support for the idea became Government policy, and over the best part of a decade the seeds of a National Institute took root.

It's now led by a director, Patricia O'Brien from New Zealand. It's supported by Government and by philanthropy. It's researching and developing best practice. It's gradually building its capacity to disseminate information. It's working with parents (Frieda now helps to run a programme in that area) and professionals.

But, most important of all, it's enabling its first cohort of full-time students, twenty adults with an intellectual disability, to undertake the first course of its kind in Ireland, the Certificate in Contemporary Living. Formally approved by Trinity College, the Certificate is taught over two years and has ten demanding modules in the social sciences and the expressive arts. CCL students – that's what they're called – are full and equal students of Trinity College.

The National Institute for Intellectual Disability was formally opened this week, in its own premises near the front gate of Trinity, by the Minister for Education Mary Hanafin. It took more than a decade of campaigning to bring it from the mad idea of two mothers to something that Mary Hanafin described as being capable of making a profound difference. There's a lot to be said, isn't there, for never giving up!

At the opening ceremony, they showed a short video about the Institute, narrated by the poet and Trinity lecturer Brendan Kennelly. At the end of the video he recited a poem, in that warm voice we all associate with him. At first I thought he might have written it about the struggle that Frieda and Mary had undertaken to get the Institute established. It turned out to be a poem, written by one of the students on the new course, about the hope and struggle of a college student's life.

> *As one door closes after me*
> *I open a door to the future*
> *Full of challenges and experiences*
> *Bravery, determination*
> *The next door I open*
> *Shows a bumpy road ahead*
> *And it becomes steeper and harder to walk*
> *Till I reach the top*
> *Then I come down followed by a smooth path*
> *Along the way*

After he'd read it, Kennelly paused. That poem was written, he said, by Helen Donnelly. A gifted student.

Memories Are Made of This
(2008)

My wife made one of her occasional forays to IKEA in Belfast last week. Great value to be had up there, especially with the current rate of exchange, and the quality they produce for the price is quite remarkable. Apart from the other stuff she bought, she arrived back with some flat-pack bookcases, so I could finally get the tiny room referred to as my 'office' into some sort of shape.

Big mistake. I don't mean the bookcases – even I was able to follow the instructions with relative ease and get them assembled into a fine-looking arrangement. No, the problem is with the phrase 'sorting out your office'. You know what that means, don't you? It means finding stuff you haven't seen for years. It means hours wading through old photographs, old reports, books I'd forgotten I had. I've always told people I disapprove of hoarding, and that there's no need to keep stuff that goes back to old God's time. But in emptying an old bookcase I discovered I'm just as much a hoarder as anyone else.

Why do we keep the stuff? Photographs I can understand, of wonderful holidays when the kids were young and I even had hair on my head. There's nothing quite like the pleasure, is there, in the memories that an old

128

forgotten photo can bring back? Finding them, especially out of the blue, is almost like revisiting the scene.

But the ancient old books! I can't remember now why I bought some of them, let alone why I've kept them all these years. Hidden away at the back of the old bookcase, for example, was *The World in 2030*, a dusty old hardback written by the Earl of Birkenhead. Lord Birkenhead was actually Fred Smith, a Tory politician of the old school, until he was made a viscount and then an Earl in 1922. I have no idea why he felt the need to publish *The World in 2030* in 1930 (but then, I can't imagine what possessed me to buy it at some jumble sale, and keep it all these years).

It's hilarious – and perhaps far-seeing in some ways. He predicts, for example, that by 2030 China will be an enormous economic power – to such an extent that Europe is forced to forget old enmities and unite into a federal state, which will wage war on China with the support of America. Side by side with this prediction, however, he scoffs at the idea that India could ever become independent, and guarantees that British rule in India will endure, 'as a modern example of a successful benevolent tyranny'.

The airplane had been well developed by 1930, and Birkenhead is able to predict that commercial flight will be possible in the future. But only for distances no longer than 500 miles. So, alas, transatlantic flight will never be possible, unless, of course, they build landing stations in the middle of the Atlantic. The only realistic solution for Birkenhead is the airship, and that's what he predicts will be developed. I hope he wasn't too mortified when the biggest airship ever put into service across the Atlantic (and the last) went up in flames about seven years later.

It's on the subject of women that Lord Birkenhead is funniest however. 'I do not believe,' he intones, 'that statesmanship is either congenial or indeed possible to feminine genius.' Although women might excel in the arts, or even (possibly) in business, poor old Fred could never see the remotest possibility of a woman prime minister in Britain.

But you know the sad thing about keeping loads of old stuff? Sometimes it tells you just how little has changed.

I've always had a shelf full of books and reports about disability issues. Some of them are seminal, like the *Commission on the Status of People with a Disability*. Some of them are almost curiosities now, full of language that has disappeared, and occasionally rather patronising attitudes towards 'the mentally handicapped' or 'the disabled'.

One report I opened with more than a little curiosity, however, was *Needs and Abilities*. I'd forgotten I still had it, although I can remember how significant it seemed when it was first published, all of twenty-eight years ago. It was the first attempt in a number of years to review the array of services for people with an intellectual disability, and to make recommendations about all of them. For instance, it was the first policy document I remember that recommended that we stop using the term 'mental handicap', and that people with an intellectual disability themselves should be consulted as to what was the most appropriate terminology.

The report took what would nowadays be called a 'life-cycle' approach. Its authors, who were all public servants, looked at the needs of young people, people of school age, people as they got to working age, and older. It also looked at the needs for families. And it focused on the fact that at the time, there were estimated to be upwards of 1,000 people with an intellectual disability 'in the care of the psychiatric service' – in other words, inappropriately living in surroundings that were totally non-therapeutic for them.

At the time *Needs and Abilities* was published, the main concentration was on the number of additional places it recommended as a priority. The authors of the report said that their minimum requirement was the creation of 600 residential and 1,000 day places. There was some shock in Government circles at the cost of creating these places, which was estimated at about £23 million in capital costs and £28 million in current costs. That would be a lot less, of course, than the cost of an electronic voting system today, but it was considered enormous in those days. Nevertheless, the political parties all said that *Needs and Abilities* had to be implemented.

But you know what? I don't just keep old reports in my office – I have the more up-to-date stuff too. Among them is the *Annual Report of the National Intellectual Disability Database Committee 2007*. There, on page 63, the following paragraph appears: 'The data returned in 2007 indicate that 2,430 people will require major elements of service, either a full-time residential service or a day service, or both, in the five-year period 2008–2012, an increase of 58 since 2006.'

And still, after a decade and a half of fantastic wealth accumulation, 207 people live in psychiatric hospitals who shouldn't be there. Many of those people were there in 1990, when *Needs and Abilities* was published. That's more than a life sentence, and it remains a national scandal.

Keeping old books and reports does enable the tracking of who did what, who tried to deliver on the promises of the past and who ignored them. In the twenty-eight years since *Needs and Abilities* was published, there have been some changes for the better. But despite all our wealth, we've never managed to keep vulnerable people on the priority list for long enough to eliminate some of the scandals. And that's as good a reason as any for keeping the books. After all, there are some things we should never forget.

On the Shoulders
of Giants

The Ringmaster
(2000)

William M. Tweed was a second-rate politician who moved up the ranks of Democratic Party politics in New York City in the 1850s and 1860s to become one of the most powerful men in New York City politics.

Known to all and sundry as Boss Tweed, he ruled the city with an iron hand. Initially, he was seen as 'a good thing' – jobs were created, land was developed, the city was modernised. It gradually became apparent that the jobs were being distributed on the basis of cronyism and party politics, and the Boss was giving and receiving kickbacks in respect of every piece of development in the city. Although he ran a tight and secret ring, he was undone by colleagues and cronies who turned on him, in the end betraying him for the sake of their own ambitions.

At his trial for corruption, it was alleged that Boss Tweed had enriched himself by as much as $200 million over the nearly twenty years he held sway. His headquarters in the heart of the city, Tammany Hall, became a byword and a synonym for political corruption for all time.

But that was a hundred and forty years ago. We live in different times now. There's transparency, investigative

135

reporting, laws. Decisions are made in public session, and are based in arguments thrashed out in public.

Of course it's always going to be possible for a few councillors to be amenable to friendly persuasion and political contributions. But systematic corruption of the Tammany Hall kind? How could that survive in the undergrowth?

This week we discovered that it's all too easy. Throughout the eighties and nineties, and right up to the very recent past, there was a ring. And Frank Dunlop was the ringmaster. This was no small group of grubby councillors always willing to do the right thing for a shilling. This was organised, systematic corruption.

Frank Dunlop effectively made his living by being the man you called if you wanted a decision made the right way and didn't care how it was achieved. And he never said no to a client – whatever you wanted to secure, he would look after it. That'll be another €100,000.

It's been a shocking week in all sorts of ways. Shocking in the personal sense – the sight of Frank Dunlop effectively collapsing with stress would move all but the most inhuman. The thought of the lies he has lived with for years – lies I believe he has lived with by learning to believe them himself – was sickening.

But above all that is the notion that behind Frank Dunlop, always ready to pick up the phone to him, were people who, on the one hand, were willing to sell their votes and, on the other, wanted to buy them. The sinister trade of which he became a master has done immense, perhaps irreparable damage to the political system.

It doesn't have to be so. There were honourable politicians just as there were corrupt ones. There were people who fought against the system, who tried to expose it for what it was. They didn't get much credit then, and they are not getting much now. They are all just lumped in together – the 'body politic' has been affected. And the message is that all politicians are the same.

This message only serves one set of politicians. I haven't heard Bertie Ahern saying 'members of my party disgraced themselves and let politics down'. All I hear him saying is 'some politicians let the system down'. The subliminal message in this is that the basic Fianna Fáil response is going to be to spread the blame as much as they can to muddy the waters.

Sure, they've promised to bring in emergency legislation, and they talk in grave and solemn tones about the need for an all-party response. Why should there be an all-party response to what is, in its essence, a Fianna Fáil problem? Why should other parties, especially those whose track record in relation to planning is honourable, be sucked into this miasma of self-justification? A certain culture within Fianna Fáil is at the heart of this, and it is up to that party and its leadership to root it out.

They won't do it with the legislation they have published. They're agin' corruption, but they haven't introduced any power for the Gardaí to arrest and question people who are suspected of corruption, or to seize papers and documents. In other jurisdictions, police routinely knock down office doors and impound everything inside when they are investigating this kind of crime.

Under the legislation John O'Donoghue is proposing, they will have to make an appointment with the suspects, if the suspects are willing to talk to them.

At present, in our law, bribery of a public official is a crime (including councillors). As I understand it, however, the onus of proof is on the State, except in the single instance where the payment is made by someone seeking a Government contract. If the Government was serious about rooting out corruption, it would amend the law so that every payment to a councillor or official who has influence over a decision which affects any material interest of the person making the payment would be deemed to be corrupt.

The onus of proof should be transferred to the people giving and taking the money to prove that they are not involved in corrupt transactions. Without that change, I would be ready to bet that not a single conviction will ever be secured against any corrupt developer or politician. In the more than hundred years since the legislation was first enacted, not a single conviction has happened yet.

Long before we get to the point of considering criminal punishments, however, there have to be political punishments. From what we can gather of the internal investigation carried out by Fianna Fáil, everyone is as pure as the driven snow. They know it isn't true.

The party and its leadership know now who the main suspects are. They may not have proof of corruption beyond a reasonable doubt – but they have facts available to them which establish financial corruption as a matter of the highest probability. And that's the test that Judge Flood can apply if he wishes when it comes to elaborating his findings of fact.

Bertie Ahern has that discretion too. He doesn't have to hide behind 'due process' – he can, if he wishes, tell us that he has established a high probability that several of his TDs were engaged in improper and corrupt practices. In the absence of convincing explanations from them –

convincing public explanations – he can announce that he has decided to charge them with conduct unbecoming of a member of Fianna Fáil. People have been expelled from Fianna Fáil in the past for far less reason – and with far less evidence to support the charge.

That could undermine his Government majority further, of course. But it might, just might, begin to restore some moral authority to his Government. As it is, it will become impossible to respect a Government that knows it is living with the support of votes that have already been sold to the highest bidder.

Bertie's Christmas Carol
(2000)

It was dark, and the Dublin streets were cold and covered with the first snow of the year. On the northside, the house named after a saint was quiet. The last supplicant had left, Bertie's reassurances that he'd 'do his damdest for him' still ringing in his ears.

And all Bertie had in the house was a cup of tea. He wondered should he go over the road to Fagan's. But the place'd be packed, and they'd all be hanging off him. They might look like a support group to the rest of the world, but Bertie knew there was always a price to be paid for support. No, he'd sit quiet for a while, finish the cup of tea, and make his way home in due course. The car was outside, the ever faithful Mercedes engine humming quietly. It could be peaceful here, he thought, and God knows there isn't much peace these days. In the half light, with the electric fire warming the room, you could be comfortable enough.

Who was that? Jaysus, there's still a constituent left. But how did he get in, and why is he sitting there, on the other side of the fire, just staring at me?

After a second Bertie realised there was something familiar about the other man. Those hooded eyes, the baleful stare, the hooked nose. And yet, he couldn't quite place him. He looked eerie, somehow, and sinister, and still reminded Bertie of someone a long time ago.

'Howya doin'?' Bertie managed. 'I didn't see you come in.'

'Of course not,' replied his guest, his voice rasping in a way that made Bertie's blood turn cold. 'Nobody ever sees me enter or leave – but they're always the poorer for my visits.'

Bertie knew he had to ask who his visitor was. He knew instinctively that he'd be terrified by the answer.

'I'm the ghost of Christmas past,' snarled the man with the hooded eyes as he stood up. To Bertie's astonishment, the ghost was smaller than he had been expecting. Suddenly, caught in the ghost's vice-like grip, Bertie seemed to be floating over the city. It was his city, and yet the ghost seemed to know it better. They flew over Croker and Dalyer as if they didn't exist, and suddenly they were on the southside, looking down on Government Buildings.

'Why did you bring me to my office?' Bertie asked.

'Your office?' snarled the ghost. 'This is mine, mine. I built this place, and this is where the great and the mighty came to see me. This is where I taught you everything you know ...'

Suddenly Bertie realised that he was going to be told a few things he didn't want to know at all. Still struggling to remember this strange figure, images long suppressed began coming back to him. He remembered seeing brown paper bags, and all sorts of papers and Government memoranda and decisions being handed over in corridors, and this little man with the red face and the vice-like grip was always there. But what was his name? What had he done? If only Bertie could remember ...

He woke with a start. Jaysus, he thought, it had just been a dream. Something about his past had come back to haunt him, and it wouldn't be too long before he'd be able to forget it again. But he still wasn't alone.

'Who the hell are you?' he shouted at the grinning figure standing near the window.

'Ah sure you know me Boss,' replied his latest visitor. 'Ebenezer McCreevy, ghost of Christmas present. I just wanted to show you a bit of the Dublin we've created together.'

'Shag off,' said Bertie. 'I'm not depending on you to carry me over Dublin.'

'No need for that at all Boss,' the ghost of Christmas present replied. 'I've got your man's helicopter, you know, the beef fella. It'll be grand and comfortable.'

Within seconds they were circling over row upon row of neo-Georgian houses, all looking resplendent with a light covering of snow. Each of them had two cars in the drive, and all that could be heard was the sound of tinkling mobile phones. Yes, Dublin had never looked so good.

As they got closer to the city centre, there were other figures to be seen. Dark, huddled figures, wrapped in dirty blankets, and apparently sleeping in the doorways – even in some of the better streets.

'What's that?' Bertie wanted to know.

'Don't worry your head about that, Boss,' Ebenezer reassured him. 'They're not homeless children at all, they're just propaganda images created by the poverty industry.'

So they swung around over the city, admiring the affluence and the wealth. New hotels everywhere, Christmas cranes dotting the skyline, shops open late, shopping centre car parks still full quite late at night. And at Ebenezer's urging, Bertie averted his gaze from the overcrowded hospitals, the dilapidated back streets, the women struggling to put a Christmas dinner on the table in large parts of the city.

Back in his room later, Bertie reflected that he'd much rather deal with the ghost of Christmas present than the ghost of Christmas past. You still have to turn the blind eye a lot, he thought, but at least nowadays there's some good to look at as well as bad.

He was just putting on his coat to leave when the door of the sitting room opened, and there stood a truly frightening figure. Covered from head to toe in a long grey cloak, this was a tall man, and nearly as wide as he was tall. Bertie couldn't see his face, but he knew immediately that his long night wasn't over yet.

'I am the ghost of Christmas future,' the new ghost said. 'I'm going to show you a few things you need to know.'

'Don't tell me,' Bertie said. 'You're not going to drive me all around Dublin too.'

'Oh no,' said the ghost. 'My secrets are hidden all over the place, from Albania to Liechtenstein. You'll see in due course – and you're going to be sorry you shut your eyes to this lot.'

Bertie felt himself go cold. What had happened? He knew this ghost now, knew about the millions of pounds that had been squirreled away, knew about some of the favours that had been done for this man to help him sell himself all over the place. But how was it going to come out? What was the ghost of Christmas future going to say and do? And what damage would it cause? How was Bertie going to be implicated in all this?

'Taoiseach? Are you all right?'

It was Joe, the special branch driver, shaking him by the shoulder. It had all been a dream! There were no ghosts, just a sleepy Taoiseach in a lonely room. The driver had come to wake him when he hadn't come down after the clinic ended.

Bertie shook himself, and shivered.

'You're not getting a cold I hope Taoiseach,' his ever solicitous driver enquired.

'I'm all right Joe,' replied Bertie. 'Just one of those things – a bit of a premonition about what the future might bring.'

Give Me My Coloured Coat
(2001)

Joseph – he of the amazing multi-coloured coat – was a wise and much respected leader. Although never a king of Egypt himself, he was trusted by the king to manage the most important commodity in the country, the food.

Now Joe knew the value of food. He'd lived through hard times, been hated and despised by his own, and survived to tell the tale. Although he was a man who had almost literally pulled himself up by his own bootstraps, and had learned wisdom and intellect the hard way, he was never one to lecture others or to regard others as inferior in any way, even intellectually, to him.

So clearly, if you wanted to cast a play of his life right this minute, the one person you couldn't consider is that well-known video actor, known for sauntering endlessly up and down beside the canal in his beloved County Kildare, our own inimitable Charlie McCreevy. Even though he barely fluffs a word in the video we know and love, where he exhorts us soulfully over and over again to read the euro booklet, he would be entirely inappropriate for the role of Joseph.

Don't forget old Joe's greatest achievement. Sold into slavery by jealous brothers, he lived the life of, oh let's say a Fianna Fáil backbencher, trudging to do the whip's bidding day after day, never being recognised for his talents.

Gradually rising to prominence because of his outspokenness and popularity, he was imprisoned on false charges (as a man might be if he transgressed against the Emperor Charles). But even in prison, his wisdom impressed, his farseeing utterances reaching the ear of the new king.

And so Joseph (yes, we're still talking about Joseph – stay with the plot) was put in charge of the warehouses and supplies. You might say he was made Minister for Finance. What followed was seven years of plenty, seven years of unparalleled growth in the fortunes of Ireland (sorry, Egypt – I'm losing the plot myself now). Joseph used those seven years to make sure that the warehouses were full up, ready to burst. When the seven years of plenty came to an end (as they always do) there was more than enough to see Egypt through the seven years of hard times. Joseph spent those years making sure that the poor were protected and fed. And when Joseph was finally reunited with his brothers, he was the first to recognise that by selling him into slavery in the first place, they had done him the greatest favour of his life.

Undeniable similarities between Joe and Charlie, you have to admit. A Hollywood producer reading the script might well think, 'Hmm, what about that Irish guy, the one in the video – he walks a bit like an Egyptian beside that canal there, and he was Minister for Finance ...' But the producer would have to be told. Casting our Charlie in the role of Joseph would be stretching credibility to the point of fantasy.

Because unlike in Joe's story, we had the years of hardship before the years of plenty. Charlie was in charge during some of them, although not in the Department of Finance. He was in Social Welfare then, and spent his time making sure that anyone who was poor was kept as far away as possible from the warehouses.

And then the years of plenty came, not really fuelled by anything Charlie did. He had spent his time in the outer darkness all right, after first campaigning for the old king and then criticising him, even trying to oust him from leadership. The new young king, obviously impressed by his diction and wisdom, had put him in charge of the warehouses just as the corn really started to flow.

And what did Charlie do? He spent the next few years handing out amazing technicolour dreamcoats to everyone. The richer the citizen, the more splendid the coat they got. (Mind you, the poor, the sick and the handicapped were still told to stay back from the doors of the warehouses, although there were a few more crumbs around in the good days, and by and large they learned to be content with them.)

If the new king, who was always busy elsewhere, had a question mark in his mind about Charlie's judgement, he kept it to himself. Even when Charlie wanted to give the gaudiest coat of all to a fellow wise man who had resigned from the courts under a cloud, and the people rose up in revolt, the king never uttered a word of rebuke. Even when Charlie would round on the few who were impertinent enough to offer a word of criticism, and dismiss them with a few sneers like 'poverty industry' and 'left-wing pinkos', the young king seemed to approve.

But now, suddenly, the seven years of prosperity have come to an end. At the very least, they have been interrupted, and it may be that we are in for a few tough years.

And guess what? The warehouses are empty. Many of us have our multi-coloured coats, all right, but if we take them out and have a look at them, we will all discover that the material is too light to keep us warm for the winter. And as for those who never got a coat – it's really going to be a tough winter for them.

All through the years he has been in charge, when the opportunity existed to make sure the warehouses were full, Charlie and his amazing technicolour dreamcoat were having a party. The party's over, and it's us, the people around Charlie, who are going to have the hangover.

Charlie (and the king) are hoping that we won't notice. And we mightn't. Our little corner of the world is still in party mood, and likely to remain so for a while. But no thanks are due to Charlie. Instead it's because we have been hearing tales of great heroism and derring-do from the East. We sent another of our heroes over there – Mick, accompanied by a small but merry band – and they managed to break down the last barriers between us and the Far East.

And so we will spend the next few months getting ready, the excitement building all the time, to follow the further adventures of Mick and his merry men in the Far East, not this time in multi-colours but all dressed in green.

And if the warehouses are empty, with the doors hanging off and blowing in the wind, who's going to notice while Mick and his jolly green army are captivating us? When the election happens shortly before the Far East adventure, we'll all be full of good feeling because of the excitement to come.

But when the Far Eastern adventure is over (and let's hope Mick and his men come home with the honour they deserve), that's when we will all discover that we've been fooled by Charlie and the king. By then, they will have been installed for another five years, because we will all have been too busy to notice how they had left nothing in the larder for any years of hardship to come.

Another Christmas Carol
(2002)

I wasn't alone. I thought I had settled down by the fire for a pleasant doze, the dog at my feet, sparks drifting up the chimney. But there was a chill in the room, as if a window had blown open. And a strange foreboding, brought on by the sudden realisation that I was in the presence of an unwelcome stranger.

But who was it? Who was that ghostly figure in the corner, his face hidden by the shadows cast by the firelight? Why was he so still, so silent? It's Christmas Eve, after all, a time of good cheer, a time to reflect on the year just passed. It's a time for friendly faces, and heaven knows there are a lot of them around. Where had this gloomy creature come from, and what had I done to deserve this unwelcome intrusion?

I should have known, of course. Ever since the Budget, I've had Ebenezer Scrooge on my mind. It was by far the worst Budget in my political lifetime in terms of public spending and the social consequences of so many cutbacks in real terms, and I've spent a lot time since then thinking about the meanness of it all.

So perhaps I shouldn't have been surprised, just when I was ready to let the season of goodwill take over, to receive a visit from one of Ebenezer's friends. Before the night was over, I was to meet many more.

'I am the ghost of Christmas future,' the hooded figure intoned when I asked him who he was and what he was doing in my room, 'and I've come to show you the next twelve months. Your commentary in the *Irish Examiner* has been so unpatriotic, so determined to undermine the great national work of the Government, that you must be shown the error of your ways.'

And then, before I could protest, he had swept me up, and we were flying, yes flying, over the streets and houses of the city. I have to admit that once my first fear of flying subsided, the sensation was not unpleasant.

It wasn't long before we spotted a familiar figure, hunched over a desk in a little house on the southside of the city, his handsome if perhaps dissolute profile silhouetted by a guttering candle.

'It's Uriah McDowell,' I exclaimed. 'But what are all those bundles of papers all around him?'

'They are the eighty-four bills he will introduce to the Dáil in the new year,' the ghost explained. 'All written by himself, all beautiful and elegant. He will confound you with his genius when you see the fruits of his work.'

'But what are they about?'

'Oh, everything,' said the ghost. 'From the forced repatriation of malcontents to the ritual public humiliation of left-wingers. Before the year is out, our great justice minister will put the economy to rights as well. That large volume you see him working at now – that's his major work on uncovering the alchemist's secret. Yes, he will shortly show us all how to turn base metal into gold.'

'Perhaps I've misjudged him over the years,' I murmured.

'You have indeed,' the ghost told me, 'although he is too wise and farseeing to be bothered by the likes of you. But you have more to see – and if you have the wit, more to learn.'

'Who is that down there?' I cried, pointing at the old curiosity shop just below us.

'Ah, little Nell!' the ghost replied. 'Or Tánaiste Nell Harney to you. You see her there, knitting and sewing till her fingers bleed. But you have no appreciation of her, with all your carping criticism.'

'What is she making?' I wanted to know. 'It looks like ...'

'It is,' the ghost said. 'It is enough hats and mittens to keep the poor warm throughout the whole of next year, and inside, by day and by night, Tánaiste Nell is baking enough bread to feed every poor family in the land. Not that they need much, since her policies have encouraged so much wealth creation.'

'I always thought she was indifferent to the poor,' I said.

'But you were wrong,' the ghost told me. 'And perhaps now you will have the grace to admit what a soft and generous heart she truly has.'

Before I could reply, we were swooping down along the line of the canal, so fast it took my breath away. There below us, hopping and darting among the crowd, was the Artful Dodger, picking pockets with all the speed and deftness I had always associated with him.

'I see the Dodger McCreevy hasn't changed anyway,' I said to the ghost.

'You are wrong again,' the ghost said sharply. 'Look,

look at him. He is only picking the pockets of the rich, in the interests of social justice. And would he keep it for himself, like some begrudger or left-wing pinko? No, not the Dodger. Look!'

And as I watched, the Dodger emptied his takings into the pockets of a boy – Tiny Tim I knew immediately, whose brave little face, wracked with pain, was transformed by the kindness and goodness of the Dodger McCreevy.

But there was more. The greatest revelation of all came as we flew back up the canal, this time to the city's northside, to see the hordes of people crowding around one figure. Tall, distinguished, his nose red in the cold, his neck evidently sore from nodding and agreeing.

'It's Bertie Copperfield!' I exclaimed. 'But what are those people doing all around him?'

'They're seeking justice and truth,' the ghost replied, 'and where else would they come? Here they get clarity, understanding, wisdom.'

And it was true. As we watched, everyone who approached Bertie Copperfield seemed to come away from him smiling. Some looked perplexed, as if they hadn't been able to fully comprehend the words of wisdom he was dispensing. But in the main, people appeared to feel they had got what they deserved.

'You see now,' said the ghost. 'You see the injustice of your behaviour, of your obnoxious and unworthy criticism.'

'Take me home, ghost,' I cried. 'I repent all, I see the error of my ways. This wonderful Government, so full of mercy and wisdom, has nothing to fear from me.'

And suddenly I was back in my sitting room, the memory of the night already beginning to fade, only the dying embers of the fire a reminder that I had been away for several hours.

I struggled to remember everything I had seen – the great outpouring of genius from Uriah McDowell, the tenderness of Tánaiste Nell, the carefree, generous behaviour of the Artful Dodger McCreevy, and the wisdom and clarity of Bertie Copperfield. Shaking myself, and getting ready to go to my bed, I resolved that in future I would be a supporter, not a critic, of this wonderful Government.

But as I climbed the stairs, a nagging doubt arose. What if it had been a dream? What if, after all, the figures I had seen were just a figment of imagination? No, I thought. Never. How could all those visions have been a dream? How could they?

The Road to Damascus
(2004)

The mood in the Sycamore Room was tense. All the handlers had gathered, and both the ad agency and the market research companies had delivered their verdict.

'What are we going to tell Bertie?' one of the junior handlers asked. 'These figures are disastrous. He's going to go ballistic when he discovers that the party is polling even less than we got in the local elections.'

The senior handler thought, not for the first time, that this was a young lad who needed to know his place. Not a wet day in the place, and already referring to the Taoiseach as Bertie. Not even the Boss or the Chief. And besides, what earthly use was a handler who panicked every time he saw a set of poll figures? Didn't he know that the party had been through much worse than this? He himself had been through all the gubu years – the phone-tapping, the murderer in the Attorney General's flat, one business scandal after another. This was chicken feed by comparison.

'Lookit,' he said, 'we might start by remembering that we're working for the Taoiseach of the country. And secondly, it's our job to be offering solutions, not wetting ourselves just because we've got a bad poll.'

Mind you, the senior handler reflected to himself, this

is a bit of a mess. The problem is that Bertie's not exactly a fresh face. If the people are saying the bottom line is that they're tired of him, that probably reflects the reality of ten years in office. And it clearly shows that the reshuffle hasn't worked, at least in terms of brightening things up. It doesn't help when all the new ministers are wandering around putting their feet in it every time they open their mouths. Conor Lenihan announcing that we weren't going to meet the target for Third World aid, Mary Hanafin deciding that there was no way of getting class sizes down to the promised levels.

Still, we're not giving up without a fight. The senior handler looked around the big table in the Sycamore Room, one of the finest rooms in Government Buildings. This is ours, he thought. We've been here for the guts of twenty years, and those gobshites in Fine Gael and Labour aren't going to take it away from us. All we need is a plan.

'I know what the Taoiseach needs,' he said. Even as he spoke, he could see eyes lighting up. That's it, he thought. I've pulled the fat out of the fire before, I can do it again. I'll show these guys what a real handler is.

'A makeover,' he said. 'We'll give the Taoiseach a makeover.'

Immediately, he could see the idea was going to be a hard sell. One of his long-serving colleagues spoke up.

'Ah jaysus, SH,' he said. 'We can't do another makeover. We're going to have to come up with something different.'

'Why not?' the senior handler demanded. 'It's always worked before – and there's plenty of time to put it into effect.'

'Don't you see?' his second-in-command persisted.

'Bertie's already been everything. He's gone for every corner of the market. He's been the loyal lieutenant, the humble servant, the cunning strategist, the loner, the fixer. When the anorak worked and he wanted to be one of the lads, we invented the pint of Bass and the stool in the corner of Fagan's pub. When he needed to be a statesman, we got him into the good suits – and by the way, he needs to go up a size or two in the suits, he's bursting out of them right now. We had him go all open and transparent about the marriage, then we had the on-again, off-again relationship. We turned him into Mr Tough Guy just before the locals, telling the cabinet they'd better shape up or their jobs wouldn't be safe. And then we did the Inchydoney thing, getting him to go all caring and sharing, and that didn't work either. There's nothing left for him to be.'

'I don't agree,' the senior handler said. 'I think the problem is we haven't been radical enough. We've got to get him into a new persona, one that has a totally different appeal, and make him stick with it this time. Go for a totally different segment of the market.'

'My God, SH,' the ad man said. 'What are you thinking of – are you going to have the Taoiseach announcing he's gay?'

'That's not a bad idea, AD,' said the senior handler. 'I don't know if the Taoiseach could quite work his way through that one right now, though. We'll keep that in reserve, in case there's one last niche market we haven't covered. But I reckon the new Bertie will have to go soft on gay rights if his new persona is to fit.'

He paused, savouring the tension building in the room.

'No,' he said. 'I think we'll have to turn Bertie into a socialist.'

There was pandemonium in the room. The senior handler thought the market research guy was going to get sick. That's the trouble with these guys, he thought. They only know how to measure public opinion. They haven't a clue how to shape it.

'Have you gone mad, SH?' the second-in-command asked. 'The money guys will never stand for that. They haven't been contributing millions to the party to keep a goddam socialist in power.'

'Come off it,' the senior handler snapped. 'I'm not talking real socialism here. None of that role of the State, or redistributing wealth, or rights for the marginalised nonsense. But we'll get him to claim the ground, and we'll have a few soundbites about the poor and the weak and all that shit.'

'But what about his track record?' the junior handler said. 'Won't the media start investigating inconsistencies between what he says and what he does?'

'Yeah, right,' said the senior handler. 'Like that's ever happened.'

There was a general titter around the room, and the senior handler knew he was going to win the argument.

'There's something in it all right,' the ad man said. 'It'll frighten the life out of the PDs, and it will open up speculation about who Bertie might coalesce with after the next election. And we could have pictures of Bertie in the Botanic Gardens and Stephen's Green and other places where rich people mingle with poor people.'

'So no more private tents at the Galway Races, then, or sitting in the box in Old Trafford with JP and the lads,' said the second-in-command.

'Well, I don't know if we have to go that far,' the senior handler said. 'We can probably get one of the liberal bishops to call into the tent next year. That would soften the image a bit.'

'So it's agreed then,' said the senior handler, 'we're going to invent the first socialist Taoiseach, and we'll put a bit of extra money for social welfare and all that rubbish in the Budget. And don't forget lads – we can take the money back after the election, just like we did last time. In the meantime, let's all get used to saying Comrade Taoiseach!'

Apologies to George Orwell
(2005)

Winston Smith sat in the bar, alone as always, the glass of gin in his hand. The smells were familiar to him, the smells of boiled cabbage and damp. Even though they were unpleasant, there was something comforting about them, something that reminded him of home.

And of course, on each wall of the bar there was the poster. It depicted simply an enormous face, more than a metre wide: the face of a man of about fifty-four, with thinning blond hair, piercing eyes squinting narrowly through gold-rimmed glasses, and that vulpine smile he had known for years. The posters were everywhere – not just in the bar, but on every street corner, on every wall in every room in every public building, indeed in every building where people gathered.

Or even where they sat alone, as Winston did every night. The picture on the poster was always the same, one of those pictures so contrived that the eyes follow you about when you move. And the caption was always the same too. BIG BROTHER MICHAEL IS WATCHING YOU, it said.

He knew it was true. Not literally, of course. Big Brother Michael didn't have the time to watch everyone all the time. But his agents, known as the Garda, did. And he could demand the files. What files they were, full of the surveillance information that came from the universally positioned microphones, the two-way telescreens, the detailed reports about thoughtcrime. And of course, meticulous records about the ultimate crime, the refusal to accept the true value of newspeak, the language Big Brother Michael had invented all those years ago.

Winston had hated that language, had distrusted it. He had believed, back then, that the new language was intended to intimidate, to make it harder to debate ideas in public. Big Brother Michael's claiming of the Republic, for instance, or his insistence that inequality was good for you. Or as Big Brother would put it, everyone is equal. But some are more equal than others.

That was back then, of course. Winston had long ago learned, or perhaps more accurately been taught, that newspeak was the only true faith.

But still, he couldn't help remembering. It had started back in 2005, the triumph of newspeak. Innocent enough it had seemed at the time, a simple piece of legislation aimed at modernising what was then the police force, before it had become Big Brother Michael's Garda. And the newspapers, which back in those days were free to say whatever they wanted (as long as it wasn't too critical), had supported the legislation. Reform is urgent, they had said. You must do it now.

They hadn't paid much attention to the fact that all the changes were put through at the last minute, many of them never debated at all because the authorities closed the debate down, because the deputies were forced to pass a motion that put all of Big Brother Michael's amendments into law, even though many of them had never been debated or analysed at all. A motion with the effect of a guillotine rammed through: 'That the amendments set down by the Minister for Justice, Equality and Law Reform and not disposed of are hereby made to the Bill, Fourth Stage is hereby completed and the Bill is hereby passed.' And in this way, all the amendments put down by the opposition (yes, Winston remembered, opposition was allowed back then) were wiped out, and Big Brother's amendments were considered to have been passed into law, even the ones nobody had read.

What a clever ruse it had been, Winston thought. The press at the time had largely ignored the amendments and the new changes brought in by stealth in this way. That was because the police were under tremendous pressure. There were rumours everywhere of corruption, of policemen concocting evidence to frame people for crimes they hadn't committed. And of course innocent people had been framed, and the demand for police reform grew, so there was no real tolerance for debate or discussion.

Winston thought that someday, when the history of Big Brother's reign was written, this would be seen as the moment it had all started. Those amendments, ignored by the people, had become the buttress of his awesome power.

First of all, the arbitrary power to sack a policeman had made all the police afraid. Up to 2005, sacking a policeman was immensely difficult, and everyone agreed that was not a good thing. But after 2005 the head of the police, who of course reported directly to Big Brother, held their job security in the palm of his hand.

Then there was the awesome power given to the head of the Garda to install closed-circuit television cameras anywhere in the country he wanted to, for the 'sole or primary purpose', as the law said, 'of securing public order and safety in public places by facilitating the deterrence, prevention, detection and prosecution of offences'. It had taken a few years to put all the cameras in place, of course, but now nobody was safe from their watchful gaze. You simply never knew when anything you did was being watched and monitored in those control rooms built by Big Brother under the so-called 'decentralisation programme'.

But of course, the defining power, the one that made everything possible, was the one known as 'the duty to account'. Under this provision, another one of those never debated but passed into law anyway, the head of the Garda was made legally accountable to 'the minister and the Government' through the head of the Justice Department (that's what it was called back then, before Big Brother changed its name to the Crimes against the State Office).

Legal accountability sounded innocent enough, Winston remembered. But it included the duty to hand over any document in the Garda's possession, any file, any collection of information or pictures. And it also included a legal obligation to keep the minister, as Big Brother was known in those days, fully informed of any significant development that might affect the security of the State, including, 'whenever required by the minister', a requirement that the head of the Garda would hand over a report on 'any matters connected with the policing or security of the State'.

Yes, they were innocent days, back in June 2005. Winston and others had warned of the dangers. He, and some of his friends, had complained publicly, perhaps too much, about the potential for abuse in these hidden powers, about the danger that is always present when too much power is concentrated in too few hands.

But no one listened. And Big Brother's power grew on a daily basis. Soon, it was Winston's turn to be re-educated. He shuddered every time he thought of the dark rooms to which he had been taken, and the things he had endured there. But the re-education had been complete.

Winston gazed up at the face on the enormous poster. Many years it had taken him to learn what kind of smile was hidden beneath that thinning hairline, those close-set eyes. But the realisation had dawned. Winston didn't matter. No one else did either. Big Brother Michael was the boss now.

Old Finlay's Almanac
(January 2008)

Wise old political commentators, who made their names by predicting the outcome of elections and other momentous events, used to have a saying when things went wrong. Predictions don't always work out because politics, as we all know, isn't an exact science.

But getting things wrong never bothered a political commentator, because he (or she) could always say 'it was right when I wrote it'.

So if you don't believe my predictions about what's going to happen in 2008, I'll draw comfort from the fact that they are correct as I write them. The political ones may start to go wrong tomorrow, but as long as my sporting predictions hold good, I'll be happy.

<u>January</u>: Six cabinet ministers and four Junior ministers issue a statement announcing that if the Tribunals don't leave Bertie alone, they're all going to hold their breaths until they turn blue, and then those nasty Tribunals will be sorry.

This statement is apparently issued in response to a widely reported leak from the Mahon Tribunal. Apparently two of the Tribunal judges and three members of the legal team held a séance over Christmas, in which they managed to make direct contact with the late Charles J Haughey.

Based on the information he has given them, they have announced the setting up of eight new modules, which are scheduled to last until 2022. The media also report the coincidence that all of the legal people involved are due to retire that year. The opposition is apparently reluctant to underwrite the added cost. 'Over my dead body,' Enda Kenny is reported to have said.

February: Highlight of the month in sporting terms is Ireland winning their first three matches in the Rugby Six Nations, against Italy and Scotland in Croke Park and against France in Paris (these are my predictions, so I can dream, OK?).

Meanwhile in politics, the Progressive Democrats have a further look at their leadership rules. After none of their TDs, senators, county councillors or town councillors declares any interest in the leadership, the PDs relax the rules further. In future, they declare, anyone can be elected, so long as they're old enough to vote and not already the leader of another political party.

March: Ireland win their first Grand Slam since 1949 by beating Wales in Croke Park and then, two days before St Patrick's Day, England in Twickenham. George Hook immediately calls for the dismissal of Eddie O'Sullivan, on the grounds that he is unlikely to be able to repeat the feat in 2009.

In response to the PDs' rule change, Michael McDowell issues a statement saying that he is considering a comeback. 'It is clear that my people need me, and I will not be found wanting,' the statement concludes.

April: The PDs issue a clarifying statement, making it clear that as they had said earlier, anyone could be elected leader, provided they are neither a current nor a former leader of a political party. Michael McDowell responds by announcing his intention to join Fine Gael. 'Over my dead body,' Enda Kenny is quoted as saying.

The nation largely ignores the row, because over four sensational days Padraig Harrington wins the US Masters in Augusta. Seemingly dead after a double bogey from the left-hand bunkers on the eighteenth hole, an emotional Harrington goes on to win the title with a birdie at the third extra play-off hole.

May: The Taoiseach addresses the Joint Houses of Congress in Washington. A packed Chamber hears the Taoiseach announce that he couldn't have made peace in Northern Ireland without the help of President Bush. The President later says that he was glad to help his good friend Bertie O'Hern in whatever way he could.

Buoyed up by his rapturous reception in Washington, the Taoiseach tells correspondents that night that he is thinking of leading Fianna Fáil into the next election. At home, Charlie Bird asks Tánaiste Brian Cowen to comment. 'The Taoiseach has my full support,' the Tánaiste replies, through visibly clenched teeth. Meanwhile, Munster win the Heineken Cup in a thrilling replay of their previous visit to the Millennium Stadium in Cardiff.

June: In a startling development, the opinion polls show that the Government is likely to lose the referendum on Europe. The Taoiseach says that on reflection, he feels it's nearly time for him to move on, and that he has every confidence that his good friend Brian Cowen will do a wonderful job as Taoiseach. The Tánaiste barnstorms the country in the final week of the referendum campaign, and the Government just squeaks through.

July: The Leader of the Green Party, John Gormley, announces that in the interests of reducing Ireland's carbon footprint further, and as our contribution to end global warming, the Greens are going to drop their life-long opposition to nuclear power.

A tender competition is announced to build a nuclear power station in Mayo. 'Over my dead body,' announces Enda Kenny.

August: In an otherwise quiet month, Deputy Finian McGrath calls for the recall of the Dáil, so that he can vote against the Government on the nuclear power issue. Told that the Government has no intention of recalling the Dáil until October, he issues a statement saying that he would have voted against them if he could have, but since he can't he won't.

September: Frank Dunlop issues a statement retracting all his previous evidence to the Mahon Tribunal. He claims to have been subjected to psychological torture in secret cells below Dublin Castle, by being forced to read his own memoirs over and over again. Judge Mahon indignantly rejects the claim. 'Nobody could be that cruel,' he says.

October: It becomes clear that the Government is taking Dunlop's claims seriously, although no one else does. A motion appears on the Order Paper of the Dáil, proposing the establishment of a tribunal to inquire as a matter of urgency into the activities of the Mahon Tribunal, especially in regard to the possibility that it had used torture to extract evidence damning to the Government.

At the same time, rumours begin to circulate that the Mahon Tribunal and its legal team may have to be suspended, on full pay of course, to allow the new tribunal to do its work.

November: Former minister Ray Burke issues a statement claiming to have been fully vindicated by the Dunlop revelations. Furthermore, he says, he has strong evidence, that he will present to the new tribunal, that the late James Gogarty was both tortured and drugged by the Flood Tribunal before he alleged giving bribes to Minister Burke. The minister indicates that in the light of all these developments he may consider a return to public life.

December: The Government announces that, following a full investigation of the Frank Dunlop revelations, it has decided to suspend the Mahon Tribunal before it can issue its final report. 'Any finding of fact by this undemocratic and secretive body would now be entirely devalued,' a Government spokesman makes clear. Instead, the new tribunal, to be called the McDowell Tribunal after its chairperson, will begin its work immediately. Asked if the opposition will support these developments, Enda Kenny makes his position clear. 'Over my dead body,' he says.

The Sausage Factory

Merrion Street Confidential
(2000)

What's the worst decision the Supreme Court ever made? A decision that makes no sense at all, has no rationale to it, and is positively dangerous? A decision that surely deserves to be tested again, to make sure that their Honours weren't just having a really bad day?

No, it's not the Murphy case. There have been persistent rumours in recent weeks that a certain Attorney General, not a million miles removed from the Progressive Democrats, wants to see the Murphy case revisited. The rumour goes on to suggest that he believes the tax system has been bedevilled by the Murphy case ever since that judgment was handed down. Bad law, in the attorney's view, and long past time it was overturned.

You remember the Murphy judgement, of course. That was the case in which the court held that it was unconstitutional for two single people living together to be better off in tax terms than a married couple. Up to the time of the Murphy case, taxpayers were all treated as individuals, at least to some extent. The result was that a married couple, where only one spouse worked outside the home, were treated much less favourably than a couple 'living in sin' (what innocent times they were!).

The Supreme Court decided that was unfair, and

because the Constitution placed such store on the family, unconstitutional. A family, in the eyes of the court then and ever since, had to be based on marriage.

Undoubtedly this case *will* be revisited as a result of the individualisation measures in the Budget. It is the fact once again that a family with one spouse earning, at a certain level of income, is worse off than two people sharing a flat. Once again, the Supreme Court is likely to be asked whether that is right and fair. And we'll know whether the original decision was a bad one in the eyes of the judges themselves.

But, to go back to the beginning, there is a far worse decision. The present Attorney General (same guy) once believed it was awful. I imagine privately he still does. He could arrange for it to be re-examined. But will he? No chance!

What am I talking about? The decision on cabinet confidentiality, that's what. It arose directly out of the Beef Tribunal, and it resulted in the Supreme Court declaring that not alone had members of the Government the right to refuse to tell anyone what goes on in the Cabinet Room, they have an obligation to do so.

It's absurd, and it's patently undemocratic. The Attorney General's former party leader, Des O'Malley, always thought so. It serves no purpose – especially not the purpose for which it was ostensibly intended, the protection of collective cabinet responsibility. Anyone who believes that should have been following the activities of ministers over the last month, as they fell over themselves in their efforts to put as much space as possible between themselves, on the one hand, and Charlie McCreevy and his Budget on the other.

Hands up anyone who has heard a single interview

with a member of the Government (in either party) coming to the defence of their embattled colleague?

The purpose of the cabinet confidentiality ruling is to protect secrecy, nothing more than that. It was the logical consequence of a culture that believes transparency is what happens only on Judgement Day (and even then there'll be some lads trying to hide behind cabinet secrecy).

What has secrecy ever done for us? It was secrecy which produced the beef scandal in the first place. Secrecy which was behind all the business scandals of the early 1990s. Secrecy which enabled the late Des Traynor to build an empire of tax evasion. Secrecy which enabled Charles Haughey to profit from it. I could go on.

I worked in an office next door to the Cabinet Room for four years in the mid-1980s, and close by again in the mid-1990s. I never understood what went on behind those double doors. It was a process which defied logic sometimes, and always defied easy explanation.

I could fill this newspaper with instances of decisions made in that room which bore no relation whatever to the arguments facing the cabinet. At meeting after meeting, cabinet ministers are presented with detailed papers outlining the options they have in relation to any decision. Hours of work and analysis go into those papers – the economic and political rationale for every possible course of action is spelled out in them.

Time and again, ministers ignore them totally, and make a decision for which there is no known rationale (or in respect of which the rationale has to be constructed afterwards, to fit the decision).

I'm not arguing here that ministers should always follow the advice they get – that would be equally undemocratic. And neither am I suggesting that the decisions they make based totally on the arguments that take place in the cabinet room are corrupt or wrong – far from it. What I am saying is that the people who elect Governments are entitled to know the process by which a decision is made.

Under the cabinet confidentiality rule, we are entitled as citizens to see the bits of paper that ministers looked at. We're entitled to see the decision as it was recorded. But anyone who knows the process knows that many key decisions are made without any recourse to the papers – and sometimes in spite of the papers.

Sometimes, of course, decisions involve trade-offs and compromises – and compromises, however worthy, are easier to make in private. Sometimes decisions are the result of long and complicated negotiation, often with foreign governments. And in so far as they reflect a part of those negotiations, it can be necessary to keep the process behind such decisions secret too.

So there are some circumstances where I would readily concede the need for secrecy. What I believe is indefensible is the culture of secrecy that surrounds so much of our public life.

And it's not just in Government – I don't see, for instance, why we're not entitled to know what goes on in the chambers where the members of the Supreme Court are deliberating their weighty decisions. I don't know why we're not entitled to peep at the process by which a lot of planning decisions are made.

But I'd settle for starters for the right to know the basis on which the cabinet I help to elect makes its decisions. And after all, the present Chief Justice fought mightily against the cabinet confidentiality ruling when he was in charge of the Beef Tribunal. The present AG, as I've said, made a career out of criticising the decisions made behind closed doors – as did most of his party colleagues, now in influential positions in Government. The leader of the opposition is on record as being totally opposed to secrecy – there was even a time when he wanted everyone to reveal their sources.

Given the forces ranged in favour of transparency, surely it's only a matter of time before this absurd and dangerous decision is re-examined. Surely we shouldn't hold our breath!

A Pyrrhic Victory
(2002)

Since the abortion referendum was announced, I've written three times in the *Irish Examiner*, advocating and predicting a No vote. The longer the debate went on, the more certain I became that real and lasting harm would be done if we voted in favour of the Government's proposal.

So I should have been happy at the outcome, shouldn't I? Maybe it wasn't a landslide, but it was clear and explicit. It was roughly the same margin of votes that Eamon De Valera had over Tom O'Higgins on the last occasion that 'the long fellow' won a national election. And I'm old enough to remember Fianna Fáil claiming that as a decisive victory for them.

I'm relieved, I readily admit that. I got a bit worried last weekend, when I heard some commentators I respect predicting that the tide had turned and that the Yes vote would win in the end. I wondered where they got their information, because the only scientific data available, the opinion polls, showed a steady trend away from a Yes vote. But good political correspondents are closer to the pulse than we sometimes give them credit for, and they have to be listened to when they call the result of any electoral contest.

So it seemed as if maybe the pollsters (and me) were misreading things. Maybe the last weekend of the campaign, with its concerted message from the pulpits to an audience that was more likely to vote, was going to swing it. Fortunately, it didn't.

I hope it's not an unworthy thought, but I wonder how many of the forgotten women voted? In the last ten years, between 50,000 and 70,000 Irish women went to England for an abortion. Like the rest of us, they were asked to vote for a proposal that would have had the effect of declaring what they had done a criminal act, worthy of a twelve-year jail sentence, if it was carried out in their own jurisdiction. Did they vote this week? And did they vote no? If they did, I hope they are getting little moments of quiet satisfaction this weekend at the thought that their votes were decisive in ensuring that they couldn't be bracketed as criminals.

But how do I feel apart from relieved? Mostly angry, but a bit hopeful as well. I'm angry because we should never have been asked to do this in the first place. Angry because there was a lot of hypocrisy involved in it. I'm angry because the country was, effectively, split down the middle for nothing. It resolved nothing, it made life better for no one, it solved no problem.

Of course I'm guessing – anyone who tells you that they know what the Irish people as a whole really wanted to do in this referendum would be lying. But I have a hunch that one of the reasons people turned this down was because they didn't like the look of it from the very beginning.

The people of Ireland have always had an oddly protective attitude towards the Constitution. They treat it as if they have a proprietorial stake, as of course they do.

And this awful hodge-podge of words would have involved putting a horrible scar on the document. Not only is its meaning obscure, even the very language for which we were asked to vote was ugly. My guess is that a great many people were repelled by it from the start.

Not the PDs, mind you. I saw Liz O'Donnell on the television on Thusday night, after the result was announced, asserting that the whole thing had nothing to do with politics, and they had stayed neutral throughout.

Not for the first time as I watch the PDs, I wondered who she thought she was kidding. This was the same Liz O'Donnell who was the second politician in Ireland (after the Taoiseach) to support the proposition. She attended the press conference at which the whole thing was launched, and spoke strongly in favour of it. And why wouldn't she – wasn't it her party president, Attorney General and Pooh-Bah Michael McDowell who drafted the whole thing in the first place and provided the intellectual justification for it – even down to the slithery arguments he put forward for his own conversion to the conservative pro-life position?. Ah, the joys of high office – isn't it just as well nobody is so unkind as to suggest that anyone who could travel such an intellectual journey must be morally brain dead.

And the result has been unnecessary and painful division. Unnecessary because it changed nothing, painful because the discussion has been hurtful to thousands of people. Incidentally, I got a polite letter from a priest during the week insisting that I had erred last week in suggesting that the Catholic Church didn't always recognise the spiritual dimension of stillborn babies. If I did err, I'm sorry – the news that the church welcomes stillborn babies home will come as a welcome relief to several families I know.

We all have a right – maybe even a duty – to be angry with the Government that sprung this on us. As the absolute figures show, we split down the middle. For nothing. And that's the Government's fault, 100 per cent. The opposition parties behaved in a disciplined and honourable way, and debated the issue trenchantly but on its own terms. Government campaigners tried to polarise the argument by personalising it, and they deserve to be punished for that.

But where's the hope in all of this? Again I'm guessing, but I have more than a hunch about it. Call it a conviction if you like, but I'm convinced the real turning point in this debate happened ten years ago, with the X case itself. It was that case which taught us all, in a way that we don't appear to have forgotten, that these things aren't black and white. Ever since then, it has not been possible to take for granted that the Irish people will vote for a dogmatic approach of any kind, or will be led by any paternal or patronising doctrine.

And the trend in the vote (as opposed to the absolute figures) shows a definite continuing movement towards more urban, liberal and modern values. It's hard to measure still, but it's real enough for all that. It means there'll be no more rolling back progress (there might be attempts, but they will fail).

And it may mean something deeper. The Yes campaign was started by the largest party in the State, and led by a Taoiseach who is seen as being urban, young, modern. In reality, the values he and his party espoused in the last month were old-fashioned, backward looking, conservative. And more than that – they were out of touch with the Ireland of today.

That may not rebound on Fianna Fáil in the short term. But everything that has happened suggests that there are undercurrents of change in Ireland. The Taoiseach did not reflect, catch or lead those undercurrents in this campaign. In a month or so, he is going to be campaigning about the Ireland of tomorrow. But in the month just past, he looked and sounded like the leader of yesterday.

Nothing to Hide
(2004)

There's a little African country, somewhere in the middle of that great continent. From everything we've heard and read about it, it fits all the stereotypes.

A governing party that masquerades as democratic, but rumours of political corruption have been established time and again to be true. Members of the government all have big houses and drive flashy cars, even though they are surrounded by poverty.

But worse than that, over the last couple of years they have been systematically dismantling the essential trappings of democracy. Parliament is being treated with disdain. It meets very seldom, and then only to rubber-stamp decisions already made by the government. There is no debate, little or no questioning, no opportunity for parliamentarians to make any real input to the law of the land.

Even though the country describes itself as a multi-party democracy, the size of the government majority is such that they can ram through anything they want to. By and large, though, they govern by making announcements, and as often as not by doing secret deals with powerful vested interests in the land.

Outside parliament, if you study the reports coming

out of this little country, you can see other troubling signs. The freedom of information legislation that used to be trumpeted as a hallmark of the country's commitment to democracy is effectively gone. The civil service, which everyone saw as a bastion of independence, is being broken up and its senior figures being dispatched to different parts of the country.

The Government has decided to change the method of recruitment to the civil service, and independent observers have described the new rules as a recipe for the gradual politicisation of the service – something people thought had been done away with years before.

The governing party has also announced that it wants to regulate press freedom. Although they have said on the record that their intention is to reform the libel laws, their essential purpose (and nobody in Government has denied this) seems to be to establish a government-controlled press council, which will not only investigate complaints against the press but will also decide on such things as what constitute good taste and standards of journalism.

The government (itself awash with cash) also wants to do away with all the previous limits on election spending and the need to account publicly for how the money was spent. There are other warning signs that point to the possibility that any future election might be run in favour of the government party.

For instance, a few years ago it was discovered that there were huge amounts of money held in bank accounts throughout the country, and many of these accounts had been completely inactive. At the same time, some of the banks had been found to have been engaged in nefarious practices in the interests of their better-off customers, helping them to evade tax. Partly as punishment for these practices, and also because it made social sense in the country, the parliament decided that the money in the inactive accounts should be effectively confiscated and put to good use.

An independent board was established, and told to distribute the money where it could do most good, especially in terms of combating educational and other forms of disadvantage. Now, however, it has been revealed that the government has changed the rules. In future, the government itself will make all final decisions on how that money should be spent. Independent observers suspect that the move, which hasn't received much publicity, is designed to effectively create a government slush fund to be spent in marginal constituencies.

And now the last straw. A senior member of the government, who happens to be the government's director of elections, has announced that in future all elections are to be conducted electronically. Government spokespeople hail the move as symbolic of the country's great push to modernisation. A massive amount of money will be spent on buying machines that people can vote on, and the results will be counted instantly.

Following a national tender competition in which many of the country's advertising agencies and public relations firms take part, a huge contract is awarded to a firm whose principals have close connections with the government party. It will be their job to educate the peasants of the country in how the system works, and to inspire trust and confidence in the system.

As the details emerge, however, all sorts of troubling questions arise. This new system has never been properly tested (the minister responsible dismisses any concerns about testing, announcing that he is very happy that the new system will work). There will be no way of verifying the results, no paper trail, no way of challenging a close result, no way of determining if the system has been interfered with or hacked into.

There won't even be a way of proving that the software wasn't deliberately interfered with to produce the right result. The company supplying the machines is highly reputable, of course, but no one knows who will ultimately control the software.

In the past, whatever about how election campaigns were conducted, and whatever the government party was able to get away with by way of phoney promises, the counting of elections throughout the country was always carried out in a pretty open way. Everyone could watch, and indeed most of the political parties had people who had become expert in counting along – to such an extent that they were able to agree on predictions long before counts were over. In future, voters will have to have blind trust in the system which determines their future. There will be opinion polling, of course, but what if there is a huge gap between what the polls predict and the outcome of the instantaneous and effectively secret count?

In setting up the system, it has also been discovered that the government has no proper proposals, for example, to restrict access to count centre PCs during the count, or to ensure that only the right software is installed on count centre PCs. There will be no independent scrutiny of the software installation. Voters will cast their votes with the help of a watching public official, and then they will have to rely on the government-controlled system to count the votes accurately. Unlike in every election since the country became independent, there will be no basis for challenge.

The concerns about democracy in this little country have now reached the floor of the European Parliament, which has every right to take an interest because Europe has been to the fore in assisting the rapid economic development of the little republic. Following a debate, it has been decided that the EU will put together a team of observers to try to investigate the situation, and to make sure that any election in the future will be free, fair, and independently run and scrutinised.

What they can't understand in Europe, though, is why Ireland has declined the prestigious offer of heading up the observer team. As one European official remarked, noting the way in which the Irish had said they were much too busy to get involved, 'it's almost like those guys had something to hide themselves'.

A Dollop of Inequality
(2004)

Isn't Michael McDowell absolutely right? Inequality is an incentive, no doubt about it. Starve the poor and they'll go and find themselves a job – or pull themselves up by their bootstraps, as his pal Charlie McCreevy would say. Ignore people with a disability and someone who cares will look after them. Provide opportunities for the rich and boy, will they take advantage of the incentives.

The only problem with incentives, of course, is that sometimes the more you have, the more you need. The first politician to really think through the whole business of giving people incentives, and really encouraging them to take risks for Ireland, was of course the great CJ Haughey. Didn't he introduce the great incentive for the bloodstock industry in Ireland (completely uninfluenced by the fact that he owned a few nags himself)?

And hasn't it been a great success, a great incentive altogether? It has made multi-millionaires out of a whole load of people, and all entirely tax free. (They're not stable lads, mind you, or the people who work on the tote for an hourly rate. But sure no doubt if they had a few bob in disposable income they'd only waste it, because they don't have the great entrepreneurial spirit that really knows how to use an incentive.)

But all of a sudden, when you look at this wonderful incentive as an example, you come up against the first riddle. How come so many of the people we gave this brilliant incentive to, enabling them to make all this tax-free dosh, don't like living in Ireland? Apparently, if you make income from one source tax free, people seem to expect income from every source to be tax free as well.

And if they don't get it, they decide to live in places where they can protect all their income from harsh and forbidding tax regimes like ours. (Although that's getting harder too, since our tax regime is one of the easiest in the world.) And then, of course, they have to spend time and effort lobbying senior politicians to get the residency laws relaxed, so they can live 'at home and abroad', minding their tax-free status but enjoying the races and the golf too.

God, it's difficult maintaining an incentive culture, isn't it? But thank God, if the bloodstock incentive won't work, we have a range of others. All these incentives are designed specifically for people of quality, people who understand the meaning of money, people who don't have to worry about ESB or phone bills but have the time to think about how they can help to build the Irish economy while keeping their own tax liabilities low. High earners, in other words – people like senior bankers, for instance.

I've written before about this, but it's worth reminding ourselves how good we are at developing these incentives, to keep the poor dears happy, and to help them keep as much as possible of their own money in their pockets. And the other great thing about these incentives is that they're legal! You can be as selfish as you like, and it's all within the law.

You can invest in a multi-storey car park, for instance,

or a hotel, or a variety of other property-based investment schemes. You can buy a nice heritage home and we'll give you a tax break for it. And the other thing you'll have noticed about all these nice incentives for investing your money is that there is virtually no risk in any of them. Imagine, we pay you to invest in bricks and mortar, and avoid paying tax that way. How could it be better?

In fact, the last time we totted it up, we (that is to say, the rest of us) paid out around €73 million on these incentives. And we paid that out so that the highest-earning people in Ireland could keep their taxes as low as possible.

And the great news is it worked. Michael is right – inequality is good, inequality produces results.

According to the Revenue Commissioners, if you look at the kind of tax rates that the 400 highest earners in Ireland have to put up with, you find that, thanks to the incentives we've built in for them, one in five of the top 400 earners had an effective rate of less than 15 per cent, and a further one in ten had an effective rate of between 15 per cent and 29 per cent.

But that's only the top 400. Within that group the Revenue had a look at the really top earners, the top 120 or so. They're really busy, and really clever – I suppose that's what makes them such high earners. A quarter of the very top earners, using the tax avoidance mechanisms we built for them, had no tax liability at all! And a further 20 per cent kept their effective tax rate below 5 per cent.

But now we come to that riddle again. The more they have, the more they want. You can bet your bottom dollar that all, or most, of the names you've been reading in the newspapers from the latest AIB scandal are in that top

400, for whom we have lashed out tens of millions in tax avoidance opportunities. And what do they do? Not content with hiding their money away in the 'legitimate' schemes, they use their wealth and influence to create new ones, of the kind that drag a national institution into truly serious disrepute.

Are they alone? Yeah, right.

Because here's the thing Michael McDowell doesn't get, and here's the reason he and his ilk are capable of so much damage, with their blind pernicious philosophy. Side by side with the culture of incentive he loves so much, with the culture of inequality he is prepared to defend, we have built a culture of mean-spirited, petty greed in Ireland. It was conceived in the policies of the late 70s and early 80s, and first burst into public view in 1989, the year of the Golden Circle, as it was called.

And it has haunted us ever since – councillors on the take, businessmen looking for the inside track, political patronage being handed to undeserving cronies, bankers doing their business offshore. Along the way, every institution of authority in Ireland has been damaged, people have become completely alienated from politics, and everyone, it seems, wants to screw whatever system they can for as much as possible.

That's the background against which McDowell sneers at the demand for a rights-based society. To be sure, an emphasis on equality can give rise to outbreaks of political correctness, of the sort that always gives smart-assed commentators the opportunity to fill acres of space with jokes. But political correctness never robbed taxpayers blind.

It's the culture of greed that has done so much damage. All that guff about how inequality is good for you, and how people need incentives in order to get on, is so obviously blind to the real world that some of our politics, and some of our politicians, have helped to create. It's a world of corruption, indifference and neglect, and the philosophy that underpins it should have the grace, at least, to stop lecturing the rest of us.

God Help the Bankers
(2004)

If any of you bankers are reading this, let me offer you my sympathy. It's an awful feeling, isn't it, being tarred with the same brush. Looking at cartoons in the papers of bankers dressed as cowboys, bankers in handcuffs, bankers robbing the till they're supposed to be in charge of.

Ye're all the bloody same, aren't ye? Just like the politicians and the priests and the builders, if one goes bad the whole tribe must be bad. Well, no, of course not. Because there were some bankers who were prepared to go to any lengths to turn in the right profit figures, that doesn't mean that everyone who works in a bank, or everyone who runs a bank, is rotten. In fact the vast majority of people who work in that profession are honest citizens.

But they're not immune to pressure. The DIRT scandal – the one that infested the entire banking community, as opposed to the NIB scandal – was occasioned in the first instance by greed, and then by competition. If one bank was offering customers an attractive service, they all had to. And they did. We know that NIB wasn't the only bank overcharging its customers. AIB would say that while NIB's overcharging was systematic and deliberate, AIB's was accidental and

193

the result of misunderstandings. It's up to you to decide what to believe.

But let's go back to the business of tarring everyone with the same brush. It's commonplace to put the words 'corruption' and 'politician' in the same sentence – linking the politician who has fought against corruption with the one who has profited by it. Priests wince at sentences that reveal the underlying assumption that all priests are complicit in child abuse; property developers hate the notion that all property development is bad and has to be bought with brown envelopes. They are all unfair generalisations, and they are corrosive.

The most corrosive effect of all these things is on trust. Authority used to be built on trust, and the authority carried by great and powerful institutions was based to a considerable degree on the fact that they were seen as incorruptible. Now, all these same institutions – and to the bankers, politicians and priests we could add the law, medicine and many of the other professions – are widely seen as self-serving, self-regarding and immune to criticism. If not corrupt, then well on the way.

How, in the space of a few short years, has this happened? When Charlie Bird and George Lee broke the NIB story in 1998, it was genuinely shocking, hard to believe that a bank would systematically, as a matter of policy and practice, engage on the one hand in ripping off its customers and on the other in facilitating their tax evasion. Banks simply didn't do that. They mightn't behave like everyone's favourite uncle, but they were certainly never going to be the black sheep of the family.

Charlie McCreevy, at the time, appeared simply not to believe it – or perhaps he simply didn't wish to dig too deeply into the whole area of tax evasion for fear of what he would find. Among other things, he told RTÉ in an interview in January 1998 that 'the sums uncovered are very small in the context of the level of tax paid each year' and that 'it is an insult to the vast majority of taxpayers to say that tax evasion is widespread'. He went on to say that people were 'going off half-cocked and making ridiculous and outlandish allegations both against the Revenue Commissioners and against others'.

It was a stupid and fatuous way to react. The breaking of the NIB story was a seminal moment in recent Irish history. Stories like that are the same as lifting stones – we might not like what crawls out, but if maggots like that are left undisturbed, they burrow away until the entire foundation is rotten.

In recent years, a number of such stones have been lifted, with equally shocking effect. The revelation of Bishop Casey's infidelity to his vows was followed in short order by a variety of other revelations about aspects of the priesthood that have shaken the authority of the Church to its roots. The original revelations about the difficulties between Larry Goodman and his bankers led to the uncovering of an incredible tale of cosy relationships, public policy disasters, tax evasion on a massive scale, and a deeply unhealthy approach to the regulation of a vital industry.

Allegations of corruption in the planning process have led to enquiries that have revealed corruption to be more widespread, deeper and more systematic than the people making the allegations ever dreamed of. Political revelations about a transaction between Charlie Haughey and a businessman have led to the discovery that a Taoiseach of Ireland, in order to enrich himself and pursue a vainglorious lifestyle, allowed himself to be entirely beholden to a range of commercial interests, rather than to the common good.

The first funny thing about all these revelations (actually, the first tragic thing) is that although they shocked us at the time, they don't shock us any more. Partly, this is because of the passage of time – or rather the spread of time within which all these revelations occurred. We set up all sorts of systems to try to produce some kind of catharsis – enquiries, tribunals, redress boards, and so on – but in reality they have all gone on so long they're like a dull ache that we just get used to, never really feeling it until we turn badly and realise it's still there.

Did you know, for instance, that last weekend was the tenth anniversary of the publication of the Beef Tribunal report, a thousand-page document that followed four years of the most painstaking investigations and astonishing revelations?

Somebody described it at the time as '60,000 lines to read between' – others as one of the great cop-outs of modern times. Certainly it will always be remembered for the fact that no one was threatened with jail arising from that report – except the journalist who broke the story in the first place.

Maybe that's Ireland for you. And here's the second tragedy. It's still going on. We have learned nothing, and we continue to regard notions like transparency and accountability as wet liberal clichés. The Government has more or less killed freedom of information, and the Government continues to operate the kind of stroke politics that has given politics such a bad name.

Posturing in the Fianna Fáil tent at the Galway Races; insisting that the coherence of the civil service will be broken up through the political stroke of decentralisation; spending millions of public money on daft and stupid projects that have never been subjected to any form of accountability – these kind of things may not represent the corruption of the old days.

But what they do reveal is a political system that has completely failed to recognise that authority is based on trust, and that trust must be earned, and earned again. A political system that refuses to recognise that it has an obligation to continually earn the trust of the people is one that is doomed to be corrupt in the end.

Up Voltaire!
(2006)

All this freedom of speech and freedom of expression stuff we've been hearing about lately. I'm up for that. You can never be sure about these things until you're really tested, but I'd like to think that I'd be prepared to go all the way with Voltaire when he said, 'I detest your views, but am prepared to die for your right to express them.'

I have written here and elsewhere that I don't equate the right to freedom of expression with the right to be offensive or stupid. And I've always believed that it is perfectly legitimate to curtail the rights of people whose motive is to inflame hatred or bigotry, or to tell lies. But there can surely be no argument against the proposition that gratuitous curbs on freedom of expression, for political or other reasons, will chip away at the cornerstones of democracy.

To this extent, I am entirely at one with the commentators, journalists and others who have appeared in print and on all of the broadcast media over the last couple of weeks in connection with the riots taking place around the world over the cartoons of Mohammed.

Yes, there is a real challenge to freedom of expression in all of this. Yes, there are important values at stake. I don't subscribe to the view that, by definition, my values are more important than anyone else's, but I do understand the passion that this entire controversy has generated.

So I have a question for all those who have so passionately defended the right to express opinions and views, even offensive ones.

My question is this. Why aren't you marching (peacefully, of course) on the Irish Broadcasting Complaints Commission? Why aren't you writing with equal passion about the way in which that body (which is a State body) and other State bodies, including RTÉ, are now interpreting the law of the land to curtail freedom of expression? And not just freedom of expression, but normal political discourse and public awareness of normal political issues.

Consider this. It's the text of a TV and radio ad run by the Interim National Consumer Agency, a body that was set up by the Government (on foot of an independent report) with a specific mandate to ensure, for the first time, that the interests of consumers are brought to the forefront of national and local decision-making in Ireland.

This was the ad they ran:

> *Do you have views on the Groceries Order which affects the price of your shopping basket? The Department of Enterprise, Trade and Employment wants to hear what consumers think about the Order before 31 July. The National Consumer Agency believes consumers should make their voices heard. To learn more go to Irishconsumer.ie or call 01 6073015.*

Seems pretty harmless, doesn't it? You could imagine an ad like that generating a few hits on the website, a few phone calls, maybe even one or two expressions of concern about the Groceries Order. That would have been roughly what the people who wrote the ad had in mind – increase public awareness a bit, spread information, maybe encourage debate.

But no. Apparently that ad was a political one. It has been outlawed, declared to be illegal. Censored, in other words, or banned, whichever you like.

RGDATA (an organisation that represents the grocery industry and was involved in a campaign to retain the Groceries Order) objected to the ad, and complained to the Broadcasting Complaints Commission. They said the ad was inaccurate and unfair and unbalanced. That's fine, as far as I'm concerned. Everyone has the right to complain and to have their complaint heard. That's freedom of expression too.

And the Broadcasting Complaints Commission upheld the complaint. But not on the grounds of inaccuracy, unfairness, lack of balance, or anything like that. They didn't even find the ad in bad taste (which would have been hard, I grant you). No, instead, they issued this finding:

> *The Commission was of the opinion that this advertisement infringed the advertising regulations and in particular ... [Section 20 of the Broadcasting Act, which] prohibits RTÉ from accepting 'any advertisement which is directed towards any religious or political end or has any relation to an industrial dispute ... The Commission was of the view that a consultation process concerning an Irish statute is a political one. Through this advertisement, the National Consumer Agency was promoting its position on the Grocery Order. The Agency was encouraging listeners to respond to a consultation*

process ... and thereby, endeavouring to influence a political decision-making process. Therefore, the Commission was of the opinion that this advertisement was directed towards a political end. Such advertisements are prohibited.

(I've shortened the finding for reasons of space, though I haven't taken it out of context. You can find the full decision on the Commission's website, www.bcc.ie.)

This is nonsense, stupid, pettifogging nonsense. But let me tell you what makes it dangerous. As an immediate response to the BCC decision in this case, RTÉ has decided it can no longer allow any ads to be broadcast that have that sort of 'political content'. An RTÉ spokesperson is quoted in the papers as saying that the BCC's 'stricter interpretation' of the law meant it was no longer in a position to air advertisements for public meetings at which 'political issues' would be discussed.

What is the 'political content' we're talking about? One ad that has had to be withdrawn was for a conference in Kildare organised by the human rights groups Afri and Frontline. The ad said there would be 'eyewitness accounts [at the conference] from the Niger Delta and Rossport, Darfur, Iraq and Shannon Airport'. Around the same time, RTÉ ordered the Irish Cancer Society to tone down a radio advert which said that the Society was 'lobbying Government to urgently implement a free nationwide cervical cancer-screening programme'.

The decision of the BCC to reinterpret the Broadcasting Act and to use that interpretation to come up with an entirely new definition of 'political end' was made on January 9th this year. It hasn't yet had time to have much effect, but its effects will build over time. The BCC used to investigate complaints only against RTÉ, but it now has the power to deal with all broadcasting complaints concerning radio and television broadcasters licensed within the Republic of Ireland. And it has extensive rights, given to it by the Broadcasting Act of 2001.

So how are we doing on freedom of expression, especially as it relates to political issues? We now have a law, a number of State bodies, and an entire structure that has decided that no one can run an ad on local or national radio or television that is critical in even the remotest degree of Government policy, or is trying to change any aspect of public policy. It affects campaigning or public awareness advertising today. What other aspect of political discourse will be affected tomorrow? What other way of discussing public policy issues will be censored or banned?

Which gives rise to two further questions to all who believe in freedom of expression. How did this happen? And isn't it time we got our marching boots on again?

€50,642,875,000 and Change
(2006)

I got the usual strong reaction to the piece I wrote last week about the cost of a new prison. Bloody liberals, some of you muttered, you're all the bloody same. Just trying to hype up the cost of keeping people in jail because you'd rather see them roaming the streets. One caller to a radio programme that followed up on the piece said he knew the way to keep prison costs down. Bring back the chain gangs.

I'm glad to say that only a small number of you seem to feel that way. But (and no disrespect is intended here) most of you who reacted to the piece missed the point just a little bit. I wasn't arguing for or against prisons as such. Yes, I believe that we should see prison as a last resort, and the fact that keeping someone in jail is so expensive simply reinforces that view. And I also believe that the proposed new prison is being built in the wrong place for the wrong reasons.

But my bigger point is about our right to know, and our right to be involved in the decision-making, at least to some extent. The prison is a project that will cost a billion euro to run over the course of a decade – but it's not the only one. Extraordinary, unimaginable amounts of money are spent every day on our behalf, by people we elected. The amounts have got so big that they're almost impossible to grasp. So we've stopped trying – and that's a recipe for disaster.

When I started working for a Government in the 1980s, the annual size of the current budget deficit was debated. Endlessly, everywhere. People knew the consequences of one figure or another, and very often knew the detail of the row going on in the cabinet about which figure it should be. Of course, in a time of difficulty and retrenchment, the size of the projected deficit determined the size of the cuts that would have to be made in spending. So the deficit wasn't a mere economic concept – it affected people's lives in real and immediate ways.

The figures were smaller too and more manageable in terms of understanding and communicating them. Even as recently as the 1980s, you could build a hundred houses for a million pounds.

But none of us have a clue now. The figures are so big and so remote that somehow it seems to have stopped mattering. And of course, cutbacks are a thing of the past anyway. We don't need to worry.

Well, fecklessness about figures got us into a lot of trouble in the first place. The budgetary miscalculations and the wild spending decisions of the late 1970s contributed to a decade and a half of real hardship. And as sure as eggs, the one sure way for ministers to start making those kind of mistakes again is for the rest of us to lose interest in what's going on. Especially in the year before an election. With billions in the kitty, and an electorate weary of calculating what it all means, the temptation to start throwing money around will be huge.

I don't object to extra money going toward the right

things – provided it's properly managed and fairly distributed. I don't want to see long-term commitments being made about short-term problems, or money being spent for no reason other than that it's being spent in a marginal constituency. What worries me – and as I said, I think the prisons argument is only one example – is that we seem to have lost interest in our right to know what's going on.

If I stopped a hundred of you in the street, and offered you a thousand pounds if you could write down – let's say to the nearest 100 million – how much our government intends to spend on our behalf this year, not one of you would win it. That's partly because the figure has become so huge we've all lost our ability to understand it. But it's also because we've stopped caring about it.

Here's what the actual figures are, and you'll see what I mean: €43,875,637,000 is what they propose to spend on current services this year – that's running the country on a day-to-day basis. And then on top of that they intend to spend a further €6,767,238,000 on capital projects. That's a total of €50,642,875,000.

When you see it written down that way, it's a bit alarming, isn't it? You begin to wonder what kind of genius is needed to manage all that, make sure it doesn't go astray, and guarantee that it's all spent wisely and well. Because here's the other thing to remember. Three-quarters of all of that comes from you. Income tax, VAT and excise taxes – the direct and indirect taxes you pay – contribute the lion's share of what's spent. You don't have to begrudge that, just insist that it's spent wisely!

But instead, we're never really told what the figures are in ways we can get our heads around. You might have read somewhere, or been told in some fashion, that expenditure this year would exceed €50 billion for the first time. But even a phrase like €50 billion sounds a bit meaningless, compared with the rather frightening figure of €50,642,875,000, doesn't it?

During the quiet weeks of the summer, I intend to look in a bit of detail at where all this money goes. Because a few things strike me as being obvious. First of all, by the time the next election comes, our Government will have been in office ten years, give or take. That means that in current terms they will have spent, over the years they have been there, more than €500 billion – or €500,000,000,000 if you like – on providing the economic and social services, the security and governance, and the infrastructural development we have needed. On the one hand, it's perhaps not surprising that they can claim (as they do) to have achieved so much, given that astonishing amount of spending in a decade. On the other, why does there still seem to be so much to do?

And secondly, we know there has been some wasted money. Electronic voting, health service computer systems, a number of other mismanaged projects. Taken all together, they might have cost us, that we know of, €500 million. A vast amount of money, to be sure, but as a total of all spending over the decade it's around a tenth of 1 per cent.

You know what that means? No, it almost certainly doesn't mean that the Government has been unfairly criticised for waste. It means there's a huge amount more to be uncovered, because the truth is we don't know the half of what has gone on.

Knowing what goes on with our money, how it's managed and spent, and being entitled to assume that someone is accountable for it all – they are democratic rights. We know that our right to accountability hasn't been exercised very much, if at all. But you know what? We don't just have a right to know, we also have a duty to care. And if that disappears, we're all in trouble.

Phishing and Pharming
(2007)

Have you ever heard of phishing? Or pharming? No, this isn't me misspelling words you know well. Both these words describe new techniques available to people who want to use the internet for improper or illegal purposes. Phishers and pharmers are potential criminals – and they are a potential threat to your family.

Phishing is a criminal activity that uses different techniques to get hold of personal information about people using the internet. Phishers attempt to acquire sensitive information, such as usernames, passwords and credit card details, by pretending to be someone you can trust if you get an e-mail from them, or if you meet them in a chat room. Pharming is a more elaborate technique that seeks to direct the traffic to a website to a different false website that the pharmer has set up.

People who are skilled in both techniques use them to steal the identity of other people. Most often, the techniques have been used in the past to get hold of banking information, in order, obviously, to commit fraud. But the techniques are increasingly in use in another evil world, the world of the child abuser. And what is most frightening about this new use of the internet is how little we know about it.

Just this week, a police operation led by the UK Child Exploitation and Online Protection Agency, and involving police in 35 countries, appeared to crack yet another paedophile ring. The UK body, known as the CEOP, rescued 76 children from abusive environments in its first year of operation, and its work resulted in the arrests of 83 child sex offenders. The CEOP brings together police officers, computer experts and children's defence groups. In its first year they have already identified and dismantled three international paedophile rings – all with UK connections. And all active on the internet.

In the main, paedophiles use the internet to communicate with each other. But the techniques now available, which are easily learned and applied, have enabled them also to use the internet for grooming their victims.

Grooming sounds like an innocent term. It isn't. Grooming is a process by which sex abusers identify young people who are vulnerable – perhaps lonely, perhaps emotionally fragile – and systematically set about earning their trust. They want to build up a relationship of dependence and control, and they have several purposes in mind. First they want to make the young person amenable to abuse, and secondly they want to ensure that the young person won't tell – or even if they do, that they will be less inclined to reveal the identity of the abuser.

That's where the internet comes in. Now, I don't want to give the impression that the internet is in itself a dangerous place. It can be, but there is no reason why it should be. And I also don't want to give the impression that abuse only happens on or through the internet. The vast majority of young people who suffer abuse know, and often trust, their abuser. We know that for far too many young people, sex abuse happens within the family.

But access to the internet, and the freedom with which we all use it, has also made it a sort of devil's playground for abusers.

When a young person first joins one of the internet chat rooms, they're generally encouraged to keep their identity private. And most young people use made-up names and passwords to protect their identity. If they think that makes them safe, they're wrong.

Here's how phishing works. The predator picks a range of possible victims, picks a location, adds one of the internet servers that young people enjoy, and then uses the Google search engine, or any of the other search engines on the web, to collect a group of potential victims. Let's say, for example, he enters 'Bebo Newcastle male'. He will instantly find a collection of people, all identifying themselves as male and from Newcastle, and all available to chat to on the web.

Now, of course, they haven't given their real names. But what they have done, without meaning to, is scattered clues all over the place about their identity and their interests. The names of their friends, the school they go to, the name of their teachers, favourite bands, foods, sports. The patient predator will assemble these clues, and use them to start conversations on the web with as many young people as he wants to.

Let's assume that one of the potential victims is called John (though his Bebo ID is Shearer, after his football hero). John is a Newcastle United fanatic, and a big follower of Oasis. His new friend on the web pretends to share these interests, and sends John a couple of internet links that contain fascinating gossip about his favourite team. But when John tries to open the links (which are spurious), he is told that he needs an additional piece of software to access them. His friend helpfully sends him the software, and it takes John no more than a couple of seconds to download it and install it.

The 'new software' still doesn't work. His friend apologies profusely, and explains that it must have been corrupted. But it wasn't corrupted. It was a piece of software know as a Trojan – once installed in John's computer, it begins to capture every bit of data about John and his family that exists on the computer, and it can send that data to a source on the internet under the control of the attacker. Credit cards, transaction details, banking logins, address books, private e-mails, any usernames and passwords that might be there. Suddenly, the predator knows everything he needs to know about his potential victim.

The key to grooming is knowledge. The predator who knows someone's innermost thoughts – the kind that might be guessed at from knowing the websites they go to, or reading their e-mails – is in a strong position to begin the process of manipulation that can end in abuse. A determined predator doesn't have to be a computer expert, because a lot of the software necessary for this level of access and control is fairly easily available.

Speaking at the publication of the CEOP's first annual report a couple of weeks ago, its chief executive Jim Gamble described the challenge they face in the UK. Based on analysis of information from 6,000 children, he reported that up to one in four of them are meeting people offline who they initially engaged with online. 'Many of them,' he said, 'are bringing a friend along and therefore putting more children at risk. This is backed up by analysis of our reporting mechanism that shows online chat and instant messenger are still the most reported area of abuse and that grooming is the most frequently reported activity.'

Use of the web is growing every day. Some – not all – of the young people who use it most are lonely, vulnerable and deeply at risk. But even those who think they have it sussed can be taken in by the highly skilled predators who have learned how to use the internet for evil purposes. It's time we woke up to the risk.

Yes to Lisbon
(2008)

Do you remember the currency crisis at the end of 1992? Well, I'll never forget it. I took out a mortgage in the month it started. Like most of us, it was more than I could afford, and the first mortgage payment was about double the rent I had been paying in the month before that.

I consoled myself with the thought that the tax relief would help, and anyway, I was buying an asset now, instead of pouring money down the drain in rent. That was small consolation when, under the pressure of rapidly increasing interest rates, my second mortgage payment was £250 higher than the first, and the third payment was a further £200 higher again.

I was saved from bankruptcy only when the Department of Finance, after stubbornly resisting for weeks, devalued the punt at the start of February 1993. The Department had argued fiercely that there was no reason to devalue. Ireland was running a current budget surplus at the time; inflation was low; economic growth was running ahead of target. The economy had clearly turned a corner from the disastrous 1980s – as all the experts said at the time (and they still use that awful phrase), the economic fundamentals were sound.

But none of that prevented the speculators from making money on our currency. In a bid to stave off devaluation, interest rates went up by nearly 40 per cent during the three months of the crisis, and it didn't do any good. In the end, the crisis of 1992 gave a huge added impetus to the creation of the euro and the European-wide fiscal system that underpins it.

I don't pretend to understand that system, and I'm certainly not going to try to explain it. But as we read about the madness in worldwide stock markets and watch the frenzy on television, night after night, all I can say is thank God for the euro. With all this incredible speculation going on, with people and businesses in a constant state of panic, can you imagine what could happen if some super-rich speculator was once again in a position to start attacking our currency? We might be a much stronger economy today than we were in 1992 – our economic fundamentals are even sounder – but we're still small, and could not afford to allow our currency to be exposed to that kind of speculation ever again.

I can remember another occasion, a few years later. In the days immediately after the first IRA ceasefire, I accompanied Dick Spring on a long and exhausting trip, first to meet Bill Clinton in the United States, and then immediately on to meet a man called Klaus Kinkel. Kinkel was Germany's foreign minister and Vice-Chancellor, but more to the point, because Germany held the Presidency of the EU at the time, he was President of the Council of Ministers.

The purpose of both visits – to Clinton and to Kinkel – was to try to establish how much financial support could be garnered for the peace process. It was a central objective of that process to demonstrate that democratic activity produces results, and an immediate response by the rest of the world to the ceasefire, in terms of aid and investment for Northern Ireland, would be a massive foundation on which to build further progress.

We knew, of course, of Clinton's support for and commitment to the process. But the immediately positive reaction of the German foreign minister, and his commitment to bring a package of support measures to the Council of Ministers immediately, was a huge encouragement to the whole process at a critical time.

Both of those stories are part of the reason I will be voting yes in the Lisbon referendum. There are things I don't like about Europe, and the Lisbon Treaty, it seems to me, hasn't really addressed them adequately – the lack of transparency, the incredible bureaucracy, the remoteness of all of the institutions from the citizens they seek to serve.

But Europe, at the end of the day, is about people sticking together. The currency crisis of 1992 has always demonstrated to me that Ireland is much better off being part of a strong system. And the reaction of Europe to the first ceasefire in Ireland has always seemed to me to show that European solidarity is real, meaningful and significant.

Our elders and betters in the Government and elsewhere will be telling us, in the weeks and months ahead, that we should be grateful to Europe, that we 'owe it' to Europe to vote yes. Nonsense. Sticking together is in Europe's interests as much as it's in ours. Europe works best when the whole is bigger than the sum of the parts. That's why it makes sense for Europe to invest in its poorer members, as it did in Ireland since the beginning. You grow the economy of Europe as a whole by growing its component parts, by linking them together through trade and infrastructure, by helping each bit of the equation to be as productive and competitive as every other bit. European investment in higher standards within Europe is not philanthropy for which we should be grateful – it's just good sense.

In all sorts of ways, Europe is a friend for us. For example, when we joined Europe, Irish women were the subject of institutionalised and almost casual discrimination in nearly every area of their lives. Irish women have used the conventions and standards and norms found throughout Europe in the battle against discrimination. The European Courts have found again and again in favour of minorities here, and have been powerful allies on behalf of everyone who believes in greater equality and opportunity.

Having said all that, of course, there is a real danger that we will all end up too confused – or maybe feeling too hostile to the Government – to be able to vote yes. Although last weekend's opinion polls suggested a majority in favour of the Treaty among those who intend to vote, there is clearly both apathy and confusion.

If there is still apathy and confusion by polling day, whenever that is, the three parties in government will be 100 per cent responsible. Ever since the McKenna judgement, it hasn't been possible to spend public money on promoting a referendum, and so responsibility falls on the political parties to do it out of their own resources.

Even with the support of the opposition, you can't win a referendum on the cheap. The political parties supporting the government have an absolute obligation to put campaigns together that demonstrate not just their commitment to the cause, but their passion for it.

Already you can hear government ministers on the radio and television calling for reasoned debate, and promising to put the facts in front of the people. The usual old guff, in other words. Reasoned debate is no substitute for a committed, energetic campaign aimed at getting clear and honest messages to the maximum number of people. Our politicians are great at running that sort of campaign when their own survival is at stake. We need to see the same sort of energy for the European ideal in the months ahead. And it needs to start soon.

Denis the Menace
(2008)

I know I'm only supposed to do begrudgery on this page. I'm supposed to get angry about the uneven distribution of wealth in Ireland, the immorality of policies that favour the rich, the injustice and unfairness that so many people suffer from. I do, often, feel that kind of anger, and to be honest I don't regard it as begrudgery at all to point out some of the injustices that destroy people's lives in our rich country.

When you're trying to do something about some of those injustices, you get help from all sorts of quarters. There is one person more likely to be willing to put his shoulder to the wheel than a lot of others, and he is just as capable, despite his own wealth, of feeling anger about injustice when he encounters it. His name is Denis O'Brien.

Let me declare an interest where Denis O'Brien is concerned. I have witnessed and been the recipient of Denis O'Brien's decency, not in a personal way but in a variety of ways that matter, over the last few years.

So I have a certain view of the man. But I cannot understand how, in any terms, he can be criticised for wanting to help the Irish international football team be as good as it can be.

And yet we've had to listen to, and read, acres of

rubbish in the past week about Denis O'Brien and his gesture to the FAI. To listen to some of it, you'd think there was some kind of sinister conspiracy, not too far removed from the assassination of President Kennedy, about his decision to offer to help fund a top-class manager for the Irish team.

There was even a couple of pages in one of the Sunday papers about how it represented the death of the integrity of the FAI. Mother of God! The FAI has taken money from sponsors for years, and it has been involved in all sorts of political deals, in the interests as they see it of their sport. Now suddenly, taking money from an individual for exactly the same reason has some sort of evil connotation.

He's not trying to bend any rules, or attach any conditions. He's probably just trying to help recapture those magnificent days when the entire nation was carried along on the shoulders of an Irish team that was doing us proud on the world and European stage.

And wouldn't it be fantastic if we were all able to get totally wrapped up in the next World Cup, instead of the permanent relegation to non-qualifying status that has become our lot in the last few years under a succession of unfortunate or unlucky managers?

Of course Denis O'Brien can be criticised, if you want to, because he opted to become a sort of tax exile after he made all that money on the sale of Esat. He made a lot of money on that sale, and avoided paying tax here because he was resident in Portugal for tax purposes at the time.

Would it have been better, in all sorts of ways, if he had paid the tax? Of course it would. It would have been better in principle, better for Ireland – and I reckon it would have been better for him too. I don't suppose he was in any better position than the rest of us are to know what the future might bring, but his subsequent investments have been so enormously successful that the tax due on his first big deal would look like a drop in the ocean now.

I've often felt, though, that there is little point in criticising people who take advantage of the tax laws we put in place. It's our own fault. It's the governments we elect, after all, that have designed a tax system over the years that is heavily unbalanced in favour of the wealthy. It's so unbalanced, in fact, you'd wonder why anyone would ever want to become a tax exile.

For instance, do you remember that report a few years ago, when the statistics branch of the Revenue listed the top 400 earners in Ireland (without naming them, of course) and established what their effective tax rates were? Fifty-one of those high earners, or just over one in eight, had an effective tax rate of less than 5 per cent! Nearly a fifth of the top 400 had an effective tax rate of less than 15 per cent.

When the Revenue examined the tax situation of the very top earners in the country – the highest 117 people – they discovered that twenty-nine of them (exactly a quarter) had no tax liability at all, and more than half of them had a tax liability of less than 10 per cent. And it was all because of the enormous number of tax shelters we provided at the time – multi-storey car parks, hotels and a wide variety of property-based capital allowance schemes. If Denis O'Brien had chosen that route, he would never be criticised for being a tax exile – although he probably would have saved just as much tax.

I've no idea why he chose the particular form of tax avoidance he used. The one thing I would be reasonably certain of, however, is that his decision had nothing whatever to do with personal greed. I have to say the impression I've formed of him, over a number of years, is of someone who is inspired by imaginative ways of doing things, turned on by good ideas, utterly impatient with bureaucracy, and driven by a will to win.

I've never detected any airs or graces about him, and I've seen a sufficient number of examples to know that he is a man who is more motivated by generosity than most people. I suspect if everything he has given away were totted up, it would come to far more – a multiple, probably – of the tax he didn't pay on the Esat transaction.

Actually, to say he gives it away is probably an exaggeration. Insofar as I can judge, he seems to want to invest in ideas – and they tend to be ideas that are a bit ahead of the posse. There are a number of organisations I know, doing vital and important things, that have good reason to be grateful to Denis O'Brien's enthusiasm. Imaginative and brave approaches – the kind of things that governments don't want to support until they're already successful – seem to be the kind of things O'Brien is willing to take a risk with. He expects a return on the investment he makes – not a financial return, but results in terms of lives turned around for the better. That's as it should be, in my book.

I'm sure Denis O'Brien is no saint. He's made his mistakes like everyone else, and he's still waiting to find out what the Moriarty Tribunal thinks of him. He's a rich man who enjoys his money, takes occasional business risks, and is more than willing to give some of it back to people who will never have as much as he does. And by the way, in giving the FAI a nudge to go after a top-class manager, he did us all a favour.

Blessed Be *All* the Peacemakers
(2008)

Is it just me, or is anyone else getting a bit tired of the endless round of celebrations of the only true peace-makers? I know it's the tenth anniversary of the Good Friday Agreement, and I know that Bertie Ahern and Tony Blair deserve full credit for their part in bringing that agreement to a conclusion.

And I don't for a moment begrudge either of them the honours that have been bestowed on them. But they were never alone. The Good Friday Agreement itself was not exactly a stand-alone event, but the culmination of a process that had many milestones. Each of those milestones represented a significant increment on the road to peace and progress.

But I don't remember tenth anniversary celebrations for the Anglo-Irish Agreement, or the Downing Street Declaration, or the Joint Framework Documents. And I don't see the likes of Garret Fitzgerald, John Bruton, Peter Barry, Albert Reynolds or Dick Spring ever being invited to the events at which the peacemakers are honoured as indispensable and heroic.

Apart from the Good Friday Agreement, the only other event along the way that seems to benefit from sponsored celebrations and anniversaries is the IRA ceasefire. Of course the decision of the IRA to stop shooting and bombing people, after thirty years of sometimes horrible and cold-blooded atrocity, was welcome and historic in its own terms.

But the anniversary of that decision is never allowed to pass without comment on the courage and sacrifice of the volunteers, and the bravery and determination of the leadership in committing itself to peaceful and democratic means. I have to admit that every time I see the propaganda use of that ceasefire in action, to paint a subliminal picture of frustrated peacemakers waiting for their moment to bring peace to Ireland, it sends a chill through my heart.

Because I remember Warrington. I remember Enniskillen. I remember Shankill. I remember a peace process that went on despite the atrocities. That peace process was often a lonely business, and a business that had to be conducted away from the cold light of day. Perhaps that's why it isn't celebrated so much nowadays.

Or maybe there are things about what happened back then that are a bit uncomfortable to remember. When Garret Fitzgerald was doing his damndest to deal with the intransigence of Mrs Thatcher, for instance, the bipartisan approach that became a feature of the peace process was noticeably absent. Fitzgerald was pilloried by the Fianna Fáil opposition in the aftermath of Thatcher's famous 'out, out, out' speech, and was roundly mocked when he determined to press ahead.

And when he did achieve the breakthrough and persuaded Mrs Thatcher to sign the Anglo-Irish Agreement in Hillsborough Castle (with Ian Paisley bellowing at the gate and the IRA leadership planning more murder), he was utterly opposed at home. Charles

Haughey's first reaction was to send his Foreign Affairs spokesperson, Brian Lenihan, to the United States to try to persuade leaders and public opinion there that the Anglo-Irish Agreement was a sell-out.

Indeed, in his own contribution to the debate on the Anglo-Irish Agreement in the Dáil, Bertie Ahern described it as a fundamental threat to Irish sovereignty, and went on to say that in negotiating the Agreement, the government of the day 'have wantonly squandered our deepest aspirations'.

Of course, many years later (and perhaps somewhat wiser) Bertie Ahern described the Anglo-Irish Agreement as 'a shaft of light at a time of despair with no end to the violence in sight'.

Albert Reynolds' principal objective as a peacemaker was to end the violence, and thereby enable negotiation and discussion to begin. He was of course hugely successful in ending the violence, but not without taking his own risks, and often feeling very lonely in the process.

In pursuing his singular ambition of removing the violence from the conflict, Albert Reynolds was forced into doing unpalatable things in the immediate aftermath of the Warrington bomb. When Gerry Adams carried the coffin of the bomber who had committed the Shankill massacre, Albert Reynolds believed that the demands of peace obliged him to shrug his shoulders and refuse to condemn Adams. And when John Major told Reynolds that he could never negotiate about a piece of paper that had Adams' fingerprints on it, the then Taoiseach, in the interests of peace, disowned what was known as the Hume/Adams process, and left John Hume feeling utterly isolated.

None of these were easy decisions at the time. Had

any of them gone wrong, Albert Reynolds would never have established a reputation as a peacemaker. But he made the calls, often alone, and it worked.

Dick Spring was his deputy in those years. He saw it as his job, as part of keeping violence out of the conflict, to help develop a template that could be used for longer-lasting progress. Working with Reynolds, and subsequently with John Bruton, he negotiated the Joint Framework Document with Patrick Mayhew and John Major's Government. And he did so at a time when that was a minority Government, relying heavily on Unionist support.

Bill Clinton described the Joint Framework Document at the time as 'another significant step forward in the peace process'. He said 'the Framework Document lays the foundation for all-party talks among the British and Irish Governments and the political parties in Northern Ireland. The talks are intended to be all-inclusive, with all issues on the table ...'

It took several years more to get those talks under way – largely because of the decommissioning issue which was eventually resolved with the help of a process also designed and proposed by Dick Spring (and it was that process that introduced George Mitchell to the peace arena). By the time the Joint Framework Document developed into a real agenda, Albert Reynolds and John Major had moved on. Tony Blair and Bertie Ahern were now in charge, with secure political majorities, huge public support, and an enormous amount of groundwork done by those who went before.

Of course, historians will see things differently, and hopefully in a more fully rounded way. I was lucky enough to have been involved at a number of different times in the entire process, and to observe it in action. One thing that constantly amazes me about the tribute business is how many other people there are who deserve tribute but never get it. Public servants like Sean O'Huiginn, Paddy Teahon, Dermot Gallagher, Noel Dorr, Tim Dalton – the craftsmen and drafters of the process. Priests like Alec Reid and others who even to this day can't be mentioned in public. Dozens more men and women whose motivation from the very beginning was peace and a new, just beginning.

And that's just on the Irish side. In Britain and in Northern Ireland there is a substantial list of people motivated by the same concern, and determined to ultimately assert that democratic means work.

So maybe we could move on now. Maybe we could begin to recognise that peace is not the preserve of any one individual. The peace process in Ireland has been a seamless struggle, conducted by democrats on behalf of all of us. We should find a way to honour them all.

Share the Feeling!

Just Take Her Home

(Written by Fergus and Frieda – published by the Irish Examiner *in association with the Special Olympics World Summer Games in Dublin in the summer of 2003)*

'Just take her home. She'll never amount to much, but she shouldn't cause you too much trouble either.'

They were the two sentences that defined us. Not immediately, but over time they turned Frieda and me into often reluctant, usually frustrated, and frequently very angry members of the disability movement.

We don't have a disability, either of us. At least I don't think so. But we have frequently been spoken to by experts in words of one syllable. We've sat in front of them with that sinking feeling, the realisation that this person thinks we're not the full shilling. We've been patronised by politicians, had all sorts of assumptions made about our backgrounds (particularly the assumption, which has only sometimes been true, that we are 'socio-economically deprived'), told that we had been given a special gift, and promised the sun, moon and stars by every government minister we've ever met.

What we do have is a daughter with a disability. Mandy, to be precise. Now thirty-one years of age. And her disability is Down's Syndrome. It's an incurable

229

condition, but that didn't stop the system calling her for an annual check-up in case we had found the cure and were keeping it to ourselves.

Its essential symptoms are a dulling of the central nervous system – children with Down's Syndrome are hard to tickle and they don't feel the cold or heat as much as other children – and mental handicap. Or learning disability as we have come to call it lately. (That's why they talk to us slowly and carefully a lot of the time. Over the years we have come to realise that this is a part of the subconscious training of experts, this tacit assumption that if your child has a learning disability, you're probably a bit simple too. The fact that it has no relation whatsoever to the truth doesn't prevent an awful lot of 'professionals' imbibing it.)

Whatever name we apply now, I didn't know what to call it when Mandy was born. In 1972, in the middle of the summer, Frieda had gone into hospital for our first baby, not knowing anything of what was to happen. I went too, but was told I would be hanging around for hours, as a first labour can last forever. So I left the hospital, leaving the number of a friend's house so I could be called when things started in earnest.

Things started in earnest almost as soon as I left. Frieda was told that the baby was very distressed – no reason given – and an immediate Caesarean section would be essential. She was whipped up to the theatre, on her own, and anaesthetised. Whoever was minding the phone number I had given them forgot it. And Mandy was born with her father missing and her mother all alone and very groggy.

Maybe that was why they decided not to tell anyone that night. When I arrived, as Frieda was coming out of the anaesthetic, everything seemed all right. Much better than all right, actually. More than thirty years later, I can still remember the sense I had, when I arrived back in the lobby of the hospital, that Frieda was calling me from the third floor. Without being told, I knew a baby had arrived. I knew that Frieda needed me. I didn't need any further invitation to race up the six flights of stairs to where she was. And as I raced, a lot of things I don't need to go into here simply disappeared, to be replaced by the magic and power of the thing we had done together. We had made a baby girl.

They knew immediately, of course, in the hospital. All we saw was a beautiful, delicate, porcelain doll. We didn't know the tell-tale signs they know – the floppy muscles, the flattened nose, and the fact that Down's Syndrome babies, strangely enough, have only one life-line right across the palms of their hands.

Anyway, they told me the following day. A nurse was either deputed to do the job or took it on herself.

'Mr Finlay, I'm sorry to have to tell you that your daughter has Down's Syndrome.'

'Oh right. Is that serious?'

'Well – do you know what Down's Syndrome is?'

'No, I'm afraid I never heard of it.'

'Well, have you ever heard of mongolism?'

And then I knew. But I still knew nothing. A doctor would be able to explain it to me. But it was Sunday, and he was terribly busy (as they always are on a Sunday, apparently). I would have to make some sort of fist of telling Frieda myself.

Nowadays, Frieda often talks to experts – at least, when they are being formed, as students, she and some other parents try to get through to them that these are all issues that affect people. They do it by telling their own stories, and this is how Frieda has described her own reaction to the news of Mandy's condition in one of the talks she has written:

> *When I was young, I was scared of people with learning disabilities – mentally handicapped people as we called them, or even mentally retarded people.*
>
> *They really frightened me. As I grew older, I was less scared, but also, I couldn't care less – and I certainly wasn't planning to have anything to do with them.*
>
> *During my first pregnancy, I had dreams about my wonderful child, and all that he or she would do and be. I had an emergency Caesarean section, so I was told Mandy had Down's Syndrome before I saw her.*
>
> *All I could imagine through my shock was a wizened, shuffling, snotty-nosed, young, old-looking adult. My life was shattered; my rejection was instant; I was scared of my monster baby. Of course, I had never seen a baby with Down's Syndrome.*
>
> *When I saw her, she looked quite beautiful, like a little doll. But that was no consolation. I felt imperfect, and not a proper woman. I wanted to hide her. There was something wrong with me – what would people think – after all, if I had all these attitudes about people with a mental handicap, weren't people going to have the same attitude about me and my child?*

Some did have attitudes, of course. Not the doctor we eventually got to see. He couldn't have been more casual, more laid-back, more brutal.

'Just take her home. She'll never amount to much, but she shouldn't cause you too much trouble either.'

Over the years, though, Mandy caused a lot of trouble. Bits of pain too. Here's Frieda's account again:

> *I can also remember when she was a toddler, the first time we took her for a walk up Killiney Hill. I think every bouncing healthy child in Dublin, from 1 to 12, was out there that day. And it hurt. Again it brought home the reality of my situation. You live coming to terms with it every second day.*
>
> *Don't ever think that parents get used to having a child with a disability. We don't. We develop enough scar tissue to stop us bleeding in public, and to carry on some kind of normal life.*
>
> *Even though I have been campaigning for many years for her rights, and shouting about the importance of equality, it was only recently I realised how equal my daughter really is. It is very important to understand how we perceived our child who has a disability.*
>
> *Two years after Mandy I had another daughter, yes she was perfect, then my third daughter was born, again it was, 'How is she, she's perfect', what a relief.*
>
> *And so with my fourth daughter, 'yes she's perfect too'. Now, those three beauties range in age from 25 to 22 to 19, and I can assure you they are far from being perfect! On that realisation I now see my daughter Mandy in a very different way.*

But that took a long time, for both of us. Unconsciously, we blamed her for her disability. We blamed her for the fact that other kids were making better progress, were walking and talking before Mandy. We blamed her for the pity we seemed to attract, and even, as she got older, for the fact that her identity in some ways was stronger than ours. We were the parents of the Down's Syndrome girl.

As time went by, however, we discovered we weren't alone. We weren't alone in a number of ways – society as a whole, for instance, holds people with a disability responsible for their shortcomings. That's why we went through a period when all our kids with a disability needed to be 'normalised'. Later, when society came to realise that normalisation mightn't be too easy, our kids needed to be 'integrated'.

'I'll tell you about integration,' I heard a mother say at a meeting one night. 'My son has a job in the local supermarket – he's integrated with the other boys. At lunchtime they play soccer in the yard, you can see them any day. The boy on his own, with no one talking to him, sitting on the steps watching the others play ball – that's my integrated son.'

The buzzwords were only part of the stupidity, only part of the way in which people with disabilities are at fault. The annual check-ups to be sure we hadn't invented a cure. The fact that when Mandy was in a school with brighter kids she couldn't speak as well as them – and so she got priority for speech therapy. When she was in a school with kids of her own ability they all spoke the same – so none of them got speech therapy. The fact that your role as parents was to take a tin cup once a year and stand outside the church, so people could go out of their way to make themselves feel better by giving you their small change. And you'd stand there mumbling thank you while your daughter was receiving charity.

At different stages, different issues had an impact. Frieda co-operated with RTÉ on a little news item in which Mandy and her boyfriend at the time walked arm in arm down the street and cuddled each other. The item was to promote a conference and it caused a storm – not

so much among the outside world, but among parents
who had been in denial for years about their own children's sexuality.

It hadn't come easy to Frieda either, as she explained:

*You can see sexuality flourish in every teenager – but
it happens with a layer of religion, attitudes,
education, and discrimination. Mandy had none of
these – that's what made the sexuality so frightening.
Looking back on it now, I realised that I dumped all
my fears and anxieties on her.*

*When she reached thirteen years of age, and started
to develop physically into a young woman, I just
wanted it all to stop. I wasn't ready – she wasn't ready
– her mental ability ranged between five and ten years
– this wasn't right. After all, sexuality was all in the
mind – an adult thing.*

*I didn't like it. She couldn't grow this way. Nobody
had said anything about this. After all, she was always
going to have the mind of a child. Why should she be
getting the body of an adult? I remembered somebody
said to me when my daughter was about seven – 'What
are you going to do when she grows up – are you going
to put her on the Pill?' That really depressed me.*

*Sexuality didn't matter for people with a mental
handicap. I would always be there to protect her. But
she was growing up, and I didn't like it. I didn't like
her, and I took it out on her. Nobody had prepared me,
or rather, I had never allowed myself to think about
my daughter becoming a woman.*

*Again, I totally rejected her. I couldn't see any
reason or purpose for her sexuality – a feeling that I
would never have had about any of my other
daughters. It has taken me years to weave my way
through all these thoughts and fears, and to realise that*

not only may my daughter have a good and happy future, but also that she is entitled to it.

What you do come to realise, perhaps over more years than it should take, is that disability isn't an issue of fault. At least if it is, the fault doesn't lie with the person with a disability. Disability is a barrier, or a series of them, and those barriers are erected by all of us.

Frieda began dealing with those barriers by finding other parents – Mary Boyd, Jean Spain – and people of great character such as Deirdre Carroll, and working with them.

And all the time determined to do what they can to tear those barriers down. I got involved through politics, trying (and usually failing) to persuade people that disability is the last great civil rights issue.

Until we got involved in Special Olympics, we believed there was no limit to human potential. But we also thought it was a kind of cliché. Special Olympics taught us it was true.

In the last century, all the great stories were of people overcoming. Women overcoming the barriers to equality, from the struggle to be allowed to vote right through to the liberation movement. The struggle for civil rights in black America, and the inspirational leadership of people like Martin Luther King. (The theme song of the movement – 'We Shall Overcome'.) The even harsher struggle for freedom in South Africa, and the monumental and historic role of Nelson Mandela. And the fall of the Berlin Wall, typifying for many of us the final collapse of some of the most cruel barriers to freedom.

But at every Special Olympics event, you can see

people overcoming. You can see grace and dignity in the face of adversity. You can see people aiming for a genuine and clean sporting ideal. And you can't fail to be drawn into that, almost against your will.

It happened to us the first time we went to an international sporting event. (We had been at local competitions in Dunmore House, where we knew all the competitors and spent all day cheering them on. But you always do that when it's your own local club, don't you?)

The international event we went to was the World Summer Games in 1995, in New Haven, Connecticut. The reason we went was Mandy, who was picked on the Irish basketball team for the Games. (Remember the doctor saying 'She'll never amount to much ...')

Mandy was twenty-two when she became the first member of her family to represent her country abroad, and to wear the green blazer with pride.

The week of the 1995 Special Olympics was a revelation. I can still remember thinking how corny it was when I heard the athlete's oath for the first time – 'Let me win. But if I cannot win, let me be brave in the attempt.'

The following week taught me that it might be corny. But when the athletes say it, they mean it. And they are as brave as anything you will ever see.

In the middle of that week, we went to the athletics, to see how the Irish team were doing. They were doing well, and went on to win quite a few medals in track and field. But it was one of the heats in the 1500 metres that I will never forget.

They were lining up for the event as we took our seats. In the outside lane, so close to us I could see his eyes, was a black athlete. The eyes were dull, slightly unfocused.

And he had only one leg – he was using an old-fashioned wooden crutch.

He was slower than all the rest to start, and by the end of the first lap it was clear that he was in trouble, without the remotest chance of qualifying for the next round. By the time seven of the eight competitors had finished the heat, he still had more than a lap to go. And he was hobbling badly.

But he never stopped. More than that, he never faltered. Although from where we sat it looked as if each step was more painful for him than the previous one, he was determined to finish.

And little by little it became clear that the entire crowd was determined to help. As he eventually crossed the line, collapsing into the arms of his coach, 2,500 people gave him a standing ovation. None of them, I'll bet, could remember who had won the heat. And none of them will ever forget the way that African athlete overcame that day.

Mandy and her teammates, by the way, came fifth in the world in the basketball – as she put it herself, up there with Michael Jordan. And the proud supporters of the Irish basketball team cheered to the echo when they were presented with their ribbons.

That World Games in 1995 taught those of us who were there something else as well – anything Connecticut could do, we could do better. The idea of bringing the Games to Ireland started in New Haven, and it was Irish families that began the movement that culminated in 2003 in the never-to-be forgotten Special Olympics World Summer Games in Dublin, bringing 7,000 athletes and their families to Ireland.

But most of all, that week in Connecticut showed us

that courage and grace are no clichés. They are more alive in the Special Olympics movement than almost anywhere else.

The South African song about apartheid – 'the higher you build your barriers, the faster I will run' – might have been written for our athletes.

As Frieda says:

> But we're still building the barriers. We're still expecting people with disabilities to overcome every day, without the sort of back-up we take for granted. Isn't it just as well they have grit and determination, even if we can't see it?
>
> Mandy is a woman now, and she lives independently about half the time, with a number of her friends in a community that is protected. She didn't get there as a right, in fact she has no rights. There is no law that says we should all take some responsibility for the barriers that are put in the way of people with disabilities.
>
> They've just published a Disability Bill, and it doesn't give people like Mandy rights either. In fact, it erects a huge bureaucratic maze that they have to work their way through to get any services at all. We're now promised a well-funded Disability Strategy. We'll see how long that lasts.
>
> What we know is the potential that people like Mandy have. What we want to see is the political will to enable them to unlock that potential. That's why we argue for rights. And we will go on arguing until they finally have the rights the rest of us take for granted.

Lighting the Flame
(2003)

I want to suggest a compromise between what seems like two entrenched positions. The Government has apparently set its face against legally enforceable rights for people with disabilities. The disability movement refuses to rely any more on the promise of charity or goodwill, and is adamant that a culture of rights must replace the broken promises of the past.

A compromise is possible. It mightn't be my place to suggest it, and it is entirely possible that the disability movement mightn't accept it. But we mustn't end the year of People with Disabilities without this issue being resolved. After this fortnight, we cannot go back to the way things were.

We know now what people with disabilities can do. We know how they can contribute. We know how they can move and inspire us, leave us breathless even. We know that courage and good humour are possible in the face of any adversity, how what Eunice Kennedy Shriver calls the 'unquenchable spirit' of people with disabilities can overcome.

No one who was present in Croke Park on Saturday night will ever forget the occasion. I don't think I have the words to describe the emotion I felt when the Olympic flame was lit. Everyone I have met since, whether they were there or had watched it on television, was transfixed. There was, and is, a huge degree of pride that Ireland can put on a show like that for the world, that Ireland can make so many people welcome, that Ireland can be so professional when the occasion demands it.

But underneath that there is a strong sense of awareness of what this is all about. Behind the spectacle there was years of preparation. Throughout this week there will be intense hard work by thousands of volunteers, all of them making sacrifices to do fairly humdrum and tiring things. Throughout last week and this, thousands of families opened their homes to athletes from all over the world.

They all – volunteers, staff, families – have an abiding memory that they have been dealing with people in respect of whom it is a cliché to say that their determination, concentration and courage are second to none. It takes real guts to sit on a horse in competition when you are visually impaired and your limbs don't do what they're told. Swimming two laps of an Olympic-size pool requires considerable determination when one of the symptoms of your disability is a difficulty in controlling breathing. Only the most determined will steer a heavy bowling ball to a strike or a spare when the muscles of your body aren't well coordinated.

Most of the athletes who compete this week have been in training for years to get where they are. None of them have started with natural advantages – no naturally gifted runners or jumpers, no natural gift of hand–eye co-ordination. Everything they do has been learned with the help of volunteers, learned by doing it again and again. The process of learning is difficult and requires considerable patience on the part of both student and teacher. Progress is often made in the tiniest of increments. When some of these athletes win medals this week – indeed, when some stand proud on the starting line in their events – those closest to them will remember a lifetime of hard, intense preparation.

The achievement of participating in these Games is an achievement against the odds. It's hard enough to deal with a disability sometimes without being dismissed. Overcoming disability to participate often represents an incredible achievement, but the barriers you have to climb to take part in the Special Olympics can be as nothing compared to the barriers that people with disabilities encounter all their lives.

There is a disability magazine called *Insight* which in its current issue features an article by Michael McDowell under the heading 'Confronting the rhetoric of rights'. He begins the piece by saying, 'It seems to me that personal responsibility is something we have surrendered to a view of the world that implies the individual is owed a duty by someone else. I see in this development grave consequences for the future development of our society. Because inherent in such a societal make-up is, in my view, an absence of initiative and enterprise, a diminution of the "can-do" self-reliant spirit, that it characterised by people taking responsibility, rather than expecting there is something owed them.'

Inherent in this argument (which I regard as pompous claptrap, but leave that to one side) is the notion that if we go down the slippery slope of rights, we will end up, not with a more equal and participative society, but with a sort of layabout, couldn't care less about anything sort of society (like, say, Sweden?).

But the Taoiseach sees it differently. He believes that everyone should have rights, he's all for that, but if they're legally enforceable people will be running to the courts all the time, and all the money will be eaten up by lawyers.

He has told us again and again that he's not opposed to rights, but he doesn't see how they can be enforced in a practical sense.

People with disabilities, on the other hand, know only too well that without rights, they will go to the end of every queue. It has been that way for years. In the Celtic Tiger, resources were put in – not enough, but some; but the moment things became a little slower, the resources were totally cut off. That has been the experience of their lifetimes.

What rights are they looking for? The right to an assessment of their condition. The right to a statement of needs arising from that assessment. The right to be included in decisions made about them. The right to basic services that promote dignity. The right not to always have to wait in a queue.

Does anyone really believe that enshrining such rights in law, for people who have huge barriers to confront, would rob society of its can-do spirit? Does anyone really believe that people with disabilities want to be running to the Four Courts?

In case they do, here is one alternative. Put the rights in law. And give people with disabilities a Disability Ombudsman instead of a courtroom. That Ombudsman must be entirely independent, appointed by the President on the nomination of the Oireachtas, free to investigate and report in public. He or she must have the power to compel an assessment to be carried out, and the power to represent people with disabilities in their dealings with agencies. He or she must be an advocate as well as a judge, and the Disability Ombudsman's office should have the power to establish an advocacy service. In cases of last resort, the Ombudsman should have the power to initiate legal proceedings, because there are situations where the exercise of moral authority isn't enough.

A Disability Ombudsman, with real resources and influence, can be a vehicle for turning the aspiration to rights into reality. And it's not beyond our wit and intelligence to achieve the goal of justice and dignity for people with disabilities. If this week proves anything, it proves how much they are entitled to that.

Shiga Kogan
(2005)

Yamanouchi is a Japanese word that means 'middle of the mountains'. It's the name of a place of great and challenging beauty, one of the world capitals of skiing. Right in the heart of the middle of the mountains is the ski resort named after Shiga Kogan.

Shiga Kogan is a volcano, with naturally heated springs side by side with tremendous snow falls and temperatures of minus twelve to fifteen degrees at this time of year. The skiing is accessible by a winding, twisting mountain road, where the buses have to stop half-way up so chains can be put on the tyres.

And the buses are crowded because Shiga Kogan, at the heart of Yamanouchi, is a mecca for skiers. The slopes are steep, wide and uninterrupted, and the snow is fast. Those who know about these things say it is the fastest snow in the world, especially when it is fresh. And it is always fresh because it snows every day – some days as much as two feet of snow can build up.

It's a long, long way from there to here: 6,500 miles, fourteen hours in the air from Dublin to Tokyo, five hours by bus from Tokyo to Nagano city, a further two hours to Shiga Kogan, high in the mountains at the centre of the Japanese province of Honshu. And it's not just miles.

Language, culture, food, habits are all totally different. All require a capacity to adapt and to see the world through different eyes.

And it was there, last week, that eight Irish athletes took on the best in the world at their levels. They were there to compete in the Winter Olympics, the pinnacle of their sport. All alpine skiers, four of them from the Republic and four from Northern Ireland, they made their way to Shiga Kogan, looked up at the daunting slopes, and got on with the job.

They had a few disadvantages to overcome. It won't have escaped your attention that Ireland is not exactly a skiing capital. Our skiers have learned everything they know on a nylon slope in Kiltiernan, and on a smaller one in Craigavon. Apart from some practice in Austria in the final run-up to the Winter Olympics, many of them had little or no experience of skiing, and especially competitive skiing, on real, fast, driving snow.

And that's before you take account of the difficulties involved in the events themselves. All require an ability to slalom, and to slalom without error. If you miss one gate on these slopes, you simply go to the tail of the competition. There's no way to catch up. So a slalom run means forty seconds of going as hard as you can, downhill with the snow driving into your face, but concentrating totally on the gates and turns.

Strength and speed are vital, but so are technique and concentration. Each competition involves two runs, both against the clock. And you mustn't miss a gate. Miss one and you're out. No allowances can be made. The rules are the same in each of the divisions – novice, intermediate and advanced. To a non-skier, they seem harsh, but the skiers accept them.

The point about this, of course, is that you're not just competing against people of similar talent and ability. Unlike a lot of, say, track and field events, when you're skiing you are skiing against the course. No matter what anyone else does, when you stand at the start of a slalom course, the only one who can beat you is you.

And so the athletes prepared for five days of tough competition, the toughest in their lives. Some had family with them, but the families had to stay separately, seeing their athletes only at the competitions. And a small contingent of incredible Irish volunteers, who were in Nagano to work (at their own expense) on the Healthy Athlete Programme run by Special Olympics, made the long journey to the slopes every day they weren't working to cheer the Irish team on.

On day one of competition, they faced the downhill runs – more emphasis on speed, fewer and wider gates. Not our favourite competition. But Ryan Hill from Armagh flew through his race to pick up a bronze. It was to be the first of three medals over the following five days for Ryan, who finished the Games with a gold, silver and bronze. Our cheering had hardly died away when Finbarr Hughes, who has lived with his sister in County Tyrone since his parents died seventeen years ago, glided through his division for a second bronze.

Two of our athletes had now won medals, in the discipline that was their least favourite.

Day two was the start of the Giant Slalom competition, with the finals on day three. Each day, two races against the clock, with aggregate time counting provided no gates were missed. And not one gate was – at least, not by the Irish.

Fiona Bryson from Stillorgan, the tiniest, quietest and

most determined member of the team, won a brilliant bronze. Liam Weir from Dungannon, who had been looking grimly anxious, broke into a giant smile when he flew over the line in his division for gold – and the smile didn't disappear for the rest of the week. Ryan added silver to his bronze of the first day. And then Lorraine Whelan skied the slalom of her life, pure grace on skis, to cap the day with a wonderful gold medal.

But there was some disappointment among the skiers themselves. Over the days of preparation and competition, this team had bonded in the most incredible way. Partly this was down to coaching – there is no sport in Ireland that has wiser or better coaches than Eddie and Kathleen Sythes, who built this team – but no member of the team was going to be happy until every member had skied his or her best.

If it was to happen, it had to happen on day five, the finals of the most difficult competition of the three, the Slalom event (more gates and tighter turns than either the Downhill or Giant Slalom). Cyril Walker from Armagh had had a fourth and a fifth in the earlier events, and was a bit down in the dumps. That ended when he put in one of the best performances of his life, in his first Olympics, to take bronze in the novice class.

All eyes were on the intermediate slopes now – a high start, a constant and speedy descent, and some of the trickiest gates right at the end. In his first run, Warren Tate from Stillorgan, Ireland's leading Manchester United fan, had skied a silver medal time, and just needed to avoid mistakes to make sure of his medal. Avoid mistakes? He nailed the second run, fast, stylish and flawless, with absolutely perfect discipline, and then led the loudest cheers of the day.

But there was worrying news from the start gate. Cormac Maguire from Ballinteer was now the only Irish skier who hadn't won a medal. He had skied steadily throughout, and was lying in fourth position after his first run in the final. But he wasn't well. He had thrown up earlier, and was reported to be lying down at the start. His mother, Kay, who in her own words 'had Padre Pio worn out', was surrounded by all of us at the finish line. This mattered. None of us, and none of his fellow skiers, wanted Cormac to miss out. But if he was to improve on his fourth position, a tummy bug was the last thing he needed.

And then he was at the start gate. And he was flying. Lorraine Whelan's dad, Brendan, an experienced skier himself, gasped that Cormac was going too fast – he'd never make all the gates at that speed. But if anything, Cormac seemed to get faster, and he was scything his way through the gates. And then he was over the line, after one of the fastest runs anyone had ever seen. The fourth was turned to gold, Cormac was crying tears of pure joy (along with more than a few of the rest of us), and Kay announced that Padre Pio could have the rest of the week off.

Eight Irish skiers, every one a winner after a week of intense competition and high drama. Each of them has a giant heart and an incredible personality, and each of them has an intellectual disability. But they overcame enormous distances. They faced a climate they had never experienced in their lives. They adapted to different food, culture and habits. They raced in conditions normally experienced by world-class international skiers. They became part of a team that was tight and brilliantly coached.

Above all they showed huge reserves of discipline, concentration, skill, grace and courage. They won twelve medals altogether. And in the process they showed that intellectual disability is just one more of life's hurdles. Nothing that can't be overcome.

China Goes Green
(2007)

It's almost impossible to describe Shanghai. A city of 20 million people that seems to go on forever.

Thousands of skyscrapers, many of them built to fantastic designs and brilliantly lit at night. A wide river where the endless shipping traffic runs in three lanes in each direction. A constant buzz of activity in factories, shops, offices and on the streets. Markets where the range of incredible goods and designer labels is only matched by the never-ending hum of loud haggling and bargaining – bargaining that usually results in designer handbags or watches changing hands for €30 or less. They're fake, of course, but they're about the only thing about this astonishing city that is.

And everywhere you go here, Shanghai has gone a bit green. For the Special Olympics World Games, Ireland has sent its largest ever delegation abroad. As a proportion of our population, we have the largest delegation at the Games by far. The vast majority of them have paid their own way to be here – many of them raising money for Special Olympics in the process. Nearly 1,000 of us are here, primarily to support our athletes but also to help out in the overall organising of the Games. And to have a whale of a time in the process.

A lot of the families and volunteers came out to Shanghai, I suspect, with no little trepidation. The language and culture barriers are huge – if you get lost here, you get really lost, and there's no point in trying to find helpful street signs. The people are very helpful, but only a tiny smattering of this enormous population speaks English. But if there's an Irish team that needs support, anywhere in the world, you'll find Irish supporters willing to do whatever it takes to rally around them.

So the Irish delegation has turned the Equatorial Hotel into a little bit of Ireland. There's an Irish cottage in the lobby that serves as a centre for information and direction, rostering volunteers, guiding parents and organising transport to each of the sporting venues. From this hub, every day, the Irish set out to gather the stories of the Games.

And what stories are emerging. Oliver Doherty is the incoming captain of his local golf club in Donegal and the proud representative of the North West Special Olympics Club. As an outstanding golfer, he was expected to put in a great performance on the championship course being used here. Despite the incredible humidity of the past few days – humidity well in excess of anything an Irish golfer would be used to – he has played out of his skin, and is in prime position for a good medal. But the entire Irish golf team has astonished its mentors. Each of them, male and female, has battled their way into the premier divisions of the golf, and they are all playing the golf of their lives.

In the aquatics, we've had personal best after personal best. Perhaps the story of the swimming so far has been Ryan Archibold, from Ballymoney in County Antrim. The nature of his disability means that he relies exclusively on upper body strength to compete with great swimmers from around the world. On Saturday he was on his last chance for a medal, having come fourth and fifth in two previous events.

I watched the tension build on the faces of his parents as they watched him on the starting blocks, and then we all roared ourselves hoarse as he powered his way to an astonishing bronze in the 100-metre freestyle event, well within his previous best time. Later, he posed for pictures with Ruth Swann from Craigavon and Paddy Monaghan from Dublin, both of whom won silver medals. The smiles in those pictures would provide enough power for any of Shanghai's skyscrapers.

It's the same story everywhere you go. It's difficult sometimes to keep track, because local politics decreed that the venues for these games would be spread across Shanghai's 19 districts (each of them almost big enough to be an Irish county), but the football team is going like a train, the equestrian team is notching up medal after medal, Ireland's bowlers and bocce players are all flying, the basketball teams are doing brilliantly, and we have won gold in badminton. In sports that Irish athletes mightn't normally be expected to shine, this team has already exceeded all sorts of expectations.

An awful lot of medals will be decided over the next couple of days, but one athlete in particular might end up coming home as the medal star of the games. Una McGarry from Belfast has already won two golds and two bronze medals in a variety of demanding and intricate disciplines of gymnastics. Her attitude to her medal haul, though, is typical of all the other athletes. She's here for the team, and she won't be going home happy unless everyone does well. But the performances across the board have already been so good that this team will be going home very happy indeed. And they will be going home having represented their country, in a faraway and strange land, with huge distinction.

Special Olympics, of course, is about more than medals. One of the other challenges the movement takes on is to try to change hearts and minds where the whole issue of disability is concerned. Many people feel that this is a particularly difficult challenge where China is concerned.

The history of China and disability has not been a proud one – several Chinese people have told me here that, before the Games began, they had never, for example, seen or met a person with Down's Syndrome, because disability usually means institutionalisation.

But you can see the signs of change everywhere. The sight of Chinese President Hu Jintao, who presided over the opening ceremony and was shown in a video working with people with disabilities, has astonished the Chinese people. He, and Prime Minister Wen Jiabao, have made a number of speeches, and allowed articles to be published, which demonstrate a new commitment to integration of people with a disability into mainstream Chinese society.

Posters of people with disabilities have sprung up all over the city and, in all of them, the message is the same. The slogan for the Games – 'I know I can' – has become a byword for a new understanding about disability here.

It's a step forward – and it may be too soon to tell how much of a step it is. A society of more than a billion people, with a history and culture that were flourishing long before Newgrange was built, takes time to change. And change often only comes in tiny increments.

China defies our understanding in many ways but, right now, it seems, this is a country determined to take its place in the world. In economic and strategic terms, that will be a powerful place; economic growth is rapidly positioning the country as a world leader.

If these Special Olympics World Games play their part in helping to finally include people with disabilities in China's future – and of course that's a big if, with no certain outcome – that will be the ultimate victory.

The Other Side
of the Tiger

Bowling Almost Alone
(2001)

'Most Americans watch *Friends* rather than have friends nowadays.' That's a quote from Professor Robert D. Putnam of Harvard University, who was in Dublin over the last couple of days to address Irish non-governmental organisations and volunteer groups to mark the UN Year of the Volunteer.

Professor Putnam is a professor of public policy in Harvard, and the author of a dozen books on democracy and the role of society. His message, familiar to millions of Americans, is that civic engagement – the neighbourhood friendships, the dinner parties, the group discussions, the club memberships, the church committees, the political participation; all the involvements, even the street protests, that make a democracy work – has declined over the last thirty years. And he made the point that it could happen here in Ireland – indeed, that it was well under way here.

At the conference, he and several other social policy experts expounded the theory of 'social capital'. Dr Putnam said the theory recognised that social networks and interactions had significant value, and declining social contact damaged social and economic well-being.

What intrigued me about his message was two things.

First, the fact that it was being said at all, and by someone with at least the academic credentials to demand he be listened to. And second (at least according to the newspaper account I read), he said it at a conference organised by the Taoiseach's Department.

In fact, the Taoiseach addressed the conference too, and in welcoming Dr Putnam's comments said he believed social capital 'has the potential to be a very positive influence in public policy development in this country. It puts communities at the centre of our debates.'

He also acknowledged that many forces affecting the State's prosperity had profoundly affected the ways we interacted. He included urbanisation, a growing acceptance of diversity and in-home mass entertainment. 'If we only look at Ireland in the last few years, we can see the sort of dramatic change which can occur,' he said.

At around the same time, the Tánaiste Mary Harney was addressing a lunch of financiers, also in Dublin. After dealing with the success of the IFSC and other developments, all contributing to growing prosperity, she offered a personal view of the necessary philosophy to keep it all going.

'The liberal, pro-competition, open market political outlook is present in the European Union, in the liberal democratic grouping,' she said. 'It is important that we continue to develop and press the liberal democratic point of view, the one that I believe serves Ireland, Europe and its citizens best. In Ireland, we must press the case for an open, liberal Europe that has a low burden of tax and regulation on enterprise because that is the best way to secure employment and prosperity. That is what we are implementing in Ireland. It is also my priority in Europe.'

Indeed. No doubt both points of view – the

Taoiseach's and the Tánaiste's – are both sincerely held and expressed. It doesn't take a genius to recognise that there is a considerable contrast between them, amounting to a fundamental ideological conflict.

You might argue that in the Ireland of today, ideological conflict doesn't matter. It does. People get hurt by it – especially when the ideology that is supreme is one that is essentially designed to hurt people and damage communities. Because the bad news for Bertie – and the rest of us – is that in the real ideological battle that is going on, the Tánaiste's philosophy (which she shares with the Minister for Finance) is winning. To see the consequences, think about another contrast for a minute. This contrast is between Jamie Sinnott and the Finance Bill.

The Finance Bill has now passed all stages in the Dáil and Seanad. Among other things (and believe me, the following list is not exhaustive), it provided for:

–£1.2 billion in tax reductions, a significant proportion of which went to reduce the top tax rate
–Cuts in indirect taxation
–New and very substantial tax breaks for share options
–Significant tax cuts for people who want to give some of their disposable income to charity
–Expansion of tax relief for third-level fees
–Extension of tax relief for health insurance
–Widening of medical expenses relief
–Tax incentives for landlords and tenants
–Capital allowances for taxi licences
–A major new Savings Incentive Scheme
–Reductions in stamp duty rates

–Abandonment of the new anti-speculative tax announced last summer
–Tax relief for premia for insurance for long-term care with the benefits of the policy exempt from taxation
–Major new tax breaks for people who invest in private hospitals
–Relaxation of the rules relating to tax returns.

Look at all these things. I'm not saying they're necessarily good or bad – but I am telling you they are the fruits of an ideology, and they are all pointed in one direction. The beneficiaries of these measures, without exception, are people with middle and better incomes.

This was the week this Bill passed through the Dáil. It was the week the Taoiseach worried publicly about the impact of prosperity on communities and society. It was the week the Tánaiste sought to press the case for 'an open, liberal Europe that has a low burden of tax and regulation on enterprise'.

And it was also the week that the State they are supposed to govern tried to take back most of the damages awarded to Jamie Sinnott's mother, and to deny him the recognition that he had a constitutional right as a citizen – a citizen with autism – to an education.

At the start of the twenty-first century, the State's arguments in the case were chilling. They were prepared to provide for Jamie, but not as a matter of right. They were prepared to 'bend over backwards' for people with disabilities, by not cutting off their constitutional rights until they were eighteen. They had to protect the Exchequer from abuse by others who might argue they still needed an education.

Where have we heard these arguments before? In poor law times, in systems where the starving ended up in workhouses, the well-to-do sometimes gave of their plenty. But it was intolerable that anyone should have the temerity to assert a right.

Who does the State represent when it argues that Jamie Sinnott – and thousands like him – should depend on charity and goodwill (because that is the only alternative to a legal right)? Who does the State represent when in one week it gives away not millions, but billions, to those who have plenty, and tries to take back £40,000 from a woman whose crime is that she fought for the rights of her son? Not me, and not many, I suspect.

But a state which gives to the well-off with one hand, and seeks to take from the vulnerable with the other, represents something. It represents an ideology – and that ideology is all too visible now. If and when society does begin to break down, if and when community does begin to mean less and less, the Taoiseach who has allowed that ideology free rein, even if he doesn't believe in it, might have cause to reflect.

Dublin in Despair
(2001)

Do you remember that old song – 'Dublin can be heaven, with coffee at eleven, and a stroll through Stephen's Green'? It's still true, you know.

I left my office last evening, to take advantage of late-night opening in the shops, and walked over to Grafton Street and the Green. It was lovely – there is surely no other capital city in the world where you can hear birdsong above the noise of the traffic in the heart of town. Grafton Street itself was packed, full of those extraordinarily talented buskers. It seemed to be mostly young people, younger than me anyway (everybody is these days), and they were happy, busy, excited looking.

The shops were full between six and seven, and there seemed to be no shortage of money. Most of the pubs were allowing their patrons to stand outside in the evening sun, and some had even set chairs and tables. The city felt like Paris.

And it's like that a lot these days. It is undeniable that the Celtic Tiger, even if it seems to be losing a tooth or two recently, has created a great deal of wealth and excitement. Up to a few months ago (and the change is visible), it was hard to be unemployed if you had experience or a degree or even looked the part.

I used to think that my generation, the one that left university in the late sixties and early seventies, before the first oil shock, was the last generation that would be able to experience that ease. We walked out of school and into jobs, and after us that didn't happen again for more than thirty years.

My youngest daughter Sarah has just finished the Leaving Cert, and we're all on tenterhooks at home waiting for the points to come out. She's looking for a lot of them, in order to open up the range of choices she wants to pursue. They get tired of me telling them that in my day, we wandered up to college on the opening day, with our two honours under our arms, and more or less decided there and then what we were going to have a go at. To this day I'm convinced that more people chose Arts than anything else because it began with an A, the table was positioned near the front of the hall as a result, and it didn't sound too hard.

But the point I'm making is in sympathy with them. Part of the reason, I believe, why economic competitiveness has become almost second nature to us as a nation is that we enrol our kids in the most highly competitive race they are ever going to have to run when they are eleven years of age, and we keep them at it for six years until the points are published.

One could argue that it's not doing them harm, just as the point could be made that the ethos we have now is probably an improvement on the ethos we had then. An awful lot of what I do in my normal working life involves trying to promote the excellence of the things we manufacture and sell. There was a time when you promoted Ireland on the basis of *craic* and hospitality, and not a lot else.

But I wonder about the balance. The hard work and the pressure on our kids are turning out a lot of well-educated (and well-trained) young people. But there is a disturbingly high suicide rate, especially among boys. Our educated kids can go to the top. But the ones who don't get in can stay stuck at the bottom.

In the recent ESRI report, *Monitoring Poverty Trends and Exploring Poverty Dynamics in Ireland*, the dynamics of poverty in Ireland are examined by means of a detailed survey which tracked people's financial circumstances from year to year.

The ESRI discovered in its research that there is considerable income mobility, so substantially more people experienced low income at some point over the five-year period from 1994 to 1998 than in any one year. About one-quarter of the sample of people surveyed were below half the average income for two or more of the five years.

That is important because the more years one is on low income, the lower the probability of escaping it: about one in five people escape from poverty after one year on low income, but only about one in fifteen do so after four years. People who are unemployed, lone parents, people in unskilled manual occupations, and those without educational qualifications are most likely to experience long periods on low income.

And of course, the longer low income persists, the greater the damage to the living standards of the household and the well-being of the people in it. In the dry language of the press release accompanying the ESRI report, 'levels of strain, psychological distress and fatalism are highest among those who remain persistently on low income'. The ESRI, and everyone else who has studied poverty, has identified three core solutions: education, education, and education. It is the greatest investment any society can make in its people and in itself.

As I walked back from Grafton Street, and began to realise (and then count) the number of people begging for money, the number who were shivering rather than basking in the evening sun, it became more and more obvious that the growth of the last seven or eight years hasn't solved all our problems.

Regular readers of this column will know, I hope, that I believe the reason is the choices we have made. The ESRI finds that in our prosperity, we have made some inroads into poverty, but not nearly enough. Particularly where the hard, grinding poverty that gets passed from generation to generation is concerned, the years of growth have nearly passed without anything being done.

And the choices we make are never debated. The points system, for instance, is no indicator of merit. Sure, the best competitors will get the highest points. But the system itself is only a regulator of supply and demand. You don't need higher points to get into some courses because you have to be brighter to survive. You need them only because there aren't enough places on the course.

In our prosperity, that is surely something that a Government with foresight would have rectified over the last five years. If we can't fix third level, surely in this rich country we can ensure that no one leaves school without the basic tools to break free of poverty?

I know a stroll around Stephen's Green, especially on the nicest evening of the year, shouldn't induce despair. But it is possible now to see the Celtic Tiger beginning to slip away. Maybe, before too long, there'll be nothing left but a swish of its tail. Then, when it's too late, we might remember what the Taoiseach said on Thursday evening, when he was asked to respond to the accusation that the Programme for Prosperity and Fairness had brought plenty of prosperity, but not enough fairness. 'We'll keep working on those issues,' he said, 'as resources are there.'

Now where have we heard that before?

Bah! Humbug!
(January 2002)

Humbug. I've been trying to think of a better word to describe the key events of the week, and I've failed. The only word that suits is humbug. According to my dictionary, it means 'something intended to deceive; a hoax or fraud, nonsense; rubbish, pretence; deception'. Taking all those definitions together, you might come to the conclusion that I have strong feelings about some of the things that happened this week. And you'd be right.

By far the biggest example of humbug on display was Michael Noonan's promise to give a tax break to anyone who lost money on eircom shares. This shallow piece of populism has surely robbed the leader of the opposition of all credibility. It was sugar-coated humbug, and even more sickening for all that.

It wasn't the only example of humbug this week – we'll talk about the PDs later – but it was stark. And it was thrown into even sharper relief by the opinion poll on Friday which demonstrated the value of credibility, as opposed to humbug. The MRBI poll showed that Bertie Ahern has credibility in the eyes of the electorate, and Michael Noonan has none.

That might sound a bit surprising, coming from me. To be honest, I've surprised myself by writing it down. I

269

don't suppose my best friends would describe me as a fan of the Fianna Fáil Party, and in fact I want to see Fine Gael in Government after the election.

But the thing I share with the great majority of the Irish people is that I no longer have any great interest in seeing Michael Noonan as Taoiseach. I would find it difficult, if not impossible, to vote for any Fine Gael candidate (at any level of preference) as long as that shamefully irresponsible promise remains on the books.

They just don't seem to get it, do they? We have surely more than enough evidence to conclude that people want to see something they can admire and respect, or at least like, in their leaders. Instead they see Michael Noonan pandering and wheedling. And they think it's pathetic.

As for the promise itself, I cannot see how they can find the remotest justification for it. If the entire Irish nation was duped into buying eircom shares, as Fine Gael seem to believe, they must also believe that the entire Irish nation are imbeciles. There was a debate at the time – not all commentators advocated buying the shares – and there was certainly plenty of understanding of the central fact that shares go down as well as up.

But all sorts of myths have been allowed to grow up since, and now Fine Gael are pandering to the myths. Myth one is that the shares were over-priced. If that is true, why did they shoot up immediately after the flotation, and stay above the sale price for months? Myth two is that it was some act of Government policy that drove the shares down again. These people seem to have closed their eyes entirely to the world-wide downturn in telecoms shares, of which eircom was only one victim.

There are other myths surrounding the eircom saga. But what they add up to is this – if it is justified to give a tax break to people who took a punt on eircom shares and lost, it is equally justified to offer a tax break to everyone who loses money on the next Grand National. No amount of huffing and puffing will alter that fact.

When I wrote here about the eircom flotation – before it happened – I predicted that the shares would rise in the short term, but I also said it could end in tears. And I added that if it did go wrong, 'don't be at all surprised if there isn't a mass middle-class movement demanding compensation for lost profits'.

Mind you, I never realised that the leader of Fine Gael would be part of it. Or that Fine Gael would be insisting that those of us who didn't invest in eircom shares should now be the ones to compensate those who did. Will Mr Noonan insist that the people who got out quick, and made handsome profits on their eircom shares, should now make a contribution to the losers? Will he what!

There is a considerable number of credible, serious people in Fine Gael – people who are healthily ambitious to be in office again, but not at any price. The likes of Alan Dukes and John Bruton must be cringing at the carry-on of the moment. It's time they reined their leader in, and explained to him that he will never get elected Taoiseach by making a laughing stock of his party.

The other arch humbug of the week, though for a different reason, was the PDs in general, and Michael McDowell in particular. What kind of party are they now? One day they recruit Tom Parlon, a man who clearly believes in the maximum degree of state intervention in the interests of his members. Presumably, he will adopt the same approach to the needs of his constituents if elected. Farmers and their leaders have always had the capacity to preach individualism and demand a collective response to their every need.

But a couple of days after recruiting the country's leading interventionist, the PDs announce the return of the country's leading free marketer, Michael McDowell. When Tom Parlon is leading the next highly vocal demand for more public spending and tax resources to be used for farmers, will Michael McDowell be telling him that competition and the free market are the answers? Will he what!

The same Michael McDowell celebrated his return to active politics (I gather he's thinking of using the humble campaign slogan 'I've neglected my constituents too long') by being interviewed on Eamon Dunphy's Last Word programme. When Eamon quizzed him about his role in appealing the Jamie Sinnott judgement to the Supreme Court, he readily admitted that he had been active in the case.

If he hadn't, he told us all – if he had allowed himself to be brow-beaten into allowing Jamie Sinnott's legal right to an education to stand unchallenged – he would have been contributing to the undermining of the separation of powers. And, in that way, he would have compromised one of the cornerstones of our liberty, something he courageously wasn't prepared to do.

Three cheers for Michael McDowell. He has defended our liberty against Jamie Sinnott. What perfect, complete humbug, delivered with the grandiose authority we expect from we-know-best lawyers. Most of us believe that the Supreme Court should have decided to protect Jamie Sinnott's constitutional right to an education appropriate to his needs. Earlier Supreme Courts would have – because they believed that the constitution was about people. If the present court had found for Jamie, are we really expected to believe that our basic liberties would have been eroded by that decision?

Give us a break from this kind of humbug. Think, just for one second, of the liberty enjoyed by Jamie Sinnott today as a result of the appeal. Then ask yourself if we really need such a champion of liberty as once and future Deputy McDowell. Do we what!

106 Mercedes
(2002)

Here's a health warning. Don't be surprised if you come across references to this article as begrudgery, and the politics of envy. It's only a few facts, but they're about something we're not supposed to talk about in Ireland.

Two friends of mine were driving home to Thomastown in County Kilkenny last Friday. It's a place that has seen its fair share of excitement recently, with the All-Ireland Hurling Final a fortnight ago and the visit of Tiger Woods this past weekend to nearby Mount Juliet.

The traffic got heavier as they got nearer – mostly drivers coming the other way, presumably on their way home from the golf. One of my friends remarked to the other on the number of new Mercedes cars that were passing them, heading towards Dublin. To while away the time in the slow-moving traffic, one of them started counting Mercs. To make it easy, she only counted 00, 01 and 02 mercs – nothing older than two years.

In the time it took them to drive from Casteldermot in Carlow to Thomastown, they counted 106 new Mercs going the opposite direction. Later they made a rough calculation, and worked out that that represented €7 million worth of shiny new cars.

And yet, if this weekend's papers are to be believed,

we are going to cut aid to the developing world again next year.

What in the name of God are we becoming under this backward and reactionary Government?

Or to be more precise, where are they trying to lead us? I didn't see the *Late Late Show* on Friday night, but several people who did told me that Charlie McCreevy was roundly booed on the show.

So there is some hope for us yet. We may have seen through McCreevy a bit late, but at least he has been found out at last. Others will surely follow.

I know I'm repeating myself, but isn't it surely time that in addition to kicking Fianna Fáil around, we all wised up to the pernicious and nasty trap they have us boxed into? The 'secret memos' revealed in some of the Sunday newspapers talk about cuts, cuts, cuts. We are doomed if we don't cut. Unemployment and emigration will start to rise if we don't cut.

I'm afraid there is no other word for it – and you know I never like to see language in the *Irish Examiner* – but horseshit. Even after a couple of years in which spending was allowed to rise very rapidly – in the case of some areas for purely electoral purposes – Ireland still has one of the lowest rates of public spending in the European Union. We can't be 100 per cent sure what the up-to-date comparisons are, but these are the most recent ones available.

They are compiled by Eurostat, the European Union's statistics agency, and they show public spending in each country as a proportion of that country's national wealth. Here are the figures at the end of the year 2000 (and I'm only going to list a few of the comparisons):

Ireland: 32%
Belgium: 49.9%

Denmark: 53.5%
Germany: 45.9%
United Kingdom: 40.2%
Sweden: 58.1%
France: 52.8%

The average across the entire EU is 47 per cent, and the average within the eleven countries in the euro is 47.3 per cent.

Just look at those figures for a minute. If I listed every country in the EU, you would see that we spend less as a proportion of our national wealth on public services than any other country. Yes – less than the United Kingdom, and miles less than France or Germany or any of the others.

And yet, right now, we are richer than any of them.

I'm sorry about the figures, but really, we have to ask ourselves what's going on here. Why are we being told by these chancers we call a Government, day after day, that we have to cut back? If you look at a few more figures gathered by Eurostat, you'll quickly see that we have cut back quite a lot already.

Here, for example, is the amount of money spent on social protection on each member of the population throughout Europe (social protection is broadly defined as the range of payments and services for people who are unemployed, sick, pensioned, disabled, etc.).

Ireland spends 3,339 ecu per head of the population.
Belgium: 6,040
Denmark: 8,784
Germany: 6,865
United Kingdom: 5,717
Sweden: 7,980
France: 6,696

The EU average is 5,601 and the average within the

eurozone is 5,558. If I listed all the countries, you would see that there are a few countries that spend somewhat less on social protection than Ireland. They are Greece, Spain and Portugal – where at least poor people have the comfort of a warm climate!

So it is possible to see at least one of the reasons why, despite all the propaganda, public spending is so low in Ireland by comparison to all our neighbours. We spend less on protecting vulnerable people than our neighbours do. Of course there are other reasons too – we spend less on our army than some, for instance.

But look around you – at one of the richest countries in the world. Look at the traffic jams, the queues for housing, the overworked hospital staff, the derelict playgrounds, the potholes, the pensioners in fear, the children who still go to bed hungry.

And look again at the Mercs, the BMWs, the amazing houses. You don't have to begrudge them, but you do have to realise one thing.

Our leaders have made a choice for us in Ireland. They never really debated it with us, they just put the propaganda in place to make sure we would see things their way. And the choice they have made for us is this. Everything that can be done to facilitate the growth of private wealth and consumption has been done. Everything that can be done to make sure that no sense of community obligation interferes with that growth of private wealth has been done.

That's what Charlie McCreevy, Bertie Ahern and Mary Harney are about. That's what they have achieved. That's why there are so many Mercs and so many potholes, so many amazing houses and so many people without a home.

And that's why every time they tell you we have to cut back on public spending, they are telling you lies. What they really mean is that if we look after the more vulnerable of our citizens the way we should, it might mean there is less wealth to be consumed at the other end. In almost the richest country in the world, the key choice at the heart of public policy is to encourage and facilitate the rich as they get richer.

This is the great unmentionable, of course, the thing never spoken about. We mustn't, at all costs, let the people know that all public policy is directed at encouraging the consumption of private wealth. If we did that, the people might do more than boo when they see government ministers on the telly. So call it begrudgery and envy. That way you don't have to deal with the truth.

No Room at the Inn
(December 2002)

No room at the inn. That's the phrase running through my head this past week or so. I've read it in several different places, and I've heard it used in conversation.

No room at the inn. In one of the four or five richest countries in the world. A country whose economy is still growing, whose inflation rate is manageable, whose debt is coming down. A country whose society is young, articulate, gifted, and the best educated in our long history.

No room at the inn. It's a phrase that paints a picture. A picture of a mean, cold and bitter place. A place where plenty doesn't guarantee a welcome. Where prosperity is not meant to be shared. Where those most at risk must fend for themselves.

Is that what we are becoming? Are we becoming the sort of place where to be poor is to be hunted, where to be in pain is to be alone? Or are our political leaders just trying to lead us down that mean little cul-de-sac?

The thought is prompted by a number of news stories and images. Of course the most powerful image, but by no means the only one, is of the devastated face of Denise Livingstone on the *Late Late Show*, as she pleaded with our Government not to let more tragedies happen in Monaghan.

This week, Denise's baby, Bronagh, died. She was born in an ambulance, because her mother was turned away from one hospital and sent to another. Had Bronagh been born on the way to Monaghan rather than on the ambulance trip to Cavan, she would have been admitted to Monaghan, and been in the best hands when an emergency struck. But she wasn't.

Because our system decreed she shouldn't be born in Monaghan Hospital. And our system decreed that there should not be adequate investment in the support and back-up that Denise and her baby needed on that dreadful journey.

Who is to blame? No doubt there will be someone to scapegoat in due course. But in all the recrimination let's not forget one thing. For the last few weeks two government ministers have been bickering in semi-public, through the use of judiciously placed leaks. One (Finance) has poured scorn on the efforts of the other to manage money. He has poured billions into health, he says, and it's all squandered. The other (Health) has said he is determined to get value for money. He wants us to think of it as the taxpayers' health service, rather than the patients' health service.

But Monaghan was one place they both agreed that money could be saved. All the reports and studies were there to back up and justify the choice they wanted to make. And that's the thing you have to remember. The downgrading of Monaghan was a political choice – not something forced on the system, but something the system was only too willing to accommodate.

Nobody wanted Bronagh Livingstone to die. That

was nobody's choice. But she died as a consequence of a political choice anyway. In the one place that could be safely downgraded to save money and prevent waste. Somehow or other, it never occurred to people who thought money was the only thing that mattered that people could end up suffering.

But it's not the only image. Look at all the other choices that have been publicised in the last week or so. Will no one suffer as a consequence of those? Are those choices too designed to lock the door of the inn, to nail the sign that says 'no room here' outside?

For example, this headline from a few days ago is a less dramatic sign perhaps, but just as meaningful. 'Cheaper housing plan abandoned' – the story of how the Government has capitulated to one of the most powerful vested interests in the land, and significantly watered down one of its own (very rare) progressive ideas.

The 20 per cent requirement on builders to include affordable housing within their developments was hated by the industry. But it was beginning to work – even in some of the most 'salubrious' developments. Now it's gone, and over time, despite protestations, the old order will reassert itself. The sign saying 'local authority tenants not wanted here' can be erected again.

And the Government has admitted that it intends to 'review' the number of special needs teachers it employs. 'We may be more generous in the Republic regarding special needs and over-generous in the interpretation of Department circulars,' a Department of Education spokeswoman is quoted as saying.

Really? Tell that to the several hundred parents who still have to sue the State to get any education at all for their children. Tell it to the youngsters in a three-year queue for speech therapy, or a five-year queue for psychological assessment.

It's about saving money. About ensuring that one more group won't gain admission to the inn, because they might be a bit expensive. Expensive because we've neglected their needs for far too long. The minister will reassure us, no doubt, that he has no intention of firing any special education teachers. But what of the 800 or so additional teachers due to be recruited this year? Guess what – their letters of appointment might just be suspended (for, say, a year or so) while the situation is being investigated.

Meanwhile, plans are well advanced to save between thirty and fifty million euro by slashing the numbers of people who can benefit from two more schemes. No, no, no – we're not talking about tax breaks which favour the idle rich here. We'll save the money by radically reducing the number of unemployed people who can benefit from the Back to Work Allowance Scheme, and by radically cutting the number of unemployed people who can be hired on community employment schemes.

These schemes worked for people. They worked very well, and they were cost effective. Only thing is, they might have given people ideas above their station. They might have persuaded them that long-term unemployment doesn't have to be that way.

So the schemes are being removed, little by remorseless little.

I could go on. We are, it seems, going to have tighter controls on 'would-be' refugees. Our Minister for Justice has decided that anyone wishing to claim refugee status should in future do so at the airport or port where they land.

And if they do, will there be resources at hand to ensure that they get fair treatment? Will individuals or groups concerned for the rights of refugees, and for due process, be allowed ready access to them? Or will the majority of applicants be summarily dealt with on the spot, packed back onto the plane or boat they just got off, without any of us being any the wiser? What practice do you think is likely to prevail in the fullness of time?

Because despite what I've said, this is after all Ireland of the Welcomes. A place where we are only too glad to share. A place where we are conscious of the plight of our neighbour, and willing to look after our own. A place where there is always room at the inn. Isn't that right?

The iPod Generation
(2006)

One point two million. That's how many children there are in Ireland (if you count eighteen-year-olds as children). Just under half are girls, and they constitute about 30 per cent of our population. According to the last census, about 90 cent of them were born in Ireland. They are being born into smaller families – the average size of a family has halved in thirty years, from four children to two.

I know all this because I was asked to speak about 'the child in the twenty-first century' to the Irish Primary Principals Network last week. You might have noticed the Minister for Education on television at the weekend urging them to stop moaning about their lot. I think she must have been at a different conference – far from moaning, the people I met were committed and concerned professionals, determined to get the most from the education system for the kids they worked with.

It was when I began researching the subject about which I was asked to speak that I discovered there is actually a wealth of information, in all sorts of different places, that add up to a fascinating picture of our kids. It's a good news, bad news kind of picture, that makes you wonder sometimes how well the next few generations are going to do.

We know that one in seven children grow up with one parent only, usually a mother, and that those children are at a significantly greater risk of poverty. And we know too that one in seven of all children in Ireland now live in consistent poverty. There is of course significant overlap between those figures.

On the good news side, more than 80 per cent of boys and girls report themselves as being in good or excellent health. The 2002 *Health Behaviour of Schoolchildren* study reports that Irish schoolchildren score highly on the happiness index, with around 90 per cent of them reporting that they feel quite happy or very happy with life. They are idealistic, with thousands of them being willing to take part in voluntary activity. They are close to their parents, and close to siblings.

They are key consumers, or at least a key target for those interested in marketing. The published marketing studies almost all refer to eighteen- to twenty-four-year-olds, not children but still very much the next generation. Nine in every ten young people have their own mobile phones, and they send an average of thirty-seven text messages a week. They tend to be somewhat disparaging of the interest of other young people in brands, but more than half derive a strong sense of belonging themselves from the ownership and use of branded products. The iPod generation needs to own trainers with a logo on them, telephones capable of doing almost anything, and their own personal DVD players. (They might be taking a lead from their parents in that regard – none of us seem able to watch a television any more unless the screen is as a wide as a house.)

They are starved of time, these young people, although by no means starved of alcohol, with plenty of manufacturers willing to invest large amounts of money in inventing and marketing drinks specifically for them. Some of the alcohol manufacturers are a bit queasy about referring to their marketing plans for children, so they tend to refer to children as MLDAs. The acronym stands for 'minimum legal drinking age'. Many young people, of course, start drinking long before they reach the so-called MLDA, and around one in ten young people report taking an illegal drug, usually cannabis or ecstasy, within the last year.

Have these young people ambitions? The marketers certainly hope so. Based on their surveys they have concluded that more than half want to own a car soon. Slightly less than that want to own a credit card. Sadly, only around one in fourteen intend to join a political party – around a third of the number that want to experience bungee-jumping.

Nearly 200,000 children in Ireland suffer some form of mental distress. One in ten children in Ireland suffers from mental illness severe enough to cause them some level of impairment, and one in fifty suffers severe and disabling mental illness. Between 1998 and 2000, for instance, 2,650 children and teenagers were admitted to adult psychiatric hospitals and units – 200 of them were fifteen years of age and younger. Most starkly of all, the incidence of suicide among young people has risen by a quarter in the last ten years. In the last twenty years or so, fifty-five Irish children between the ages of five and fourteen took their own lives.

It's a mixed picture, isn't it? All the studies of children show that there is a strong link between education and a variety of different levels of fulfilment. At least our education system is geared to maximising the chances and opportunities for children, right? Alas, not so.

Almost 1,000 pupils per year fail to make the transition between primary and secondary school. One in three children in disadvantaged areas suffer severe literacy problems, three times the national average. Early school leaving is estimated to affect nearly one in five young people in Ireland. Fifteen per cent of young people leave school without a Leaving Certificate and 3 per cent with no qualification at all. One in five students from disadvantaged areas miss more than twenty days in primary and secondary school in a given year.

Ireland had a pupil to teacher ratio of 19.5 at primary education level in 2001/2002. This was the third highest ratio in the EU. We spent €5,000 per pupil at primary level, €6,788 at secondary level and €8,914 at third level in the 2003 academic year.

Regular national assessments of English reading levels in Irish primary schools have been conducted since 1972. The results of the most recent test carried out in 2004 were recently released. This has concluded that little or no change in national reading standards has occurred since 1980. In particular the levels of reading difficulties in areas and schools designated as disadvantaged remains consistently at 30 per cent.

Children from lone-parent families, from large families, from families who had medical cards, from the Traveller community, from families with unemployed parents and whose parents themselves have low educational achievement are consistently represented among that 30 per cent. In fact, they are children with the same family profile as children found to be in consistent poverty.

One striking bit of additional background is that most of the children of Ireland are citizens of a very affluent republic indeed. There are, of course (and there will be more), a great many children in Ireland for whom citizenship will be an aspiration rather than an entitlement, even if they have been born here. There are, and there will be more, many children here whose skin colour and whose language would not have been familiar to the men and women of 1916, when they pledged to cherish all the children of the nation equally.

Still, for the last ninety years, we've been committed, at least rhetorically, to doing just that. Have we done OK? Or is it possible, in this really rich country of ours, that we could do a bit better?

A Letter to Bertie
(2006)

Dear Taoiseach,

I hope you don't mind my writing to you about this, because it's something I really feel strongly about. You spoke very effectively, I'm told, at the conference in Croke Park organised by the Commission for Justice and Social Affairs during the week. I wasn't there myself, but I've spoken to a number of people who were, and they were very impressed by your take on the Church's impact on Irish social policy.

What really seemed to make an impact on people was your expression of a personal philosophy and set of values that were, in your own words, bound up with the dignity of the person. The expression of human dignity as a core value for a powerful man was an important milestone, many felt.

Incidentally, Taoiseach, I don't know whether you're aware of this, but I have a feeling there may be a nasty little conspiracy to prevent your core values being more widely available for study. When I went looking for the full text of your speech, it wasn't on the Fianna Fáil website, and even more surprisingly, it wasn't on the Government website.

In fact, in your own Department they haven't put any of your speeches on the web since the middle of February. So while I was able to find your remarks at the opening of the new All-Weather Pitch and Clubhouse Extension at Round Towers GAA Club in Lusk, and the speech you made at the launch of the Revenue Commissioners' brand new Container Scanner, they're a while back, and not nearly so uplifting. So I have had to rely on media reports of the speech I wanted to read, where you outlined some clearly deeply held values.

But I'm taking those reports at face value. As Taoiseach, your commitment is to human dignity. In fact, when I did go to the FF website, I found a very well-produced video there, where you also spoke effectively about the dignity of work, the strong community ethos you value, the sense of togetherness that is so important to the fabric of that community. There were lots of shots of green fields, busy roads, happy children waving tri-colours, and perhaps incongruously, the port tunnel.

Again and again throughout the video the refrain was the same – keeping prosperity strong to build strong communities, to enable Ireland to be everything it can be.

There's a problem, Taoiseach. Not with the vision, but with the reality. Yes, we have a strong economy. But the dignity of the person? The strength of the community? Surely it's becoming clearer and clearer that dignity in Ireland, in this rich and prosperous country, is more and more a matter of income. In a week when one Irishman was able to bid €16 million for an untried horse, apparently only because he wanted to best a rival, let me tell you a couple of stories about the dignity of the person. They're true stories, and they are happening right now in the transformed Ireland you speak about.

Chloe is two years old. She lives with her mum and dad in a one-bed basement flat. There are a few pieces of furniture in the dark flat. Chloe hasn't had a chance to meet other children or to play outside. Chloe's lived in this flat for a year now, after moving around hostel accommodation and temporary accommodation for the first year of her life.

Her mum and dad are young and both grew up with serious family problems. Her dad spent a lot of time in the care system and both her parents were sexually abused as children. They turned to drugs to dampen the chaos and hurt inflicted on them in their young lives. Now they are both stable on a methadone programme. But the family is isolated. They are living in appalling conditions of poverty and Chloe's health has suffered. She is underweight, had head lice and skin rashes like ringworm. Chloe's speech and language are delayed.

Chloe isn't an emergency – which is to say that the social services that should be available to her are simply too hard-pressed to be able to reach out and provide her with the help she needs. As you know, Taoiseach, despite all the representation made about the subject over the years, it will be a long time before Chloe can get to the top of a waiting list for speech and language therapy – perhaps the one thing that could really change her life permanently. If she had money, it would be different.

The good news for Chloe is that her mum and dad, despite their own problems, both love her. They know they need help for her, and they came to a voluntary organisation looking for it. Between her parents and the voluntary organisation, Chloe will get a break. But that voluntary organisation, despite its best efforts, can only scratch the surface. There are too many Chloes.

Annie, on the other hand, is now in her late eighties. She depends on her pension, and as you know, it's pretty modest, despite the increases of recent years. Mentally alert and proud, she is alone in the world, and suffers from a number of physical ailments – not the result of years of hard work, but the result of raising a large family. Many of them emigrated in the bad times, and those few who are still at home find it tough to make ends meet themselves.

They were doing what they could, with frequent visits, but everyone, including Annie, was relieved when a place was eventually (after a long wait) found for her in a public bed in a nursing home.

And then, under the regulations that your Government brought in last year, every penny of her pension was taken from her. She had to sign over the whole lot, and has been living ever since on the €35 a week that the State – your State and mine, Taoiseach – has decided she should have.

In the fairly recent past, a couple of her grandchildren celebrated their Holy Communion. Their parents gave them some money and said it was from Granny. If one of her grandchildren has a birthday, Annie has to choose between a present or her favourite brand of breakfast cereal.

She's had to abandon the habits of a lifetime – she can no longer afford to buy a daily newspaper, and she totally depends on visitors to think of bringing her occasional flowers, though she always had them around the house – when she had a house.

She won't ask, of course, because as you know Taoiseach, that generation of Irish people – the ones who knew the hard times while they were building our rich country – are fierce about their independence. When that goes, dignity goes.

It's not too late, I think, to start putting sincerely held values into practice. When the dignity of a child depends on speech and language training, and some help with diet and nutrition, dignity shouldn't be hard to find. When the dignity of an old person depends on her independence being respected, that shouldn't be beyond us. If it is, then all our commitment to core values about dignity surely ring very hollow indeed.

Yours sincerely,
Fergus Finlay

New Religious Icons
(2006)

Have you noticed, on your travels around Ireland these days, that virtually every town in the country has acquired three things in common with every other town? No matter where you go, on the Cork to Dublin road, through the towns in the midlands or the west or the north-east, down south of Limerick and into Kerry, or through Carlow, Kilkenny and into the south-east, they're all the same.

Every single town has a brand new hotel on its outskirts, sometimes one on each corner of the town. And all the hotels have enormous signs outside, advertising the cheapest prices you've ever seen and the most attractive possible amenities. After you've seen the signs, you'd never want to stay anywhere else – until you see the next sign.

And every town is ringed by new apartment blocks. They're all luxurious, they're all exclusive, they're all dripping with prestige. You have to be ready to snap them up, because they're all 'almost' sold out. Generally speaking, they tend to be surrounded by scaffolding, and they're usually built so close to the road that that it's hard to visualise the gardens and the play areas that must be associated with such luxury and prestige. But sure, no doubt all that is coming.

And the third thing you see at the edge of every town you drive into now are the new cathedrals. New places of worship, built on a scale we've never seen before. Humbling in their majesty, awe inspiring in their magnificence. What new gods, you wonder, have come to inhabit the earth? Who could possibly deserve a home made with such a lavish outpouring of glass and steel, such vaulted ceilings, such an abundance of light that they can be seen from miles away?

And then you draw a little closer, and see the signs over these wonderful basilicas. Honda. Mitsubishi. Volvo. Ford. And slowly it dawns on you. It's not gods that live here, nor even people of high rank. These homes were built for cars, to keep them dry, warm and shiny, and to enable us to gaze on them with wonder. It's one of the great manifestations of the new religion of consumerism – materialism made flesh.

And it must have cost millions. All over the country we have built huge shrines to new cars. Nobody lives there except the cars, and yet they're lit through the night. They look warm and comfortable, the cars all beautifully looked after. There are places in our larger cities where there are whole streets of these cathedrals, lined up one after the other, each one more magnificent than the next. Liffey Valley in Dublin, Mahon Point in Cork, and a dozen places in between have whole villages of car basilicas. In all our lifetimes there has never been anything like it. Palaces for cars. Magnificent surroundings to make sure they feel at home.

Sister Stanislaus Kennedy, writing in the annual report of Focus Ireland, describes home this way: 'Home is a place in which to feel safe and secure, warm and dry. A place to rest, eat, sleep and entertain, find solitude, pray, love, laugh, argue and cry. A place to read a book, share a meal, watch a television programme, play an instrument, do a bit of gardening, play with the children, get the housework done and the bills paid, be at ease with oneself and with friends and family, in safety and security without fear of interference or intrusion.'

And she goes on to say that the need for a place like that is deep and urgent in all of us. 'The desire for a place called home is the deepest need in every human heart and perhaps the least recognised,' she says. I'm sure the cars feel the same.

We started building these mausoleums in the early 1990s, as the Celtic Tiger started to roar. Back in 1995, for example, we bought almost 83,000 cars brand new. By 2005 that number had increased to 166,000 – exactly double the number we bought a mere decade earlier.

(The number of second-hand cars we've been buying has actually declined a bit in the same period. There wouldn't be room for them in the motor cathedrals. On the other hand, the number of cars that are big and powerful, as well as shiny, has gone up by a factor of six.)

But here's an odd thing. Back in 1996, again a decade ago, the number of people who were homeless in Ireland was almost exactly 2,500. The most recent official figure was 5,581. The number of shiny new cars we own has doubled in a decade. So has the number of people who have nowhere to live.

Nowhere to live? There are different definitions of homelessness. Focus Ireland includes three categories in their definition of homelessness: Visible Homelessness (sleeping rough or living in emergency shelters); Hidden Homelessness (involuntarily sharing with family and friends or living in housing that is woefully inadequate);

and At risk of Homelessness (likely to become homeless due to economic difficulties, too high a rent burden, insecure tenure or health difficulties). The official doubling of homelessness during the busiest years of the Celtic Tiger was in the 'visible homelessness' category.

There are other ways to measure the need for a home of your own. The most common and often used is by counting the number of people on the waiting lists for local authority housing. And guess what? A decade ago, there were about 25,000 families on the waiting lists, and now it's just short of 50,000. Doubled again.

It's strange, isn't it? All these cars, living in their wonderful showrooms. The rest of us with our faces pressed against the glass. Those of us who have a second-hand car want a new one. Those with a new one want a bigger one. Few of us are content with one car – the number of two- and three-car families in Ireland has also, you guessed it, doubled in the last decade.

Over the weekend, I read a couple of newspaper columnists in the Sunday papers, including some who ought to know better, having a bit of a cut at the 'poverty industry'. The headlines, of course, were full of the news (if it is news and not just speculation) that Brian Cowen is going to cut the top rate of tax in tomorrow's Budget. There's good news for us all – we'll be able to pop around to the local car showroom and admire the glossy brochures. By this time next year, if the good news keeps rolling, another 100,000 new cars will have left their shiny palaces in order to transport us in the luxury to which we have become accustomed.

And a few more people will join the housing waiting lists, only to discover that the great Irish dream of a home of your own is slipping further and further away. A few more people will become homeless altogether. A few more will be unable to cope with the pressures of the modern world. We might even find some sleeping rough in the doorways of the new cathedrals. Looking for sanctuary, maybe, at the mercy of the new religion.

High on the Hog
(2007)

Have you any idea how much a Harley Davidson costs? I was dying to find out, because there was a time when you simply wouldn't see one on Ireland's roads, but recently I've been seeing a lot of them.

The 'hog', as it's known, was something we all associated with the USA. Remember that movie *Easy Rider*, with Peter Fonda and Denis Hopper? It changed the culture in America, introducing two pot-smoking anti-heroes to an entire generation of young people. The real stars of the movie, of course, were the Harley Davidson bikes on which Fonda and Hopper explored the deep South.

Ever since then, the Harley Davidson has been the bike most associated with an alternative lifestyle. Very few drop-outs, of course, can afford one nowadays. According to my researches, an UltraClassic Electra Glide touring bike will set you back just under a cool €30,000. That's roughly the same price as a new Volvo S40 or a top-of-the-range Toyota Avensis.

But guess what? Thirty-nine of you bought Harley Davidsons in the month of June this year – that's about one in ten of all motorbikes bought in the country. Assuming that proportion remains more or less constant each month, so far this year about 212 of the hogs have been bought in Ireland.

And they are big bikes, as well as being expensive. The vast majority of the Harleys on the road are over 1,000cc. But big and brash is what we like when it comes to buying any kind of wheels nowadays. Take our ever-increasing love affair with the car, for instance. The figures for the month of June alone show that we bought 15,472 cars (almost 140,000 so far this year). Of those cars, 55 per cent of them had engines bigger than 1,500cc. And the total included – just for one month – 368 Mercs, 729 BMWs (BMW is now the sixth most popular make of car in Ireland!), 467 Audis and 135 Lexuses. There's no doubt about it, we like a lot of power under us.

And of course, the BMW or the Merc is almost certainly not the only car in the driveway (now that most of us have converted our garages to studies or TV rooms). Ten years ago, one in every seven households in Ireland had two or more cars. In a decade, that number has more than doubled, to the point where one household in every three has a second car or more.

There's progress for you. And it's only part of the story. More than twice as many households have tumble dryers, dishwashers and microwave ovens as had them ten years ago. More than three times as many have home computers and burglar alarms. When the Central Statistics Office was conducting its household survey in the mid-90s (from which all these figures come), the number of mobile phones wasn't even worth recording. Now, 85 per cent of households have at least one. And nearly half of all households have internet access, something else which didn't exist, for all practical purposes, a decade ago.

With all this fantastic stuff around us, it's surprising that we need holidays. But we do. The average Irish household spent a total of €1,727.24 on holidays in 2004 –2005, which was almost 46% higher than the €1,183.63 recorded five years earlier. Oddly enough, those of us who live in towns and cities seem to need to spend twice as much on our holidays – €2,122.54 – as those who live in the country. We urban dwellers also spend twice as much on wine as our rural counterparts. Must be all the stress caused by all the commuting caused by all the traffic caused by all the cars on the road!

I suppose the question has to be asked – how come we're managing to afford all these holidays and cars and microwave ovens? There's more good news on this front. According to the CSO, average household income has only shot up since the last time the Household Budget Survey was conducted.

The average gross weekly household income for the State in 2004-2005 was €989.53, which was 48.4% higher than the €666.72 recorded five years earlier. Disposable income, which is arrived at after the deduction of income tax and social insurance, increased by almost 53 per cent from €551.60 to €842.06 and now represents just over 85 per cent of gross income for all households in the State. (On average, that means our total direct tax burden as families is about 15 per cent of income – and we're supposed to be crippled by tax!)

And remember, those figures are just the average. The top 10 per cent of households, God bless them, have seen their disposable income increase by more than half since the last survey, and now have €2,233 a week to spend. But of course, the more you have, the more you need. It is, after all, those in the highest 10 per cent who are keeping the travel agents and the Harley Davidson suppliers in business. And look at all the jobs that involves.

People in the lowest income category, after all, don't have much to contribute to our free market economy. How could they, with weekly disposable incomes of €157 a week – especially when they have to spend more than a third of that on food, fuel and light. The higher-income groups spend only half of what the poor spend on these commodities, so naturally they are going to have more to spare for the finer things of life.

A lot of the people in the lower-income brackets are pensioners, but not all of them are. In the annual review we published in Barnardos a couple of weeks ago, we told the (true) story of just one low-income family. I hope you don't mind if I repeat it.

Three years ago, Ciara's mum was hurt when a stolen car crashed into her. She has severe brain injury. She finds day-to-day tasks impossible. She can't walk without help and has moved into the living room. The toilet is upstairs, so Ciara and her dad take turns to help her to the bathroom.

Ciara is twelve, but already she has the responsibilities of a mother. She makes sure her brothers and sisters get up for school and gets them dressed. When her dad is busy she looks after her little brother Cian. Ciara doesn't want to go to school any more. It is the last place she wants to be. She has missed so many days in school that she feels stupid when the teacher asks her to read out loud.

The washing machine in the house is broken so she has to hand-wash her uniform. That takes ages. Sometimes the other girls say she smells. Ciara hates them for making fun of her.

The days Ciara makes it to school she finds it really hard to concentrate, as she worries about her mum. Will she be OK by herself? Is her dad going to be home early to look after her? Sometimes Ciara wishes it was her that had been hit by the car. Then her mum could look after them all. Then maybe they wouldn't be in the bottom 10 per cent when the next survey is done.

Sneaking in the Cuts
(2008)

This is always how the squeeze begins. In stealth. Usually accompanied by jargon and gobbledegook. Almost never accompanied by a straightforward announcement. A hidden circular, a secret letter, a coded message. Nobody ever stands up and says, 'The Department of Finance has told us that we have to cut back this year, because they're not going to reach their targets.'

But that's what all these announcements and letters mean. We are going to see a period of cutbacks now. The squeeze has begun. And guess what? The cutbacks are going to be crude and simple. And they're going to hurt people who have no one to speak up for them. And they're going to be counterproductive.

Example 1:

An announcement appears on the Department of Education website. It's not simple, nor accessible. It's to be found under the list of circulars they send out constantly, listed as circular number 0010/2008, and it's called 'Regulations governing the appointment and retention of teachers in primary schools for the school year 2008/09'. At first glance it seems anodyne, harmless. There is no accompanying press release – the newspapers have to find out about it for themselves.

But when it's translated into English, and when principals begin to apply it to the situations in their schools, the real meaning becomes clear. Nearly 150 schools will lose teachers in the new academic year. Many more, who were expecting to be able to appoint an extra teacher because enrolment is growing, find they won't be able to after all. The plan to reduce class sizes in primary schools is gone.

It wasn't so much a plan, more a very specific commitment. It's there, on page 42 of the Programme for Government. Because, it says, 'this Government sees education as central to achieving our goals of protecting and growing Ireland's prosperity and ensuring greater social inclusion', almost the first commitment the Programme makes is this.

> *We will increase the number of primary teachers by at least 4,000. This will enable us to reduce class sizes. The staffing schedule will be reduced from a general rule of at least one teacher for every 27 pupils in 2007/08, by one point a year, to one for every 24 children by 2010/11.*

That commitment, and the Programme, was signed by three people. Bertie Ahern. Mary Harney. And Trevor Sargent (remember him?). None of them have had a word to say about the abandonment of that promise. Their real message, of course, is simple enough.

'Sorry. Not going to happen. We know it was only last year – actually only nine months ago. We know we agonised for several weeks over the Programme for Government, and there was great fanfare when we signed it. We know the ink isn't even dry on the document. But that promise is gone now, and there'll be more. Cutbacks, you know. You didn't really think we were serious about the Programme for Government, did you?'

And by the way, they could add, if they were willing to, that they also know that cutbacks that damage primary education are particularly counter-productive, because they have knock-on effects on children and young people right through all the years of their education. But cutbacks in Ireland never have logic to them.

Example 2:

The Secretary General of the Department of Health writes to the head of the HSE, Professor Brendan Drumm. The letter is written in January, but of course is not intended for publication. It takes several months for this letter to find its way into the newspapers.

It's written in classic civil service gobbledegook, using language like 'the financial framework which accompanied the HSE national service plan'; 'we are all agreed that your 2008 national service plan has been prepared on the basis that the planned level of services can be delivered within your allocation'. The Department indicates in the letter that it has, in its own view, provided enough funding for a 'demographically adjusted existing level of service'.

When all that is translated into English, it transpires that the HSE told the Department that it would need €450 million more in 2008 to maintain services at the level of 2007 – and the 2007 services already included cutbacks. The Department replies that they know all that, but tough. The HSE isn't getting it. Naturally, of course, this correspondence isn't accompanied by a press release either.

When you go back to the Programme for Government, that document signed with all the fanfare nine months ago, you find that a full seven pages are devoted to health care. There's going to be new investment in this, that and the other thing. Every problem known to man, and ventilated during the election campaign, is going to be sorted. No mention anywhere of frozen budgets, of the HSE being unable to fill a single vacancy, of two years of cutbacks starting almost the moment the Programme for Government was signed. No mention anywhere of a financial squeeze that would force the HSE to start contemplating the closure of A&E units (imagine if that had been announced during the election!), or reducing elective surgery and outpatient clinics by about 20 per cent in some hospitals.

Isn't it astonishing? The election was held ten months ago. In terms of issues, it was dominated by health care almost from start to finish. You can search the media coverage of the general election from start to finish, and you won't find a single reference to the fact that once the election is out of the way, the real intention is to start squeezing as hard as possible on the HSE's budget.

Nor will you find it in the other place you might expect to see a change in direction like this, the Minister for Finance's Budget speech. I went back and re-read that the other night, looking for some indication of the cutbacks ahead. Instead I found the minister setting out his personal priorities for this year, including as priority number one 'to protect the weaker in society through maintaining a high level of social spending'.

Under the heading of 'Health', Brian Cowen had this to say: 'Much of the public debate about health services is focussed on the increased cost involved. While there are valid concerns about the growth of health spending, both nationally and internationally, the proper context for this debate is one which views health spending as delivering benefits as well as accruing costs.'

Somewhere in that couple of sentences, there must be a code. If we could all figure it out, we'd have a better idea of when to look out for the cutbacks. At almost the precise moment that the Minister for Finance was talking about 'valid concerns', the Secretary General of the Department of Health was telling the HSE its budget was going to be squeezed.

We'll be back to this subject throughout the year. You can be absolutely certain that now we are once again in an era when cutbacks are to be the order of the day, it will be people who are elderly, disabled, ill or otherwise vulnerable who will suffer most. That's another reason they don't like talking about them. And another reason you need to be updated regularly.

The Recession Arrives
(2008)

I hope you remember that you read it here first. Last March, I told you the cutbacks were beginning. I warned you it would start with stealth cutbacks, in the hope you wouldn't really notice. But as the slowdown in the economy begins to bite, the appetite for cuts within the system will grow.

Nobody took a whole lot of notice of that warning, three months ago. But suddenly, the warning signs have started going off like a fireworks display. Last week we had the Minister for Finance sounding like someone who has just realised he has taken a real hospital pass. I don't know whether he was blaming Bertie Ahern for resigning as Taoiseach, or Brian Cowen for handing him the promotion, but there was no doubt that Brian Lenihan was suddenly confronted by the horrible reality that he is unlikely to be a popular Minister for Finance.

And then there were this weekend's Sunday papers. the *Sunday Business Post* was pretty direct. 'The government is preparing plans for a significant curtailment of public spending,' it said, 'involving cutbacks in some areas and the postponement of planned projects, amid a worsening economic outlook.'

And the lead story went on, 'Officials in the

Department of Finance are finalising the annual budget strategy memo, stipulating what the government can afford to spend next year. It will be circulated to ministers in the coming days and formally discussed at a cabinet meeting on July 9, and again a week later. But the *Sunday Business Post* understands that ministers have already discussed the worsening economic situation at cabinet last week, where the prospect of cuts to public spending plans was raised.'

Hidden away in the business news of the *Sunday Tribune* was part of the reason behind this apparent panic. 'Central Bank set to slash economic growth forecast' was the headline, and the story went on to say that 'the Central Bank are set to slash their economic growth forecasts for Ireland to between 0% and 1.5% as the property market and construction sectors continue to decline and bank credit remains constrained'.

You might well wonder why a story like this wasn't the lead story in the newspaper. If the Central Bank is really looking at a growth figure at or close to zero, that is huge news. It will send shivers through every market, and you'll be able to see politicians and senior civil servants ageing before your very eyes. A zero growth rate hasn't been recorded in Ireland for more than fifteen years – a generation in political or economic terms. We simply won't know how to cope.

And then there is today's news. Elsewhere in this paper today, you'll probably be able to read about the latest forecasts for the economy by the ESRI, whose quarterly economic bulletin is likely to contain more bad news. I'm writing this, naturally, before the ESRI report is published, and I seem to have mislaid my crystal ball. But it wouldn't surprise me in the slightest if every news bulletin for the remainder of the day was dominated by their gloomy, not to say dire, predictions. By the end of the day, zero growth in the economy – maybe even the dread word 'recession' – will have become a reality rather than a prediction.

What does surprise me is that anyone should be too surprised. The reality is that there's never been an economic cycle in the history of the world, going back to the Bible, that didn't slow down or stop, if only for a time. Remember the seven years of plenty followed by the seven years of famine?

But if we're really headed for zero growth, even for a period, the one thing we shouldn't do is precisely the thing we're most likely to do. Panic.

We've been through zero growth before – even negative growth. And we know what it can do. People are forced to emigrate. Factories close. Investment goes elsewhere. And the poor carried the lion's share of the burden.

But that happened in different times. We were a poor country that had experienced little except stagnation and recession for the best part of thirty years. Now, we're a rich country, with one of the lowest national debts in the developed world. We have assets beyond our wildest dreams a generation ago. We have more than enough to tide us over a period of uncertainty if we keep our heads.

But we're not great at that, are we? Our political masters always seem to know only one response when a squeeze comes on. And the clue to that response is in this sentence from the *Sunday Business Post* story. 'Department of Finance briefing documents obtained under the Freedom of Information Act show that officials have been warning about spending pressures in the three key departments of education, health and social welfare.'

Over the next month or so, while the rest of us are trying to enjoy whatever decent weather materialises for the rest of the summer, senior civil servants and their political masters will be engaging in the annual ritual dance known as the 'estimates campaign'. Against the backdrop of all these awful predictions, the Department of Finance will send out their round-robin letter to all the other government departments and key state agencies, like the HSE. It will turn the blood cold of everyone who reads it. But its real message will be that they intend to cut everything they possibly can at the margins of public expenditure.

That's the key thing. It's all going to happen at the margins. Ninety per cent, perhaps more, of next year's public expenditure bill is decided before the process even gets under way. The big projects on which contracts are signed, the vast bulk of the public service pay bill (including public servants' increments), the amount that is going to be set aside for debt repayments and pension provision, the cost of maintaining most things more or less as they are. All that is settled already, and either can't or won't be interfered with. The estimates campaign, in that sense, is more than a bit phoney, because everyone involved knows that it's only the extra little bits that are vulnerable, the bits that are left over.

So what is left over? What's left is what's at the margins. Anything new or different. Our allocation to the developing world. Anything that might count as an improvement on a pretty bad service. All that kind of stuff. And one other thing – services to people whose votes won't make a difference. Homeless people. Frail elderly people. People with mental health problems.

312

People with disabilities. Lone parents. People in run-down housing estates.

So you can get one thing clear. When you start reading all the predictions about public spending cuts, you don't need to worry too much. The services you need – the teachers, the guards, the soldiers, the bin collections, the street lighting – they won't really be affected. Whatever the Department of Finance says, all that public spending is pretty well committed. You'll be all right.

Unless, of course, you live at the margins too. Then you'd better get used to carrying the burden for the rest of us.

Drivetime

He's Going to Be Great!

When our first daughter was born in Holles Street Hospital, and diagnosed with Down's Syndrome, we didn't even know what the words meant. That was 1972, and one of the staff of the hospital had to ask us if we were familiar with the word 'mongoloid' before we realised the condition Mandy had.

We left Holles Street with a baby who had a disability, and no help whatsoever to deal with the challenges we faced. We were given a five-minute audience with a consultant paediatrician, who said, 'Just take her home and mind her. She'll never amount to much, but she won't cause you too much trouble either.' He probably thought he was being cruel to be kind. I thought he was just a brute.

Over the years since, we've met a few people like that. Experts, people who know best. They don't know how to listen, to spend time. They don't respect the talent and experience of people – especially mothers – who have devoted years and years to the extra support that's necessary if a child with Down's Syndrome is to grow into a fulfilled and capable adult.

I have to add that we've met lots of great professionals too, but I've never forgotten the words used by that consultant, nearly thirty-five years ago. And I've often reflected on them. Never more so than when Mandy became the first and so far the only member of her family to represent her country, when she played basketball for Ireland in the Special Olympics World Summer Games in New Haven, Connecticut in 1995. It was no expert who brought her to that point. No, it was her own deter-mination, the skills and talents of her mother, and the support of the Special Olympics organisation. Unlike some of the experts, Special Olympics believes passion-ately that there are no limits to human potential, apart from the limits we put on people.

We've never been to Holles Street since the day we left with Mandy. But we were back there this week, to visit our first grandchild, who was born there a week ago today.

The building is still the same, but things have changed a lot inside. Our second daughter, Vicky, had a long and difficult labour before giving birth by Caesarean section to a bouncing, and perfectly healthy, baby boy. The hard work involved lasted well over two days, and throughout every minute of that time Vicky told us she felt supported by staff who were completely committed to her. Nursing, midwives and medical staff were all superbly professional.

But none of them pretended they knew best. They consulted Vicky and they respected her, as they respect all the mothers in the hospital. After the baby was born they made sure that Vicky had the space and time to recover and to get to know her son. They even helped and encouraged Tony, Vicky's husband, to take the steps necessary to physically bond with the baby.

We've spent most of the week since alternating between bursting with pride for Vicky and being besotted by the new arrival she has brought us. But I do think it is worth recording that some things have improved in our health service. The care and professionalism of nurses and doctors are second to none, especially when it's delivered under pressure as it usually is, and in my view they deserve any reward they get. If nothing else, their care and their respect helped erase a memory of Holles Street that has lasted an awful long time.

By the way, Vicky and Tony have decided to call their son Ross. Ross Whelan, that's his name. You might want to file it away for future reference. He's my grandson, and he's going to be great!

Justice Is Blind –
and It's Sometimes Deaf Too

I don't want to use her real name, but Mary is twenty. She has Down's Syndrome and she is bright as a button. Two years ago, she was sexually assaulted.

Despite her own sense of horror at what had happened, Mary knew she had done no wrong. She was determined to tell her story, and she did, honestly and always consistently. First to her family, then to the guards, then to lawyers, and finally to a judge. Bravely, clearly, and in necessary detail.

And the judge decided she wasn't competent to tell her story to a jury.

He decided this after submitting her to a test of her ability, in court, with the assistance of the prosecution lawyers. Mary's family was ordered out of the court for the duration of the test, although the person accused of assaulting her, together with his lawyers, remained behind and watched Mary answer questions.

I don't know on what basis the judge decided that Mary wasn't competent to tell the truth to a jury. I know it was a difficult decision, and that he did it reluctantly. Perhaps he had in mind that if Mary did go on to give her evidence, no matter how bravely or truthfully, she would be subject to cross-examination at the hands of a skilled lawyer. The judge would know how additionally traumatic that could be.

So the only person judged in a horrible case of sexual assault was the young woman who suffered the assault. She was judged and found wanting, because she has Down's Syndrome. And so there was no trial, no jury, no case for and against, no corroborating evidence, no conviction, no acquittal. In the absence of all those things, there was one other thing missing. There was no justice. There couldn't be.

In 1990, the Law Reform Commission published a report dealing with Child Sexual Abuse. It ran to 240 detailed pages. Among their recommendations are these:

–That expert evidence be admissible as to competence and as to children's typical behavioural and emotional reactions to sexual abuse.

–That the defendant should not be allowed to cross-examine the child at the trial without the leave of the court, which would only be given in the interests of justice and fair procedures.

–That the child should be questioned during the investigation and prosecution of these offences by disinterested but skilled child examiners, experienced in child language and psychology and appointed by the court.

In the same year, the Law Reform Commission published another report which said that these special arrangements should also be applied in the case of sexual offences against people with an intellectual disability.

We have legislated for some of these things, in a sort of a way. It is possible now to take evidence by video link, and in that situation (but only then) to use what is called an intermediary to ask the questions in a more child-friendly way. Naturally, of course, we haven't equipped our courts properly throughout the country to use video links, and it remains the case that judges are expected to know best about whether a child, or a person with an intellectual disability, is capable of telling the truth under oath. In Mary's case, although a video link was used, there was no intermediary.

Mary, you'll be glad to hear, is doing well. She knows she told the truth, and she knows her courage has made her family even more proud of her. She doesn't know, and perhaps it's just as well, that our system of justice let her down. Until we recognise that children and people with intellectual disabilities are citizens of our country too, and have a right to be properly heard, that's the way it will continue.

The Big Red Suit

My Santa suit arrived the other day. I tried it on and it's a perfect fit – jacket, pants, great big belt. Lots of ticklish fur, but I'll get used to that. For the last couple of years I've been standing in for the big fellow at some of our projects around Dublin. He always does the business himself on Christmas night, of course, but he doesn't find it easy to get around to all the pre-Christmas children's parties, so I've been giving him a dig-out.

This year I want to try to get to some of the thirty-odd projects we have outside Dublin, assuming the borrowed reindeer are up to the various journeys involved. So that's why I decided to get my own suit – a case of have beard, will travel.

The suit arrived early, but so, I suppose, has Christmas. I know the intention behind all the fairy lights in November is grimly commercial. It's supposed to encourage us all to shop earlier and more often. I'm not sure it's going to work.

From everything I'm hearing, we're all going to have a quieter Christmas this year. Office parties are being cancelled or downsized, and everyone is talking about more modest gift-giving than before. It's certainly not like the last couple of years, when people were throwing their SSIAs at the problem of what to buy for Christmas.

So I guess none of us should be too surprised if retail sales are down a bit this year, especially from last year's record high. And maybe it's no bad thing that drink sales – and the resulting hangovers – are likely to be down too. Maybe we might actually find, in a less material Christmas, more of a sense of what it should really be about. Time to reflect, maybe, time to be peaceful, time to rediscover relationships. Maybe it won't be so bad if we can't get the latest mobile phone or iPod for Christmas, just for once.

Last year, while we were all spending like mad things, there were some families who just wished, with all their hearts, that Christmas would pass them by. I met mothers last year who wondered how to put a Christmas dinner on the table, never mind how to give any sort of presents at all to their kids. Most of the kids I met when I was deputising for the man in the red suit were told that they could only ask for a surprise – because Santa wasn't going to be able to afford the bike they really wanted.

And if things were bad for some families last year, they're going to be harder in 2009, and for more people. People who were secure in their jobs a year ago are now facing their first Christmas on unemployment benefit. People who were paying a mortgage a year ago are fearful of having their houses repossessed. And people who were battered by life all through last year, in all the hidden enclaves of poverty we've built around Ireland, haven't found the going easier this year.

Organisations like mine are trying to gather up what we can, especially by way of toys, to try to ensure that Santa Clause leaves no one behind. And this year, the efforts of organisations like the St Vincent de Paul Society are really going to matter to an awful lot more people.

Their commitment, through their thousands of volunteers, to helping families have a decent Christmas, and to doing so in a way that is respectful of people's privacy and dignity, is one of the things worth honouring at this time of year. They will be starting to collect now, because they know their resources are stretched tight by the demands of this season.

So I know it's early. I know you haven't really focussed on what you're going to buy, and who's going to get what in your family this year. But when you do sit down to plan Christmas, maybe there might be a chance to factor in one suggestion.

The best Christmas present you can give your family, and yourself, is the thought that there's a child somewhere in Ireland just as excited as yours, about to open the present you made possible. When you're planning Christmas, just add the cost of one more present to the list. You'll enjoy it all the more.

Happy Christmas, Louise

He's making his list, and checking it twice. And on Wednesday night, Santa Claus will have a wonderful vantage point from which to take a long hard look at our tiny green island. From high up in the sky, his sleigh laden with presents, he will be able to see us all, and what we have become.

He's going to be busy, of course, because in our little island alone there are more than a million children to visit. And they all deserve it. Many of our children have seen hard times this year, even if many more still have reason to have high expectations of what Santa might bring.

I'm wondering if he will have time to reflect on what an ironic if beautiful country this is. We're a country that has just spent tens of millions – even though we don't have it – on bailing out the pig industry. And we're about to spend hundreds, if not thousands, of millions to protect the banking sector. All very well and necessary, no doubt, and no doubt too those hundreds of millions will be able to guarantee some children a better Christmas than they might have had otherwise.

But at exactly the same time, we have pursued one of the bravest women in Ireland to the point of emotional and financial ruin. Louise O'Keeffe, when she was a little

girl in County Cork, suffered terribly at the hands of one
of her teachers.

A good teacher will often be counted among the most
important influences that most of us can remember. But a
bad teacher can destroy lives. A teacher who uses the
authority and control their position gives them to abuse
children can, and does, leave scars that never heal. The
man who abused Louise O'Keeffe in Dunderrow National
School, near Kinsale, was a public servant employed for the
specific purpose of helping to shape her young life and
equip her for the future. His name was Leo Hickey. He
wasn't just any teacher. He was the principal of the school.

Leo Hickey was paid by the State out of taxpayers'
money. His pension was guaranteed by the State. The
resources to run his school were provided by taxpayers. In
every sense that matters, Leo Hickey was a public servant,
until he was convicted of his crimes. But then, it seems,
the State decided he had never been a public servant at all
– because technically, he was an employee of the local
school, a school that would never have existed if the State
hadn't put it there.

And our State – yours and mine – fought Louise
O'Keeffe every step of the way when she tried to make
someone admit responsibility for the abuse she had
suffered. And the technicality helped our State to win.
Having destroyed her emotionally, we are now
threatening to destroy her financially, by forcing her to
pay the State's legal bills as well as her own.

And at the same time, our State seems equally
determined to downplay, as much as we possibly can, the
consequences of an honest, damning and courageously
written report into the abuse of yet more children, this
time in the diocese of Cloyne. We now know – because

the Bishop of Cloyne has accepted the report – that in that diocese the Church, in the person of its own Bishop, failed completely to implement the Church's own procedures in relation to established abuse of children.

But again, it seems there is no question of resignation. And perhaps worse, there is no question of anyone in authority in our State – no member of our Government – having the courage to say that the resignation of a bishop is the only appropriate response. In this case, as in Louise O'Keeffe's case, the only ones who will suffer consequences are the ones who were abused in the first place.

Could it really be true that we have become a place where the State is willing to move mountains in responding to the needs of the rich and powerful, but is prepared to ignore those who have no money and no power – indeed, even to punish them for speaking out? If it is true, then surely Santa Claus, and whoever else is looking down on us from above, must be wondering when we are going to examine our consciences. Or if we have consciences.

But at least we know this. We know Santa Claus won't let the children suffer. Because Santa's outside every system. All he does is bring every child some excitement and happiness at Christmas. I hope he does that for the two children of Louise O'Keeffe.

I have other hopes, too. But they may need even more than Santa Claus to make them come true. I hope that our State finds the moral courage to make even powerful and protected people, including bishops, accountable for the abuse they should have stopped. And I hope we, the State, can find the moral generosity to tell Louise O'Keeffe that she will be punished no more for doing the right thing. The least she and her two children deserve, now and in the future, is a very Happy Christmas.

A Survivor

Around this time of year, I often think of a mother I know. Mary isn't her real name, but it will do. Mary has two children, by two different fathers. She was separated from her children when they were born, and they were each put up for adoption. They have lived their entire adult lives – they're both middle-aged parents themselves now – without knowing of Mary's existence.

That's the way Mary wants it to be. But every year, around this time, she wavers in her determination. She desperately wants them to know, in the run-up to Christmas, that their children have a grandmother, and that grandmother is still alive. But to reveal that would reveal what Mary believes to be her shame – the fact that she gave up her children for adoption in the first place. So every year, the Christmas cards she buys are never sent.

Mary was one of those kids who 'entered into care' as the expression has it, in one of our industrial homes. She never really knew her own mother, because she was either four or five when she was taken away from her family after her mother died. From that moment on, she endured most of the abuses for which our State apologised a few years ago. Along with countless others, she has told her story to the Confidential Committee that was part of the commission to enquire into child abuse in institutions

329

supported by the State over many years. That confidential commission heard the stories of more than 1,000 people, and its report is believed to be almost ready for publication now.

Apart from the time she told her story to the confidential committee, Mary has never talked much about her time there. We know from the bald recitation of facts in the Laffoy Report that abuse was commonplace and vicious. In the spare language of that report:

> *Witnesses described becoming accustomed to being hit as staff passed by, or in the classroom, as their daily lot and believed that life everywhere was like that. The complaints most often made to the Confidential Committee concerned the more extreme beatings witnesses were subjected to, or those that they were made to witness. Witnesses reported that they were hit on all areas of the body: the fingers, hands, wrists, shoulders, ears, face, head, trunk, feet, legs and thighs. Among the instruments witnesses described as being used were: canes, sticks, pointers, chair legs, sewing machine treadle belts, leather straps, rulers, scissors, keys, rosary beads, coat-hangers, hand-brushes, hairbrushes, yard-brushes, rungs of chairs, broom handles and tree branches.*

All this happened to children in Ireland, and it happened with our authority as citizens and taxpayers. Some of it, at least, happened to Mary. And when Mary was sixteen, she was put into service, where she became pregnant the first time. She saw that child only once, and the same thing happened to her when she became pregnant again. She had two children, and lost them both, by the age of nineteen. It happened because she had no training for life, no experience of the love and support every child needs.

You might think a lifetime like that would destroy a person. Well, you'd be wrong. Mary has made a good life for herself. She went and got herself an education in her twenties, and found a career in the public service. Now she's retired, and she herself would admit that she's not as strong as she once was.

She has made a will, and in that will she has left a pretty decent sum to each of the children she has never met. She has thought about them every day of her life. She has longed to meet them.

But she has never been able to overcome the conviction that they would be ashamed of her, that they wouldn't be able to understand why they were given up for adoption. Attempts to persuade her otherwise have always been rebuffed.

It's funny, isn't it, that Mary's only real experience of love has been to give it – never to feel that she deserved it herself. Throughout the years when it mattered most to her, there was no one to love her. Perhaps more than the beatings and the neglect, that left its mark on Mary, and made certain that there were some things she would always have difficulty communicating. And some times of the year more difficult than others.

The Cost-Benefit Approach to Cervical Cancer?

We had a fascinating man in Dublin last week. He came to address the Barnardos conference on tomorrow's child, and while he was here he met a number of senior policy-makers. Steve Aos is his name, and he is one of the world's leading authorities on how to get value for money from social care programmes.

Although his primary responsibility is to advise the Washington State Legislature, he has over many years found the answer to one pressing question for state governments all over the US and further afield. And the question is this – 'How can we do it better, and still get real value for money?' The answer to that question has led to prison-building programmes being cancelled or scaled down. It has encouraged governments to invest in early education. It has led to major investments in health programmes. These things have happened because he can demonstrate that the investment in alternatives will produce a better rate of return, year after year, for taxpayers' money.

I don't have time here to go into the process under-taken by Aos and his team. Suffice to say it is neutral, non-partisan, rigorous, demanding and internationally respected. But he himself would say that there are three good ways to do things better, and get real and lasting value for money. They are prevention, prevention and prevention.

Here in Ireland, we are developing our own version of Steve Aos, at least in the health sphere. It's called HIQA, the Health Information and Quality Authority. HIQA has set out to try to answer exactly the same question – how do we do it better, and get value for money. They use a process called a health technology assessment, designed to answer the question through rigorous research.

HIQA has only produced one health technology assessment so far. It was designed to answer an important question. If Ireland set out to provide a vaccination to every girl in the country against the virus that causes cervical cancer, would it be effective, and would it provide value for money?

They compared the cost and benefit of vaccination and screening against the cost and benefit of screening alone. The vaccination is against a virus called HPV, which causes 70 per cent of all cervical cancers. In 2004, ninety Irish women died of cervical cancer – on the law of averages, that means that around sixty Irish women were killed by the HPV virus.

Vaccination wasn't available when those women were children – it works best when administered to girls between the ages of ten and twelve. But vaccination is available now. The Center for Disease Control in Atlanta, the most reputable body of its kind in the world, recommended two years ago that it should routinely be given to girls – it involves three injections. And a study in the *New England Journal of Medicine*, also among the most reputable journals in the world, found that there was very significant cost-benefit associated with the vaccine.

So it's hardly surprising that HIQA found itself in a position to recommend to the Minister for Health that we should, as a matter of public policy, institute a programme of vaccination, and that we should seek to get to a point, as quickly as possible, where 80 per cent of girls of the relevant age would be vaccinated. Without wishing to go into the technicalities, HIQA found that not only would the vaccine be effective in preventing death and suffering, but the combination of vaccination and screening (which would still have to continue) would produce a substantial value-for-money return to the taxpayer.

And the cost of all this would be, according to HIQA's estimate, around €9 million a year. There would also be a once-off cost of around €30 million if the Government decided to also adopt a catch-up programme of vaccinating older girls – a measure considered desirable, although with a smaller rate of return, by HIQA.

Nine million euro a year, to save around sixty lives a year in the future. It's roughly the cost of building one mile of motorway. It's an investment in prevention that is backed by all the reputable science. And the taxpayer is ultimately the winner.

And that's why I think anyone who heard the minister say she would rather spend the admittedly scarce resources available to her on screening alone must have felt a deep pang of despair. It's hard to imagine a more short-sighted, more blinkered approach. If this is really how public policy is to be built, if people are going to be forever sacrificed to a form of stubbornness that is willing to ignore all professional advice, how can we ever build a better future in Ireland?

Unplug That Telly!

Here's a statistic that made me sit up straight. More than a quarter of children in Ireland have a television in their own rooms. And that's children between the ages of five and nine. One in seven Irish children under the age of five have TVs in their own rooms, and almost all of those toddlers have a DVD player as well.

The figures come from an independent, professionally carried out survey called Growing Up in Ireland. The survey was commissioned by Barnardos, and will be published in detail tomorrow. It represents a conscious effort by us in Barnardos to listen to parents, and to children too – because we have surveyed both – about the things that are important about childhood in Ireland today. It's a bit of a departure for us, because our main focus is, and will continue to be, working with children and families in extreme disadvantage. But as an organisation that believes passionately that a nation's best legacy is its children, it's important to us to be able to contribute what we can to a national conversation about childhood generally.

And we will be reporting a lot of good news, even if some of it has to be qualified. For many, if not most, children in Ireland, childhood is a good place to be these days. And the reasons reflect well on our commitment to strong family relationships. In most families in Ireland, it seems, both parents and children are reporting that 'quality time' is alive and well.

But statistics like the one I mentioned earlier make you wonder. A lot of Irish children feel happier – but they seem to relate their happiness in some measure at least to having access to lots of stuff, and family income is very important to them.

Of all the stuff our kids should have access to, I can't help wondering if a television and DVD player in their own rooms is the right way to go. I know only too well that there are times in every day when it comes as a blessed relief to be able to plonk a three-year-old in front of their favourite TV character. Sometimes even Barney and Dora the Explorer have their uses!

But a television in a child's own room can surely be a double-edged weapon. First of all there's the issue of how to regulate what's being watched. We live in an age where television, more than most media, reflects a rapidly changing world, a world that is becoming more violent, with more fraught relationships, with a host of life circumstances all on daily view.

There are hundreds of TV channels routinely available now, and a great many of them show material, even during the day, that can confuse and upset kids. The child on his or her own may not be able to communicate what they've seen, and may not feel encouraged to do so.

But maybe more to the point, childhood is about story time, about bath time, about cuddles and tickles and fun. A box in the corner of the room, telling its own stories and pursuing its own commercial imperatives, is a very poor substitute for a bed-time story.

I'm not saying, of course I'm not, that we should

never let our children watch telly. What I'm wondering about is whether we're allowing our kids to develop a habit of being alone, of drawing entertainment and attitudes from sources we know nothing about. A quarter of all our young children watching telly in their own rooms doesn't sound to me like a good way to build long-term relationships.

He Hit Her. Again.

Right now, we're in the middle of a campaign marking sixteen days of international action opposing violence against women. Events are going on all around Ireland to highlight a subject that we seldom seem to talk about. You may have heard the radio ad, the one featuring a little boy and girl in an adult conversation. I know I always stop what I'm doing when I hear the menace in his little voice as he snaps, 'Get me a beer, would you' at the little girl.

We know that domestic abuse can affect men as well as women. It is a fact though that women are far more likely to suffer abuse in the home, in all its forms (and there are many) than men are. But the impact on children can be profound too. For thousands of children, witnessing domestic violence can trigger the same emotional and behavioural responses as being the target of such abuse.

The majority of children who witness violence experience nightmares, spend a lot of their time afraid, and all too often blame themselves for what they have witnessed. We know that children who experience actual violence can themselves grow to perpetrate it, because they have been taught there is no other way. We know that systematic violence against a parent can undermine the relationship between them and their children. Children who struggle to understand violence in their homes can sometimes be as willing to blame the victim as they are reluctant to blame the abuser.

And we know that the incidence of domestic violence in our country has not been unduly affected by our increased prosperity. The refuges remain full. According to Women's Aid, since the beginning of 1996, 134 women have been murdered in Ireland. Of those, eighty-four were killed in their own homes. Of the cases which have been resolved, in almost exactly half of them the murder was committed by a partner or ex-partner.

Nearly 10,000 times a year the Gardaí are called to scenes involving domestic violence. One in eight women experience abuse while they are pregnant. And children were present in a significant number of all those incidents.

It's not a class-based phenomenon, not related to poverty. According to research carried out by Women's Aid, domestic violence occurs in every social and economic grouping of our community. As they put it, there is no 'type' of woman to whom it occurs, and there is no 'type' of home in which it happens. It happens everywhere, all the time. And domestic violence is not combined to physical abuse. Let me quote directly from Women's Aid: 'Sexual abuse, mental abuse and financial abuse are as common, as terrifying, and as damaging as physical abuse. But they are harder to see and may be more difficult for women to name. Many women are subjected to multiple forms of abuse at the same time.'

In Barnardos we work with children and families who have had to cope with domestic abuse, and we know the terrible scars it can leave, scars that can last long after the bruises and the broken bones have healed. We try above all to help children understand that domestic abuse is not something they have caused, that it's not their fault.

It's not their responsibility to make it stop. That responsibility belongs to all of us, and one way we can all help is by talking more openly about it. People who abuse their partners always want to do so in secrecy. The more we talk about it, the harder it is for abusers to hide behind closed doors.

Shadowboxers

As we sat in the new town square in Bray last Saturday afternoon, a strange scene unfolded in front of us. A tent, in the shape of a dome, had been erected in the centre of the square, and as we watched a group of five actors approached it. Diffidently they explored the mundane everyday objects that hung from the dome – clothes pegs, plastic bags, and the like. Little by little they felt their way around the dome, until two of them seemed to find a door. They opened it, and beckoned to us, the audience, to come in.

This was the beginning of Cloud House, described on the flyer that accompanied it as a walkabout theatre experience. Cloud House is a production of the Shadow-box Theatre Company, a tiny group of people who deserve huge support but get very little.

Inside the dome, the actors created a world unlike any that most of us had experienced. Inanimate objects became friends, to be stroked and caressed. People reached out to each other in pain, but were unable to make a connection. A tiny doll became the baby that some of the women yearned for but wouldn't have. A huge globe, made of paper and rags, became the world they could never own. Instead the world the actors lived in was a wasteland, bare and brown and ugly.

But all the time the actors moved through this world with grace and discipline. No words were used, just dance and mime and movement. A hypnotic soundtrack accompanied every scene, and facial expressions conveyed the depth of the emotional charge implicit in the unfolding story.

It sounds bleak, but it wasn't. It was spellbinding – moments of pathos, even despair, followed by playfulness. One minute you might have been watching *Waiting for Godot*, the next the three witches from *Macbeth*.

Their brilliant director, Gemma Gallagher, had devised a play about rejection and isolation. But the actors she worked with, during six weeks of hard work and preparation, had all added their own experiences. Every scene they enacted over the forty minutes or so of the production conveyed a personal experience. As the actors grew into the play, the play became their life story.

These actors, it became clear, understood very well what isolation means. They know what it's like to be outsiders, to be alone, and to feel alone. As the audience watched, we could all see that. In fact, maybe we began to understand isolation in a way we never had before.

It's really tough, doing a performance about a subject so difficult, in a small and crowded tent, with an audience that is slowly being drawn in. It requires concentration and effort on the part of the actors, who were faultless in the way they responded to the music, and passionate in the way they told their story.

Still, watching the play develop, it was impossible not to feel their sadness. The story of rejection may be a common one among Irish citizens who live on the margins. But watching it being enacted by such talented actors is hard. The audience, you could see, was moved, and some were almost angry.

So it was important, as well as being a great relief, that the actors decided to end this play with an exuberant dance. As the Tom Waits song 'Let It Rain' pounded around the Bray Civic Plaza, the actors rocked their way out of the tent, followed by an audience that was clapping and cheering.

It really is amazing that a small, under-funded theatre company can produce work like that. In forty minutes you felt you gained a huge insight into the human condition, without a word being spoken but also without a step out of place. The rehearsals, the preparation and the whole troupe's passion for their work paid off.

There were two performances last Saturday. Admission was free, but places were limited because we all had to fit into the dome. Shadowbox is going to do more performances, on the Esplanade in Bray on August 28th. You really need to go and see them at work. You'll be thrilled that you did. And I'll bet you anything that you'll watch those five actors work as a team, and completely forget the one other thing they have in common, the one thing that really makes them understand rejection and communicate it so well.

The fact that each of them, combined with the talent and the work, has an intellectual disability.

Standards for Pigs

Thank God for standards. And thank God for inspection. If it wasn't for both, we could all be eating sausages and rashers that had been contaminated with dioxins. The drama of the weekend, and the recall of all pork products in the interests of consumer safety, have made us all grateful that standards exist, and that they are properly enforced.

There are standards, of course, in relation to a lot of the food we eat. And there are safety standards, all properly enforced, in relation to a lot of the things we buy – clothes, for instance, and toys. Standards apply too to the houses we live in, and they can be enforced as well. And there are now standards, thank goodness, in relation to places where elderly and vulnerable people live. After a scandal like Leas Cross, we wouldn't expect any less, would we. And where vulnerable people are concerned, we wouldn't settle for any less, would we.

Actually, yes, we would. Just last Tuesday, the members of the Oireachtas Committee on Health and Children were shocked to discover that there are no standards whatsoever, and therefore no inspection or supervision, of residential facilities for people with an intellectual disability. The Committee was being briefed by the Health Information and Quality Authority on the work it has been doing – immensely valuable work – to try to put standards in place and to ensure that those standards are backed up in law.

And the main organisation representing people with intellectual disabilities, Inclusion Ireland, was there too, highlighting exactly what the absence of standards can mean. The chairperson of Inclusion Ireland, Bill Shorten, told the Committee that there are over 25,000 people with an intellectual disability in Ireland. About a third of them, or slightly more than 8,000, live in full-time residential settings. No standards exist in relation to where they live, and no independent inspection takes place.

The chief executive of Inclusion Ireland, Deirdre Carroll, said that Inclusion Ireland is aware of the excellent standard of service provided by many groups which are doing much good work, but through their work they are also aware of poor services, cases of neglect, poor standards, bad practice and abuse. She pointed to the absurd and scandalous position that there are approximately 400 children with disabilities in residential care, but they do not have the protection of the Office of the Social Services Inspectorate, which is offered to children without disabilities in residential care. Even though it has been well established that children with disabilities are three to seven times more likely to become victims of abuse.

But what does it mean to have standards – or rather, not to have them? A few graphic sentences from Frieda Finlay, vice-chair of Inclusion Ireland – and let it be said, related to this column by marriage – paints the picture. She told the Committee some true stories, with only the names changed.

'John is a forty-year-old man who is put to bed by staff every night at six o'clock. Mary's mother bought her some lovely clothes but every time her mother visits Mary she does not recognise the ill-fitting clothes she is wearing. Catherine had to have two nails removed when she visited the chiropodist because she is unable to look after her own nails, she does not ask for help and nobody seems to have time. Michael is twenty-eight years of age and would love to get out for just one evening a week to go to the pub, but no one else in his house wants to go so he just has to sit and watch television every night. James missed his consultant's appointment because there were no staff to bring him even though it had been written in the house book more than three months previously. Ann does not have a choice who she lives with. Eileen has to share her bedroom with a stranger. Patrick, at the age of thirty-five is still living in a ward with little or no privacy, having been told two years ago he would move to a new home. And Sarah, who has a severe disability, was slapped by a staff member.'

All these people live in residential services. In Ireland. Today. And residential services means their home – just like you and I live at home. If the standards that HIQA has developed were put into action, and properly enforced, none of these things would be regarded as acceptable practice – just as you and I wouldn't regard them as acceptable if they happened to us in our homes.

We are now all seeking and demanding the assurance that every piggery in Ireland will be properly inspected, and that only the best standards of accommodation and food will apply. Is it unreasonable to suggest that at least the same level of urgency should be applied to the places where some of Ireland's most vulnerable people live?

Theirs Is the Kingdom of Heaven

'Suffer the little children to come unto me.' That's what Jesus told some of his disciples who tried to prevent children approaching him. They didn't feel their Master should be bothered – he had too much to worry about already. He, however, was prepared to listen to the children, to make time for them and to understand them, for one simple reason he explained to his disciples: 'For theirs is the kingdom of heaven.'

How does a child feel that his is the kingdom of heaven, when at the same time he or she feels betrayed by their church?

Last week the Minister for Children published an audit of child protection practices. The audit had been carried out by the HSE, and it essentially consisted of a questionnaire being sent to all of Ireland's Catholic bishops. Simple, straightforward questions, most of them requiring no more than a box to be ticked, some requiring numbers. The bishops weren't asked to name anyone, or draw any conclusions about the guilt or innocence of any individual. In fact, they were invited by the wording of the questionnaire to protect the confidentiality of individuals.

But in respect of some of these straightforward questions the bishops were simply unable to offer any information. Questions like – please identify the number of complaints made against individuals which have been passed to the relevant authorities; the number of religious convicted of child sexual abuse; the number under investigation. They weren't even able to tell the HSE the number of allegations that had been discovered to be unfounded by the relevant authorities.

And it wasn't because the information isn't in their possession. No, the bishops told the HSE – and by implication the State – that there were insurmountable legal difficulties in the way of passing on what they knew to the State. Confidentiality – about numbers, mind you, not about names – had to be preserved.

And yet everyone says that the welfare of children must come first. If the welfare of children comes first, every bishop must be able to put his hand on his heart and say that the following statements are true. An abused person would know that his door was always open to them, and that their stories would be taken seriously. They would know that prompt action would follow complaints of serious abuse. They would know that any information – including admissions of guilt – in the possession of the Church would be handed over to the proper authorities. They would know that any priest over whom there was a cloud of suspicion would, at the very least, be removed from contact with children.

And yet, in our kingdom of heaven, after all the reports we've had, all the scandals we have uncovered, those statements are still not true for all bishops. There are honourable exceptions, of course, and the available evidence suggests that many bishops are trying very hard. But if bishops can't be open with the truth, there is always going to be a cloud.

Sexual abuse leaves terrible scars. Many of the honest and articulate people we have seen interviewed about their experiences at the hands of priests haven't recovered from their ordeal. It's just that the scar tissue is strong – it's preventing their wounds from bleeding too much. Nothing can take away those scars – but every time there is a refusal to take responsibility, the wounds are torn open again.

It's time we ended this. It's time we gave the guidelines now in place the full force of law. We need a law on mandatory reporting, and we need it urgently. In order to keep children safe, reporting known or suspected abuse should not be a matter of discretion for anyone. Instead it should be the foundation of a transparent and accountable system of child protection.

Mandatory reporting sends out a clear message on all levels that the abuse of children will not be accepted. It equips those who interact with children with a clear course of action that puts children first. It helps remove the element of discretion – a potentially important factor for someone who might want to make a report of suspected abuse but is reluctant. With mandatory reporting they can do so with the full support of the law. Mandatory reporting would also help tackle the issue of inconsistent and under-reporting of abuse and allows those investigating reports of abuse to take a more consistent approach. We need to change the law now.

Meat or Fish?

Have you ever heard of the deprivation indicators? They're a set of facts used to describe the condition known as consistent poverty. They're very useful facts, because they enable consistent poverty to be measured year on year.

Generally speaking there are eight deprivation indicators, and they can be set out very simply. The first is inability to afford a warm waterproof coat. Then there is inability to afford a meal with meat, chicken or fish every second day. There is inability to afford two pairs of strong shoes; inability to afford a roast once a week; no substantial meal on at least one day in the past two weeks; without heating at some stage in the past year; and inability to afford new (not second-hand) clothes. The final indicator happens if you have experienced debt problems arising from ordinary living expenses.

At most times in our lives, especially in the bad old days or perhaps when we were students, most of us knew times when we experienced one or other of those indicators. I can still remember, for example, a time when I couldn't afford to replace the one pair of shoes I had, even though they were badly letting in water.

That time passed though, as it did for most of us. Whatever moments of poverty we had in our lives, we had opportunities too. We had education, we came from reasonable addresses, we knew how to go about looking for jobs and building a career, we had friends and parents who were ambitious for us.

And they were the bad old days, of course. In the 1980s and before, you could almost say that the whole of Ireland suffered from the deprivation indicators. When our national debt was greater than our total wealth, and tens of thousands of people were leaving to find a better life elsewhere, there were times when it seemed like there was no hope for those of us who stayed behind, no hope of the tide ever rising.

But the tide did rise. For a whole variety of reasons, our economy began to grow. There were more jobs, and a great deal more wealth. Poverty, especially the hard grinding poverty of the past, the sort that destroys lives and locks in a generational trap, could be said to be a thing of the past.

If only it were so. The most up-to-date figures on poverty in Ireland were published recently by the Central Statistics Office. They show that one in every sixteen people in Ireland, on average, still lives in consistent poverty, still suffers from those deprivation indicators. And the number is a stubborn one – despite our hugely increased wealth, the same proportion of people is stuck in poverty.

But behind that average of one in sixteen lie some really frightening figures. For example, the consistent poverty rate for people in lone-parent households increased from about one in four in 2005 to one in three in 2006. In the same period the consistent poverty rate for children up to the age of fourteen (in all household types) actually increased too, from 10.2 per cent to 11.1 per cent.

In addition to lone-parent households, other high-risk groups were the unemployed. Almost a third of people living in households headed by an unemployed person were in consistent poverty – this compares to a figure of 2.3 per cent where the head of household was at work.

I'm sorry about all the statistics. The thing that amazes me, though, is how figures like that can go unnoticed and undebated, why there is no outcry over the continuing scandal of poverty in the midst of such affluence. We shouldn't be a country where people go hungry – we shouldn't be prepared to allow it. And we shouldn't be prepared to allow kids to be deprived, by whatever circumstance, of the best possible start in life. As long as the deprivation indicators, in all their stark simplicity, apply to so many of our population, we are all poor, in one way or another.

It Could Never Happen Here

Have you seen the photographs of Baby P? A beautiful little boy, just learning to stand when the pictures were taken, reaching up to whoever took the photograph, ready to smile.

A few months later, according to the many newspaper accounts I've read, after enduring abuse of an almost unimaginable cruelty, this little boy had been reduced to a nervous wreck, his hair shaved to the scalp and his body covered in bruises and scabs. His physical injuries included eight broken ribs and a broken back. His fingernails and the tips of his fingers had been torn off and he had been hit so hard in the face that one of his teeth was found in his stomach.

Despite it all, Baby P was said to have still attempted a smile for the nurses and doctors who tried to save his life. It was too late. Baby P died a terrible, unforgettable death at seventeen months of age.

Had he recovered from the terrible abuse he received, it would perhaps have taken years, maybe even the rest of his life, to try to heal the emotional wounds he suffered. He was terribly abused by the people he loved and trusted most.

And it happened in a civilised country, our nearest neighbour. It happened even though Baby P was visited more than sixty times by health professionals and social workers. It happened in the very place where another little girl, Victoria Climbié, was tortured to death eight years ago. It happened despite very sweeping recommendations made at the time of Victoria's death, and despite the introduction of much stronger child protection measures in Britain. It happened even though social work services are better resourced in Britain than they ever were before.

It's easy to blame in cases like these. And of course there will have to be an enquiry, to try to establish how the terrible death of Baby P could have happened under the noses of authorities whose job it was to protect him. There are disturbing indications that some warning was available, and that whistleblowers may have been silenced. All these questions will need to be answered.

But no matter what the outcome of that enquiry, some questions are simply unanswerable. What is it that makes people capable of inflicting such pain and terror on a child? How is it that sometimes those closest to the child can seem to prefer to conspire with the abuser rather than protect their child?

And there is a question we have to ask too, from our side of the Irish Sea. Could it ever happen here? Could any child in Ireland live at risk from such abuse without us knowing, and without us acting? The comforting thing to say would be that such an atrocity against a child would never happen in Ireland. We value children and childhood. We have written the special place of the family into our Constitution. We would be horrified to think that a child could be abused to the point of death in our country.

But it could happen here. And that's a fact we have to

face. Social workers all over Ireland work hard, day in and day out, to try to prevent it. They walk a fine line much of the time, trying to make decisions that will keep families together, trying to avoid too much intrusion. They know that intrusion is never welcomed by families, and attacked constantly by commentators. They know that they, and they alone, will be blamed for any wrong decision made. They get burned out trying to protect children.

Because in many cases, far too many cases, they carry too big a caseload to be as effective as they should be. And when they can't add more children to their caseloads, those children are simply not allocated to anyone. There are dozens, if not hundreds of children in Ireland, known to the system to be at risk of neglect and perhaps worse. But they haven't been allocated to a social worker, because there simply aren't enough social workers.

There is no statutory reporting. There is no out-of-hours service. There is no structured sharing of information between different authorities – the gardaí and the social work teams, for instance. There is no capacity to respond rapidly. There is no support for the people on the ground. There is no early warning system. And of course, there's no money.

Could we wake up some morning to discover a Baby P had died in Ireland in terrible circumstances? Yes, we could. Would we be filled with shame and remorse as a nation? Yes, we would. Would we demand that heads would roll and that laws and resources were put in place to ensure it never happed again? You can bank on it. But why, in the name of God, are we waiting for it to happen?

Papering the Pitch

What a match that was last Saturday. It was a thrill to be there, thanks to a couple of tickets that appeared at the last minute. And it was impossible not to reflect that an Irish team, playing with fire, passion and skill – but above all playing as a team – could achieve almost anything. The discipline on the pitch was matched only by the buzz on the streets afterwards.

I had a weird thought at halftime. I wondered how that pitch, which has generated so much revenue for the GAA while still retaining its quality, would look if it was papered with money. I looked up the dimensions of the pitch later, and did some calculations. Do you know how many fifty-euro notes it would take to paper that pitch so you couldn't see a blade of grass under all the money? Well, if you covered the entire thing with fifty-euro notes, it would cost you €57 million to do it.

Of course, no one is ever going to do that. We have far too many important other things to do with our money. Like recapitalising the banks, for instance. You know something? You could paper the entire pitch at Croke Park 140 times with the amount of money needed to recapitalise the banks. Just imagine – that huge pitch, covered to a depth of about a foot with fifty-euro notes.

And we've already committed the unimaginable sum

of half a trillion euro to guarantee the deposits of the banks. By my calculations, that would cover the pitch to the height of an average room.

Even when you try to visualise it, it's almost impossible to come to terms with money like that, isn't it? But we've made all those commitments as a nation, because we decided we had to. We didn't discuss it very much, and most of us weren't consulted. We just did it. Because we had to.

We had to, apparently, to rescue our economy. We've all bought into this idea, more or less. Of course there will be pain. A fair amount of pain for many people at work, and an awful lot of pain for people who lose their jobs, and for those whose lives depend on poorly funded and reduced State services.

Twelve months ago – even six months ago – we didn't think of having to find new billions or to pay for other people's lost billions. It is a truly remarkable turnaround that in a very short length of time, we now accept that we must find all this money for the common good, and of course for the economy.

And then one considers what would have happened if we had no crisis. Close your eyes for a second and look at the pitch in Croke Park again, still papered with fifty-euro notes, but this time only one or two deep. Focus in on a tiny little area, around any of the corner flags. That's the amount of money we needed to prevent cervical cancer a few months ago. But it simply wasn't possible. We couldn't find it. And there was no banking crisis then.

Before the crisis, there was no way our political leaders could have moved heaven and earth, holding emergency Dáil debates, to find the money to ensure that every community had a good modern school with decent facilities, to replace the ramshackle collections of prefabs and extensions with leaking roofs. Before the crisis, it wasn't possible to find the money to keep small Traveller children in school – and the amount of money involved wouldn't have covered the centre spot in Croke Park.

Isn't it one of the great ironies of our lives that before the money was gone, we couldn't find the pittance it would take to build and sustain a decent society? But after the money was gone – and gone as a result of other people's greed and recklessness – we can find more money than any of us can imagine to invest in trying to fix the problems they caused.

That Irish team last Saturday in Croke Park showed us how we can fix our problems. By working together. By never giving up. By being prepared to really go for it when opportunity arises. And when we have fixed our problems, we should make one additional resolution. We should resolve that we will never again let anyone tell us it can't be done.

That we can't prevent cervical cancer. That we can't give every child a decent start. That we can't end the exclusion of some of the most deprived people in our community. If we can cover every blade of grass in Croke Park with fifty-euro notes, to a height taller than the tallest man in Ireland, we can do anything.

Barack Obama and the Grand Slam

While I watched the match on telly last Saturday, I thought of Ryan Hill, Lorraine Whelan, Mary Foley, Brian Cork, and dozens of other athletes who have inspired me over the years. I'll tell you why in a minute.

But first, what a game of rugby, and what an occasion. In the end, it was the way the Irish team climbed the mountain that took a while to sink in. A team that over the last number of years has had to cope with its fair share of adversity finally got the triumph its work and effort deserved. And the fact that they got it the hard way, in the face of the most appalling pressure imaginable, only added to the sweetness of the moment.

During the week I heard one of the Welsh commentators, quoted on the radio, announcing that Ronan O'Gara would fold like a deckchair under pressure. As that last-minute drop goal sailed through, the thought that went through my head was, 'Some deckchair!' What was amazing was that you could see him calling for the ball – I know that I would rather walk through fire than demand to take responsibility for a nation's hopes at a moment like that.

And over months and years we have heard, and probably uttered, the criticisms that they have all had to live with – that Brian O'Driscoll was over the hill; that the

Munster/Leinster rivalry had undermined the cohesion of the team; that they were always likely to choke on the big occasion. After the last World Cup, when they returned home shattered and demoralised, there must have been a huge temptation for some of them to walk away and get on with the rest of their lives. But they managed to get over every hurdle, every obstacle, placed in their way. The courage, the concentration, the talent and the grace they showed last Saturday in Cardiff will live in the memories of all of us who saw it – on television or in the grounds – forever.

It's that thing of triumph over adversity that really gets us, isn't it? You can admire the achievements of a Tiger Woods or a Roger Federer, but somehow it's never quite the same as watching someone who has climbed a mountain to get where they are. Bernard Dunne, whose world title hopes seemed to lie in ruins only a short while ago, is yet another athlete whose ability to scale every hurdle attracts such admiration.

That's why the athletes I mentioned at the start have always inspired me – and anyone else who gets involved with them. They're all athletes who have represented their clubs and their country with great distinction, excelling in regional and national competition, and often attacking barriers of culture and language and distance to bring pride to their country in international competitions. And they are all athletes who have lived their entire lives with other kinds of adversity too. They – and dozens more I could mention – all belong to the one sporting organisation in Ireland that simply thrives on bringing out the best from adversity: Special Olympics.

Which was why it was both astonishing and disappointing that President Obama, of all people, could be so casually disparaging about Special Olympians. Appearing on a late-night talk show, the President was asked about his bowling, and admitted to having scored 129 in a recent game. 'I bowl like Special Olympics or something,' he said, a crass comment that made the audience titter.

It was revealing on two levels. First, the insensitivity of the President himself, a man who must know more than most people about the difficulties of overcoming adversity – and about how easy it is to stigmatise people. And secondly, the willingness of the audience to laugh along with a cheap crack like that. The President apologised immediately, surely itself a recognition that damage had been done.

I know it's easy to be over-sensitive about this kind of thing. We've come a long way, I guess, in our understanding of the challenges that people with an intellectual disability face. And most Special Olympic bowlers, by the way, would be genuinely mortified if they only got 129 in competition. President Obama is a good bit short of medal contention at a Special Olympics event if that's the best he can do.

But even if he was factually wrong, and quick to apologise, the ease with which jokes like that can be made proves one thing. We still have some maturing to do before we can finally say that the attitudes of old towards people with an intellectual disability – attitudes that ultimately stigmatised and diminished them, and made them safe to ignore – have disappeared.

At least I know that isn't true of the powerful athletes

who make up the Irish rugby team. Over the years, I've watched many of them – O'Connell, O'Gara, O'Driscoll, David Humphreys among many others – work with Special Olympic athletes on a basis of mutual respect. That's because they know class when they see it!